NARRATIVE MORTALITY

NARRATIVE MORTALITY

Death, Closure, and New Wave Cinemas

Catherine Russell

University of Minnesota Press

Minneapolis

London

"Wim Wenders: Film as Death at Work" was previously published in
slightly different form as "The Life and Death of Authorship in Wim
Wenders' *The State of Things,*" *Canadian Journal of Film
Studies/Revue Canadienne d'Etudes Cinématographiques*; reprinted
with permission. Parts of this book were also previously published in
Crisis Cinema: The Apocalyptic Idea in Postmodern Narrative Film,
ed. Christopher Sharrett (Washington, D.C.: Maisonneuve Press,
1993); reprinted with permission of the publisher.

Published by the University of Minnesota Press
111 Third Avenue South, Suite 290, Minneapolis, MN 55401
Printed in the United States of America on acid-free paper

Library of Congress Cataloging-in-Publication Data
Russell, Catherine, 1959–
    Narrative mortality : death, closure, and new wave cinemas /
Catherine Russell.
        p.   cm.
    Includes bibliographical references and index.
    1. Death in motion pictures.   I. Title.
    ISBN 0-8166-2485-2 (hc: acid-free paper)
    ISBN 0-8166-2486-0 (pbk: acid-free paper)
    PN1995.9.D37R87   1994
    791.43'654 — dc20   94-17542

CONTENTS

ACKNOWLEDGMENTS

Many people have been extremely helpful in the development of the work that has become this book. I cannot thank Ivone Margulies enough for her constant support, her attentive reading, and her generous criticism. Bill Simon and Bob Stam at New York University encouraged me to pursue a research project that was both ambitious and idiosyncratic. The generous, perceptive, and creative readings by Bart Testa and Paul Arthur helped me enormously to focus and structure the study. Dana Polan's input was also instrumental at an early stage in the project. Biodun Iginla at the University of Minnesota Press took an interest in the manuscript at a critical point, and both David Desser and Tom Conley offered perceptive readings. In addition, several anonymous readers provided me with helpful readings for which I am very grateful. I would also like to thank my family, my friends, and my colleagues at Queen's University and Concordia University for their support and assistance. Thanks also to Joanne Sloane, Alison Cuddy, and Angela Fong, who provided excellent assistance in preparing the manuscript.

Some of the following material has been previously published in the *Canadian Journal of Film Studies* and *Crisis Cinema: The Apocalyptic Idea in Postmodern Narrative Film,* edited by Christopher Sharrett.

The book is dedicated to the memory of my grandmother, Jean Russell, who died at the age of ninety-two in 1991.

INTRODUCTION

NARRATIVE MORTALITY

● ────────────────────────────────────

> For Death must be somewhere in a society; if it is no longer (or less
> intensely) in religion, it must be elsewhere; perhaps in this image which
> produces Death while trying to preserve life. Contemporary with the
> withdrawal of rites, Photography may correspond to the intrusion, in our
> modern society, of an asymbolic Death, outside of religion, outside of
> ritual, a kind of abrupt dive into literal Death. — ROLAND BARTHES

Death may once have been "tamed" by social representations, but it is now indisputably "wild," a signifier adrift in the cultural image bank. Death remains feared, denied, and hidden, and yet images of death are a staple of the mass media. As medical and health technologies continue to battle mortality with as little success as ever, news broadcasts prioritize stories according to the number of deaths involved. Such is the paradox of the absence of death from daily lived experience on the one hand and its omnipresence in the media on the other. Rather than regard this as a problem, though, we should be prepared to understand this wildness as an opening up of representation.

1

At the end of a feature film, where death is expected by viewers and consistently supplied by filmmakers, death is still often "tamed" by the sense of an ending. At other times it is not. This book is concerned with a cinema in which death and closure come together with difficulty, with vengeance, and with a strong sense of historical difference, a cinema that grasps death as a discourse of temporality, representation, and the body. The paradox of death—its spectacular and taboo status—will not be thereby "explained," but explored as a political terrain.

It was during the international overhaul of cinematic conventions of the 1960s and 1970s that this terrain was mapped out. The various "New Wave" cinemas of North America, Europe, Japan, and Brazil had distinctive stylistic and cultural programs, but the spectacle of death consistently overwhelmed narrative closure and destabilized representation. This book is about the ways that films of the French Nouvelle Vague, as well as the Japanese New Wave of the 1960s, and the American genre revisionism and New German Film of the 1970s, engage with the fatalism of classical representation in radical and productive ways.[1]

The term "narrative mortality" refers to the discourse of death in narrative film. It is a discourse produced by reading/viewing as much as it is by writing/filmmaking; it is both a critical method and a discursive practice. Narrative mortality is an "undoing" or "reading" of the ideological tendency of death as closure. It is a practice of resistance, with aspirations toward a radical politics of filmic narrativity. Narrative mortality is a method of understanding the function of narrative endings in the politics of representation, a means of moving beyond formalist categories of "open" and "closed" endings, as well as mythic categories of fate and romance.

The films that have been chosen for textual analysis span four decades, mapping a course through a highly intertextual and intercultural film history within which the New Wave cinemas flourished. These films are *Beyond a Reasonable Doubt* (Fritz Lang, 1956), *Lightning Over Water* (Wim Wenders, 1980), *The State of Things* (Wenders, 1982), *Cruel Story of Youth* (Oshima Nagisa, 1960), *Boy (Shonen)* (Oshima, 1969), *Le Mépris* (Jean-Luc Godard, 1963), *Pierrot le fou* (Godard, 1965), and *Nashville* (Robert Altman, 1975). These texts have been chosen for methodological reasons, as the exemplary means of indicating the scope of narrative mortality, as well as its different cultural and historical per-mutations within the various contexts of narrative and psychoanaly-sis (Lang), realism and authorship (Wenders), politics and national-ism (Oshima), intertextuality and genre (Godard), and spectacle and sacrifice (Altman—as well as Arthur Penn and Sam Peckinpah).

Mortality in these films does not provide a means of wrapping things up, but more often, a violent means of condemning "closure" as a narrative and historical event. The conventions of cinematic nar-rative, as they were developed out of the bildungsroman tradition of literary narrative, codified the desire for meaning as a desire for mean-ingful death, and the desire for ending was formalized as a desire for death.[2] The isomorphism of life and narrative in the bildungsroman tradition collapses history onto identity.[3] In an era of atomic weapons, multinational capitalism and sociocultural heterogeneity, neither "iden-tity" nor history can be so neatly parceled out. The films in question here consistently split death from closure, and prevent meaning and ending from fitting neatly together. While the death of a protagonist may often be interpreted psychologically as the loss of an ideal, the spectacular representation of violent death suggests that loss is also articulated on the level of the image and the very language of repre-sentation. Narrative mortality is thus an allegory of the limits of rep-resentation, an allegory produced through an interpretive reading of the texts in question.

Since the Second World War, narrative mortality has become an allegorical structure with a range of possibilities. The separation of death from closure has been a key means by which filmmakers have represented the social transformations of the second half of the twen-tieth century—from cold war divisiveness, through the antiauthori-tarianism of the 1960s, the "death of myth" in the 1970s, and the "death of the subject" in the 1980s. The analysis of narrative mortality en-ables us to theorize these cultural discourses within the spectacular and temporal terms of cinematic representation. As terrorism, tele-vised war, and transportation accidents have so greatly revised mor-tality on an international scale, narrative strategies conventionally in-formed by metaphysical and organic notions of mortality have also undergone revision.

From the explosive radioactive flashes at the end of *Kiss Me Deadly* (1955) and *Dr. Strangelove* (1963), and the extended slow-motion embrace of a dead killer by his brother at the end of *The American Soldier* (Fassbinder, 1970), to the afterlife of Raoul Ruiz's *Life Is a Dream* (1987) in which everyone sits around bleeding from head wounds, the coincidence of death and closure takes place on the site of a fragmentation of the filmic illusion of reality. During the second half of this century, filmmakers have exploited death in film as a privileged point of potential destabilization. The cinematic preoccupation with violence is not coincidental, and not simply historical. Both death and film are negotiations with absence: just as film is nothing but images, death is nothing except its various representations. Death is little more than the discourses around it (funeral, legal, and medical languages), and the historical and fictional narratives in which it is inevitably included.

Pulling apart death and closure is symptomatic of a larger tendency within critical theory to "deconstruct" the process of signification and place the necessity of referentiality in question. The key theoretical tools for the present project, which is at once a process of textual exegesis, historiography, and redemption, are provided by Walter Benjamin's diverse body of writing. For Benjamin, death is the emblem of historical transience, of irreversible change, and also of the singularity of historical experience. Moreover, it is in photographic reproduction that this discourse is most significantly inscribed. Benjaminian deconstruction will be developed here as a freeing of historical time from the mythic time of human mortality. Benjamin's notions of mortification, allegory, historiography, memory, and cultural practice are not, however, liberationist principles. Nor is his conception of redemption, which is above all a theory of historical imagination founded on the "ruins" of modernity, on decay and fragmentation.

Although this book draws on many of Benjamin's texts, the key source for his theory of mortality is *The Origins of German Tragic Drama*. This study of *Trauerspiel,* which was never accepted as a thesis by the faculty at Heidelberg, was written during the Weimar Republic.[4] Benjamin's challenge to Romantic literary theory was written under the sign of modernity. In his subsequent study of Baudelaire and the Paris Arcades, the theory of allegory was further developed within that modernist context. Finally, in his 1936 essay on Nicolai Lescov, Benjamin comes to understand death in narrative as the sign of history. His conception of modernity is a theory of mourning, but not one of nostalgia: "The epoch in which man could believe himself to be in harmony with nature has expired." This is the point at which "death is either the leader or the last wretched straggler."[5]

Walter Benjamin's theory of allegory presumes a theory of history in which the "temporal index" of the past is embodied in the ruin, in the photograph, and in allegorical representation.[6] If, for Benjamin, historical possibility lies in the articulation of dialectical memory, the basic structure of the cinema — in which the past (the existence of the profilmic) and the present (the time of viewing) are in continual collision — might be fundamentally allegorical. As repetition becomes a dynamic passage through history, it is emblematized in the representation of death. As a "ruin" of the performance of the body, the image is radically split between the sign of death and its referent — an idea tacked onto a body: a presence and a past. The cinematic allusion to the profilmic moment is therefore the key to historical redemption in narrative film. Narrative mortality engages the representational capacity of the cinema as a threshold of loss and redemption.

Jürgen Habermas has referred to Benjamin's historiography as a "rescuing critique," but he is skeptical of Benjamin's antievolutionary conception of history. The critique of "progress" from the perspective of historical materialism undermines the process by which social transformation might "realistically" come about. Habermas comments: "Shock is not an action, and profane illumination is not a revolutionary deed."[7] The importance of Benjamin is not the anticipation of historical catastrophe, however, but the ability to comprehend catastrophe as an allegory of history. "The notion of a present which is not a transition, but in which time stands still and has come to a stop,"[8] is only available through the mortification of teleological thought. To blast open the myth of fate is the only means of producing a dialectical image of history — an allegorical image of the impossibility of visualizing that which has yet to become history.

Habermas himself offers a way out of his own critique when he suggests that it is as criticism, as redemptive mortification, that Benjamin's thought might be reconciled with "a materialist theory of social evolution." Benjamin's "differentiated concept of progress opens a perspective" in which "the idea of the revolution as the process of forming a new subjectivity must ... be transformed."[9] In contrast to ideological critique and consciousness-raising, the Marxist cultural theories to which Habermas compares Benjamin's radical theology, "rescuing critique" enables the redemption of a cultural history that is not simply one of "affirmative culture," but that preserves the secret of historical difference necessary to utopian thought. Rather than a new subjectivity, the revolutionary moment depends on the mortification of subjectivity as the model of historical temporality.

The interpretation of films as allegories of narrative mortality is intended to realize a politics of representation implicit in the cinema of the last half of the twentieth century. Fredric Jameson has theorized the allegorical reading of culture as criticism that seeks to transform the historical real that lies outside the textual object itself.[10] He has defined allegory as the intellectual grasp of

> phenomena about which we are at least minimally agreed that no single thought or theory encompasses any of them.... Allegorical interpretation is then first and foremost an interpretive operation which begins by acknowledging the impossibility of interpretation in the older sense, and by including that impossibility in its own provisional or even aleatory movements.[11]

As a critical strategy, then, narrative mortality is an interpretation of texts that mortifies ostensible "meanings" in order to grasp their meaninglessness as semantic energy.

Cinematic mortification refers to the killing of the "eternal present tense" of cinematic realism, and is both an act of critical viewing and a stylistic effect of filmmaking. Narrative mortality refers to the effect of mortification on the construction of desire and temporality in narrative cinema. I will argue that it allows for forms of desire other than those institutionalized in patriarchal commodity culture to emerge: forms of historical temporality other than those closed by the unified subject or heterosexual couple. It allows cinematic narrative to move beyond the pleasure of "meaning" and toward other pleasures that lie beyond representation, beyond the end of the film and the known limits of history.

A familiar closure device in narrative film is the montage of images that precedes, follows, or is intercut with a character's death. The images, drawn from the narrative that has just unfolded, effectively bind the viewer's memory with the character's summing up of his or her life at the moment of death. Another conventional means of achieving this is the familiar narrative structure that opens with the death to which the narrative will return.[12] These are only two of the more familiar ways in which, at the end of a film, death has an ostensible authorization of "meaning," uniting the film's imagery into a single figuration of identity.

If the threat of death is a threat of disappearance, loss, and absence, the disavowal of death is a confirmation of presence, mastery, and meaning. Narrative mortality involves the return of the repressed fear of death, often in the form of excessive violence, outside of the parameters of "meaning," outside the existential quest for meaning. The sight of the corpse, as well as the corporeality of film — its materiality and historicity — become markers of the transience of history and the impermanence of both the "self" and the present tense.

The allegorical historiography of narrative mortality understands the textual form of history to be not only imagistic, but structural, giving shape to temporal imagination. To argue that history takes textual form in the various relations between death and ending is not to say that history is an "absent cause" of textuality.[13] The text itself must be understood as historical, as should its interpretation, and yet the methodology of allegorical criticism presented in *The Political Unconscious* remains a valuable means of negotiating historical determination and textual openness. Jameson's three stages of criticism take the critic from (1) the "act" of the text, the way that it articulates social contradictions, through (2) its status as a socially consumed "ideologeme," to (3) the identification of an ideology of form. Jameson's methodology provides an excellent model for the different levels on which narrative mortality operates as a cultural, textual, and critical phenomenon.

The Denial of Death

As a symbolic act, the representation of death in film upholds the law of the text: the believability of the image. Insofar as this belief depends on the denial of the film's celluloid status, its twenty-four-frames-a-second "mortal" state, the illusion of reality sustains itself through a strict censorship of this reminder. The denial of death is likewise a cornerstone of social institutions and practices. The contemporary denial of death is coextensive with the depletion of mythical assurances of its meaningfulness. In so many stories about victims and criminals, this meaninglessness has been codified as failure in a culture devoted to "progress."[14]

Philippe Ariès has identified five grand historical variations in the Western, Christian world in which fear and denial emerge only toward the end of the eighteenth century. By the nineteenth century, "society no longer tolerates the sight of things having to do with death, including the sight of the dead body or weeping relatives. The bereaved is crushed between the weight of his [sic] grief and the weight of the social prohibition."[15] By the late twentieth century, this contradiction has taken on the monstrous proportions of medical technology and media violence that push the mortal body and the rhetoric of mourning out of the realm of the visible.[16]

The displacement of death into discourses of excess and hysteria is a familiar strategy of melodrama, a narrative form that was refined on the nineteenth-century stage and institutionalized in Hollywood film. The "denial of death" also gives rise to existential notions of mortality as a failure of mankind to "tame" or be reconciled with nature. Ernst Becker argues that the repression of the fear of death is a repression of humanity's "creatureliness," or mortal participation in nature. For him, the denial of death is the primary stimulant of creative consciousness, the motive force behind heroism and genius in Western culture.[17] In this mind/body theory of mortality, confrontation with death is only meaningful within the convention of denial.[18]

The "denial of death" is a model of repression and liberation not unlike that which Michel Foucault has analyzed in terms of sexuality in the nineteenth century.[19] A new theory of mortality is only possible through the deconstruction of the conventions of denial. Today, in the medical industry as well as the printed and visual mass media, we have an obsession with death that corresponds to the confessionals and institutional regulations of the Victorians regarding sex, and likewise challenges any theory of its repression. Today sexuality is represented fairly freely, and death (actual as opposed to enacted) is the stuff of pornography.[20] It is hidden in the sociologists' meticulous counts of murder on prime-time TV as much as it is in the snuff film. Alongside the "pornography of death" is the legitimized discourse of its denial and obfuscation.

The taboos that mark the discourse of death are symptomatic of the way that its denial authorizes forms of empowerment. In "The Ideology of Death," Herbert Marcuse argues that "ontological necessity" has been historically grafted onto biological inevitability to the point at which the natural, organic, and individual event of dying has been entirely "appropriated":[21]

> Death is an institution and a value: the cohesion of the social order depends to a considerable extent on the effectiveness with which individuals comply with death as more than a natural necessity; on their willingness, even urge to die many deaths which are not natural; on their agreement to sacrifice themselves and not to fight death "too much." ... The established civilization does not function without a considerable degree of unfreedom; and death, the ultimate cause of all anxiety, sustains unfreedom.[22]

In Marcuse's model, the teleology of capitalism, no less than philosophical existentialism and theological redemption, alienates individuals from their own deaths. What Marcuse refers to as "ontology" and "essential necessity" in the context of the metaphysical appropriation of death is most basically the way death is situated in discourse—its various signifiers. Death is rendered as failure and sacrifice only through the narratives in which it is inscribed; narrative is the means by which Thanatos is "appropriated" by social forces. In this sense, mortality poses a major threat to medical technology and the ideology of progress that subtends it, as recent euthanasia debates have suggested.[23]

The premise of Marcuse's theory is a theology of freedom, a utopian conception of Thanatos in a nonrepressive society, and his neo-Freudanism ultimately falls to Foucault's critique of the "repressive hypothesis."[24] Although it would be easy to dispense with Marcuse's thought in a post-Marxist and post-Christian world as illusory countercultural rhetoric of the 1960s, the concept of utopia is important to retain as a sociohistorical form of desire. Jameson endorses a "hermeneutics of freedom" as a historical dialectic that "keeps alive the possibility of a world qualitatively distinct from this one and takes the form of a stubborn negation of all that is."[25] Utopian forms of historical desires were in any case vital to the aesthetics and politics of many New Wave filmmakers.

The symbolic act of death as closure mystifies utopian thinking in the form of memory, grounding the idea of utopia in the "memory of gratification"[26] (e.g., the matching of opening and closing imagery in film narrative). Its force is due to the combined mythic paradises of maternal and Edenic pleasures. Mortality is, of course, not "liberated" from discourse by the binding of Thanatos to Eros in originary myths of the mother or nature, any more than it is in Marcuse's Marxism. But even if there can be no freedom from discourse or cultural forms, as Foucault insists, I believe there can be a discourse of desire that is also a discourse of mortality. Narrative mortality is the allegorical means of wrenching memory and the structure of historical difference implicit in utopian thought from their mystification. It is not only made available in the fragmentation of narrative closure, but is written across the co-optation of desire in the commodity culture of postindustrial society.

As Marcuse's liberationist sociology was written within the historical specificity of the postwar "culture industry," Walter Benjamin's historiography was a response to the emergence of consumer culture in nineteenth-century Paris and the rise of fascism in Europe between the world wars. Benjamin's theories of allegory and mortification provide the means by which utopian ideation might be separated from the technocratic myths of progress and development that became reified in the twentieth century. In the world exhibitions of the last century, Benjamin identifies the commodity as a "dead object." As the exchange value of commodities was privileged over their use-value, the utopian element of industrial culture becomes legible as fashion, which, he says, "represents the rights of the corpse":[27] material objects allegorically separated from their symbolic function.

Benjamin's theory of history involves a grasping of mortality, not in response to its cultural repression and disavowal but to its mystification; he provides the critical tools for releasing the death drive and the power of repetition from their symbolic function in representation. Whereas repression theories of mortality are based on an ontological distinction between nature (the mortal body) and consciousness, Benjamin's theory of mortality recognizes their common forms of memory and desire. Utopian imagination, which Marcuse conceives of as a liberation from the closure of mortality, is for Benjamin a desire for the closure of mortality along with the knowledge of its impossibility. His emphasis on fashion, novelty, and commodity fetishism locates this structure of utopian imagination squarely within the phantasmagoria of modernity, of which the cinema is emblematic. The revolutionary potential of dialectical images, the shock of awakening from the dream of technology, involves not a memory of gratification but the memory of transformation, transience, and change.

As a symbolic act, the representation of death in film has two basic parameters, the political and the aesthetic, which will be introduced in chapters 1 (Lang) and 2 (Wenders), respectively. They come together through the themes of "believability" and denial. In Lang's *Beyond a Reasonable Doubt,* death will be seen to be legislated by textual and judicial paternal authorities, taking place offscreen, between frames, and just outside the frame. As the sign of censorship and repression, death figures divisively, separating individuals from society and its discourses of containment. The exclusion of the criminal/communist/delinquent from "society" is accomplished in this narrative through a radical repression of subjective desire in the repetitions of the status quo. Social and textual contradictions between viewer and text, individual and society, are apparently resolved in the instantiation of death as closure in *Beyond a Reasonable Doubt.* But at the same time, because the believability of the image is placed in question, a mortal gap is opened that lays bare the implicit strategies of containment.

A similar "act" will be identified in Oshima's film *Boy,* in which death mediates the individual's social construction and negotiates the believability of the social order. In the different perceptual apparatus of *Boy,* though, and within the different politics of representation in Japan, the inscription of subjectivity through the phenomenology of vision has a different status. Narrative mortality in this film yields a discovery of absence, not as negation but as a subject of and in discourse, and a means of resisting the process of interpellation that suicide in Japan traditionally embodies.

Oshima's protagonists learn how to die, and in doing so, their deaths become a mark of resistance produced by narrative mortality.

The enactment of narrative mortality, then, is not simply the repression of a narrative pleasure principle but its transformation. It articulates a discourse of power (death as closure) that, following Foucault, produces its opposite. In both *Beyond a Reasonable Doubt* and *Boy,* narrative mortality is articulated through repetition and stasis, specifically through the incorporation of film stills, freeze-frames, and photographic images into the film's flow. Death in film narrative can therefore be a "symbolic enactment" of the social contradictions of authoritarian societies: Lang's cold war America and Oshima's postwar Japan. In each of these films, a distance is acquired from the systems and structures of power, precisely through the production of an allegory of narrative mortality.

The aesthetic aspect of the symbolic action of narrative mortality is closely related to the photographic basis of the cinema and the believability of the cinematic illusion. In Wenders's two films about filmmaking, death negotiates the myth of authorship in postmodernity, working out the contradiction between the temporally and historically finite status of the film object and the subjective investment in the art object as an eternal vehicle of coherent identity. While the Bazinian paradox of "change mummified" is unpacked in *Lightning Over Water,* in *The State of Things* mortality is understood as a defining feature of narrative, irreparably separating fictional and documentary representation in the cinema. Death informs both realist styles, guaranteeing the "lie" of the former and the "truth" of the latter. The illusionist impression of reality in the cinema is, in this sense, narrative's disavowal of its own mortal condition as a series of discrete photographic images.

The Difference of Death

As a symbolic act, narrative mortality negotiates the contradictions between the coherent subject of "the artist" and the economic and mediated status of culture, but also between an eternal homogenous present tense and temporal heterogeneity. On the second interpretive level, as an "ideologeme" it represents these relationships in terms of loss. The director's "vision," Wenders's subjective investment in the profilmic, is sacrificed for narrative storytelling as a necessarily mediated endeavor. Wenders's loss of his romantic ideals of authorship to the industrial enterprise of filmmaking is articulated through the work of death in narrative. Narrative mortality, for Wenders, cuts film off from "life." The preservative ontology of the cinematic defense against death cannot be sustained in the age of mechanical reproduction, which inevitably situates the film text under the aegis of historical time.

On the level of cinematic representation, narrative mortality points to a lost ideal of transparency. This is perhaps most clear in Godard's and Wenders's relationships with film history and its promise of "total cinema." The struggle between narrativity and documentary realism in their work is an attempt to rescue cinematic transparency from its modernist debasement. Narrative mortality is the allegory of this possibility, insofar as it is at once a representation of time and of mediation. A sense of loss is absolutely central to the theories of both Bazin and Benjamin, and yet in Benjamin's and Godard's work it is oriented slightly differently than it is for Bazin and Wenders.

In the latter cases, it is specifically categories of subjectivity and identity that are represented as lost. For Bazin and Wenders, mortality and representation are the means by which consciousness is at once threatened and preserved in its ideal status as identity. For Wenders, especially, it seems to be fundamental to the existential preoccupations of a European "art cinema" of auteurs. However, the recovery of lost unities of subjectivity and society is equally crucial to the "thirst for redemption" that characterizes so much of American cultural production, as Rick Altman has argued for the film musical.[28] In the triumphant formation of the couple, society itself is redeemed as a utopian collectivity. Although the narrative figure of death is clearly a key signifier for the coupling of loss and promises of rebirth, in the work of Godard and Benjamin it also yields a critique of this ideology of loss, recovery, and return.

Benjamin's theory of allegory is not one of resurrection, but it implies the acquisition of a critical perspective from which to view lost unities. The work of both Godard and Oshima involves a recourse to the generic forms of popular culture as discourses of resistance. In the heteroglossia of *Cruel Story of Youth, Pierrot le fou,* and *Le Mépris,* various myths are "emptied out" and rendered inadequate, and yet the structure of the mythic imaginary is retained in narrative. Chief among these myths are those of romantic love, destiny, and heroism. In the Japanese context, especially, where suicide is mythically bound to both love and heroism, it is a complex structure that Oshima challenges. The final shots of these films, Godard's harmonious blue oceanscapes and Oshima's graphic fragmentation of narrative space, both function as allegories of redemption. They retain something of the promise of utopia in reserve, holding out the possibility that the death of the subject is the long-awaited death of the bourgeois subject, holding out, indeed, the possibility of thresholds.

As a threshold, death figures in narrative mortality as an ideologeme closely related to the theory of cultural loss that Jameson calls "ressentiment." A theory of loss and redemption, "ressentiment" binds morality to modernity in the isolation and relativity of the present against the divine right of the past.[29] Narrative mortality provides the discourse of resistance to "ressentiment": a threshold of discovery, on the brink of repetition, but also the threshold of cinematic representation. Catherine Clément describes the end of the opera as a "work of mourning,"[30] and leaving the movie theater involves a similar cathexis with the dead. Benjamin's understanding of allegory points to the fundamental relationship between this threshold that death represents, and the very process of representation.

As an ideologeme, the myth of total cinema is bound to the time of subjectivity, the "life" time that is mythically unified in and through death. Cinematic narrative mortality involves the *look* of time, but it has two faces, two appearances: the binding memory that brackets the time of the subject, the narrative, and the film from history, delimiting it as the *only* time; and an image of time as difference, in which the temporal index of memory links a multiplicity of times. Death as closure is mythic in Roland Barthes's semiological sense, "naturalizing" history by codifying death as language, as the form of closure: the means by which everything can return to whence it came. Narrative mortality, as a resistance to this mystification, recovers a historical sense of death outside language, risking perhaps a remystification of mortality as transience and change. Barthes in fact advocates such a strategy: "Truth to tell, the best weapon against myth is perhaps to mythify it in its turn, and to reproduce an *artificial myth*:

and this reconstituted myth will in fact be a mythology. Since myth robs language of something, why not rob myth?"[31]

Narrative mortality heralds the return of the repressed denial of death in order to redeem cinematic realism. Allegory, for Benjamin, is a discursive mobilization of the "fall" of language from symbolic representation. If film theory has been preoccupied with realism and its "other," allegory intercedes as a theory of ironic representation: realist discourse that knows itself to be dead. It can no longer deny its status as mechanical reproduction, but neither can it abandon the "real" of photographic indexicality. In this sense, narrative mortality runs parallel to "apparatus theory," mortifying the ideal spectator locked into the transcendental gaze of a subject without a body.

In apparatus theories of the cinema, the only locus of presence/ absence, lack and disavowal of lack, is sexual difference. Apparatus theory takes as its premise the privileged place of the phallus, which becomes the signifier of meaning, and castration the threat of meaninglessness.[32] However, if Lacanian theory is understood as existentialist as well as masculinist, the ideal subject is not only male but also mortal, and is that much closer to extinction. For Lacan, mortality is like the threat of castration in that it represents the subject's annihilation: "The phantasy of one's own death, of one's disappearance, is the first object that the subject has to bring into play in this dialectic [in the discourse of the Other]."[33] In his discussion of "the gaze," the difference between life and death is actually the foundation of signification, and only secondarily is it the phallus, which signifies this difference.[34]

Once we distinguish between the subject and the body, the mythic and the historical might also be wrenched apart. Teresa de Lauretis has described the project of semiotics as "a mapping of how the physical properties of bodies are socially assumed as signs, as vehicles for social meaning."[35] Narrative mortality is a means of shifting film-theoretical discourse away from the space of the subject to that of the body. One means of accomplishing this shift might be to conceptualize "the subject" as a mortal subject, with a correspondingly limited—as opposed to universal—relation to history. Although "the body" is typically mystified as feminine (as material support for male consciousness, and as the human reproductive link to nature), the mortal body is not gender-specific.

Hélène Cixous has argued that, because the otherness of woman is predicated on an epistemological dualism, it is as important for feminist theory to deconstruct the death drive of psychoanalysis as its phallocentrism. She speaks of "the couple" of patriarchal culture as a dizzying series of hierarchized oppositions in which "death is always at work," separating nature from culture and women from men. Meaning "only gets constituted in a movement in which one of the terms of the couple is destroyed in favour of the other."[36] Mortality and the threat of "decapitation and execution" are, for Cixous, the feminine counterpart to castration anxiety. It is imperative that women resist the economy of return and exchange that is predicated on loss, a loss that can only be a loss of life for women in patriarchy. They have nothing else to lose. Resistance consists of an "affirmation of difference" and the production of a textual body "without ending." "A feminist text goes on and on and at a certain moment the volume comes to an end but the writing continues and for the reader this means being thrust into the void."[37]

Given the maternal imagery of Benjamin's historiography, it would be a mistake to read him as a protofeminist,[38] and yet in conjunction with a feminist critique, his work might help theorize a historiography of the future. His theory of memory and his critique of progress may take the form of nostalgia, but they also involve a recognition that "there is not one moment that does not bring with it *its own* revolutionary possibility—it only wants to be defined as a specific one, namely as the chance for a totally new resolution in view of a totally new task."[39] Like Cixous's radical strategy of laughter, Benjamin advocates a "meeting of the forces of the mythical world with cunning and high spirits."[40] Cixous advocates a feminist praxis of taking up "the challenge of loss." As a hermeneutics of historical difference, narrative mortality does precisely this: it allegorizes loss as a form of historical necessity.

In shifting the emphasis of narratology from the pleasure principle to the death drive, and from the phallus to the body, there is a danger in fetishizing the body as yet another phallus. "Mortification," however, is very specifically a theory of the dead body, the corpse. Benjamin writes that the allegorization of the physis can only be carried through in all its vigour in respect of the corpse. And the characters of the *Trauerspiel* die, because it is only thus, as corpses, that they can enter the homeland of allegory. It is not for the sake of immortality that they meet their end, but for the sake of the corpse.[41]

The key difference between the corpse and the phallus, as privileged signifiers, is that the dead body is distinguished by its *lack* of symbolic unity. Its threat to cultural norms is precisely its status as an empty signifier of subjectivity, its designation of the void upon which the self is written. This is the cultural space across which theories of gender must be articulated, and the corporeality of the mortal signifier deauthorizes language and dismantles its phallic symbolic status.

This book is not about women's filmmaking, but about men's. In rethinking these filmmakers' existential anxiety as a problem of representation, the difficulty of representing desire repeatedly circulates around the bodies of women. The focus here is not, however, on this institutional victimization but on its effects on the (de)construction of male subjectivity as a discourse of desire. Reduced to allegories of fetishistic and scopophilic pleasures, the male gaze sees itself seeing in many of these films, in which desire is forced to renew itself in order to redeem cinematic vision. In the mortification of the male erotic gaze, a space is cleared for other forms of desire, which may yet include that of women.

In "What Is an Author?" Foucault claims that "where a work had the duty of creating immortality, it now attains the right to kill, to become the murder of its author."[42] It is not only the convention of antiheroism, but the very writerliness of modernist narrative by which masculinist subjectivity has performed its death throes. Maurice Blanchot has perhaps best eulogized this loss in such essays as "Literature and the Right to Death":

Death works with us in the world; it is a power that
humanizes nature, that raises existence to being.... But to die
is to shatter the world; it is the loss of the person, the
annihilation of being; and so it is also the loss of death, the
loss of what in it and for me made it death ... when I die, by
ceasing to be a man I also cease to be mortal, I am no longer

capable of dying, and my impending death horrifies me
because I see it as it is: no longer death, but the impossibility
of dying.[43]

We will see how this modernist fantasy informs a filmmaker like Wim
Wenders, and also how it can open up a space in cinematic representation through the mortification of the immortal "I." As an ideologeme of loss, narrative mortality is instrumental to the redemption of
desire in new discourses of identity.

The Excess of Closure

The threshold figured in narrative mortality is rarely actually crossed,
however, and the "look of time" is inevitably the time of a repetition
that goes nowhere. Memory secures the myth of progress from out-
stripping the limited teleology of capitalism, and the third stage of
interpretation, the "ideology of form," can be described as the spectacle for consumption that violent death is either transformed into
(in the case of news reports, snuff films, and documentaries) or produced as (in contemporary film and TV narratives). On this level of
interpretation, "formal processes" are grasped as "content in their
own right."[44] The commodification of the visible and the techniques
of visibility are crucial components of the ideology of the spectacle.
What Linda Williams has described as "the frenzy of the visible" in
the context of hard-core pornography compensates for the invisibility of female sexual pleasure.[45] The frenzy of violence likewise opens
up the possibility of resistance in its excessive overcompensation for
the unrepresentable, unknowable, and invisible event of death. And
yet, the potential of narrative mortality to open up the passage to a
different historiography is, more often than not, limited by the reify-
ing spectacle of violence.[46]

Allegory has a regressive tendency, which Benjamin identifies in
Baudelaire, whose "destructive impulse ... is nowhere interested in
getting rid of that which declines."[47] A similar tendency will be identified in the nostalgia of *Bonnie and Clyde* (1967), which involves a
resurrection of the image along with a mystification of the past. The
"progressive tendency of allegory," on the other hand, articulated
imagistically in the baroque emblems of skeletons and skulls, is to

smash false appearances, to "transfigure" and bring into visibility new possibilities of the material world. For Benjamin, it was the commodification of this material world that had emptied historical experience of its desire by designating the new as the always-the-same.[48]

In the second part of Benjamin's century, the politics of visibility and commodification have converged in the form of the spectacle. As Guy Debord put it in 1967, "The spectacle, as the present social organization of the paralysis of history and memory, of the abandonment of history built on the foundation of historical time, is the *false consciousness of time.*"[49] The difficulties encountered in a criticism of violence through its representation are amply demonstrated in *Bonnie and Clyde* and *The Wild Bunch* (1969), in which excess blood spills over into the *jouissance* of visual pleasure, and in *Nashville* it is precisely this circuit of the spectacle that is addressed. When the interpretive allegory of narrative mortality is short-circuited, and there is no spatial or temporal elsewhere besides the spectacle itself, the redemptive potential is overwhelmed by "the myth of resurrection." The closure of the spectacle is also a trap for historicity, closing off the possibility of social transformation. The allegory of narrative mortality is a means by which this commodification of history might be undone.

Benjamin's theory of allegory is not coincidentally based on baroque emblems and theater, and the "phantasmagorias" of late nineteenth-century Paris. The language of allegory finds its potential in the image world of mass culture. Narrative mortality is likewise most legible in the cinema in the challenge that death poses to visual representation, rendering signification a temporally fragmented process. We shall see how death in film can become a form of writing. Godard's tableaux of burning cars and strewn corpses in *Weekend* (1967) speak volumes about modernity, precisely in their artificiality. In *Prénom Carmen* (1983), terrorists and their victims are felled by automatic rifles, only to immediately rise and rejoin the melee. Death in fiction film always belongs to the regime of the fake, marking the very threshold of the "illusions of reality" and the myth of "total cinema": the pathos and irony of representation.

Narrative mortality may in fact be an imaginary solution to the "contagion of violence" that characterizes postwar history. While the image of apocalypse approximates the instantaneity of death as an allegory of discovery, it is also an allegory of necessity. The coincidence of death and closure is a ritual of desire, embodying the pleasure of return and the myth of fate, whereas accidental violence isolates the moment of death in historical time. Death in film has the potential of radical ambiguity precisely because it can encompass both historiographies at once and can disperse violence into a dialectic of difference and the same. The history of the future is a discourse of necessity divorced from destiny and, as will be seen in *Le Mépris,* the representation of accidental, "nonnatural" death can be an allegory of destiny, a representation of history as fragmented rather than holistic time. Its necessity is guaranteed by the natural history of decay rather than the myth of fate.

Benjamin enables us to acquire historical and critical distance from the classical thematics of fate and destiny that tend to bind form to content, and meaning to structure. As "the leader," death becomes the dynamic sign of historical transience. Narrative structures of origins and development, growth and inevitability, maturity and decadence are modeled on the organicity of the human body. The body, as the index of these structures, is in the process disavowed by the "eternal" truths that such discourse authorizes. The sense-making mechanism of death as closure — the expectations of meaning that are always anticipated, if not always delivered, by narrative — is above all a cultural strategy of coping with the contingency of daily existence. The surplus of unordered detail that is history without discourse is also the story without ending and the (dead) body without an identity. The decay of the present tense is redeemed in narrative mortality as a historiography of memory and transience.

Narrative mortality is a recovery of the body in narrative cinema, and an illumination of the fragments of history perceptible in the ruined myths of cinematic desires. We shall see how cinematic violence potentially redeems the body from its mystification, and how violence "mortifies" cinematic representation. Equally important to the present study are the aesthetics of realism. Narrative mortality is a discourse of temporality that takes very specific forms in the cinema as a medium that quite literally "takes" time. If the isomorphism of narrative and mortality has conventionally assumed a teleological representation of time, the dismantling of this relationship produces forms of temporality other than the progressive historiography of modernism. Temporal aesthetics are therefore as crucial to the variable relations between death and closure in the cinema as are the mythologies of desire.

In what is perhaps the most systematic treatment of narrative closure, Frank Kermode distinguishes between *chronos*— "passing time" or "waiting time" —and *kairos,* which is "the time of the novelist" or "the season, a point in time filled with significance, charged with a meaning derived from its relation to the end."[50] Using the model of a clock's ticktock, he says that narrative has "to maintain within that interval following *tick* a lively expectation of *tock*" because "all such plotting presupposes and requires that an end will bestow upon the whole duration and meaning" (p. 46). Insofar as time is equated with mortality in Kermode's model, it is based on an ontology of death. He notes that it was the "divine plot" of Christ that accomplished the transition from *chronos* to *kairos* as the dominant sense of temporality in Western culture, establishing "the End" as that which "changes all and produces, what in relation to it is the past" (p. 47).

The necessity of mortality is, for Kermode, constitutive of "the human mind." The limitations of his theory, belied in his denunciation of Robbe-Grillet and the American Beat writers, as against his valorization of *La Nausée,* are due to his assumption that contingency, which he equates with reality, is insufficient for narrative fiction. Contingency must always be balanced or dialectically conjoined with form, "a humanly needed shape or structure."[51] Kermode's idealist teleology of form precludes consideration of the durational strategies of "waiting" that informs so much postwar international cinema, especially Bresson, Antonioni, Ozu, Tati, Wenders, Hou, and Akerman. Within this range of "documentary" and real-time aesthetics, the mortality of the human body takes on a materiality, a corporeality, quite remote from the sense-making mechanisms of dramatic closure.

As Roland Barthes suggests in *Camera Lucida,* photographic images are themselves a form of mortality,[52] a death that is easily "hidden" in the cinematic appropriation of photography. The mortality implicit in photography is often exploited in international postwar cinema as a means of countering the teleology of Kermode's notion of narrative. Although narrative mortality is produced within narrative structures common to other media besides cinema, its allegorical potential derives from the nature of cinematic specificity and the specific relations between image and historical time constitutive of cinematic representation.[53] The indexicality of cinematic representation involves an order of temporality that is absent from literary representation, a difference between the time of shooting and that of viewing. This is one of many orders of difference that cannot be "closed" without ideological consequences.

The modernist tendency toward open-endedness, which Kermode describes as the "modern apocalypse," suggests that "our age" (*The Sense of an Ending* was written in 1965) is one of "eternal transition, perpetual crisis": "The fiction of transition is our way of registering the conviction that the end is immanent rather than imminent; it reflects our lack of confidence in ends, our mistrust of the apportioning of history to epochs of this and that" (p. 101). The analyses of films made between 1956 and 1982 should clarify the historical parameters of this form of apocalypticism, but significantly, despite the "lack of confidence" during this period, endings become endowed with an increased burden of meaningful meaninglessness. Both "the sense of an ending" and the representation of death retain a certain authority despite the relentless deconstruction of classical, conventional, and homogeneous textual practices.

The emblematic "open" endings of Antonioni's *L'Avventura* (1960), *Blow-Up* (1967), and *The Passenger* (1975) are exemplary of the pressure of mortality in open-ended narratives. Death may not necessarily "close" a narrative but in innumerable films, including *Paisà* (Rossellini, 1946), *Kiss Me Deadly* (Aldrich, 1955), *Accatone* (Pasolini, 1961), *Mouchette* (Bresson, 1967), *McCabe and Mrs. Miller* (Altman, 1971), *Fox and His Friends* (Fassbinder, 1974), and *Being There* (Ashby, 1979), it "opens up" a text by way of closure. One of the aims of this project is to compensate for the inadequacy of the terms "open" and "closed" as descriptive aesthetic vocabulary.

Using mainly David Bordwell's *Narration in the Fiction Film* as the basis for a formal model, Richard Neupert has distinguished four categories of film endings that he claims to be exhaustive and to correspond to four cinematic types, or modes of production: the Closed Text (classical Hollywood), the Open Story ("art cinema"), the Open Discourse (theoretically possible but practically/historically nonexistent), and the Open Text (avant-garde).[54] By maintaining the story/discourse separation, however, Neupert cannot address the ideological consequences of the simultaneity of "resolved" story and invisible discourse.[55] He cannot address the effects that discourse has on the story it tells, or vice versa, the effect that an inconclusive story might have on an apparently illusionist narrative voice (its potential to "crack it apart").

The "effects" of discourse are precisely the parameters of an ideology of form. The open/closed distinction becomes somewhat irrelevant if we introduce the idea of an excess of closure, which is perhaps the most appropriate description of narrative mortality in international postwar cinema. Whether this excess takes the form of meaningfulness (*Citizen Kane,* 1941) or meaninglessness (*L'Avventura,* 1960), beauty (*Imitation of Life,* 1959) or ugliness (*Eraserhead,* 1978), the difficulties of closure tend to be displaced onto a discourse of visibility and spectacle.

If the apocalyptic mythology that Kermode identifies as constitutive of narrative closure has taken on spectacular proportions, it is not incidental to the violent potential of the medium itself: its rhetoric of shooting, cutting, and "putting in the can." The representation of violent death in film constitutes a special crisis of believability, a threshold of realism and its own critique. Enacted death, bodily violence, and corporeality (such as surgical operations) are privileged points at which realism makes a firm break with the real, as the bullet-ridden corpse is at once the height of artifice and of horror. When the art of the makeup and special-effects departments is assimilated by the filmmaker, the point at which "document" and image part company is both championed and obfuscated.

The spectacle of violence produces a body in excess of subjectivity, identity, and meaning. It is an actor's body, but also the textual body of the film that is potentially in excess of the aspiration to realism. The excessive closure of international postwar cinema delineates a precarious balance, a split desire for meaningful containment and a desire to transcend the known limits of history. The notion of narrative mortality that will be developed in this book is, in keeping with the work of Walter Benjamin, unapologetically idealist in its emphasis on redemption, renewal, and social transformation. It is a historiography of transience, and to this extent is grounded in the materiality of the cinematic signifier and the indexicality of the cinematic referent.

As a double pleasure, or as a potential crisis, the representation of death in film is an uncanny mixture of fear and pleasure, the strange and the familiar. It is the fundamental ambiguity of the uncanny that gives narrative mortality, as an ideology of form, the potential of fantasy, transgression, and shock. The coincidence of image and reality that occurs in the representation of *actual* death is a harbinger of mortality, marking the transience of history. But it is also, at the same time, a means of disavowing this recognition. Unlike the still photograph, once historical specificity is taken up in moving images it is reanimated and revived, and death is effectively denied. *Enacted* death that is believable thus fixes the fiction film's "performance of time," which is what Stephen Heath describes as the "crime of the good film."[56]

Film History

In the 1960s, with the simultaneous development of mass-media criticism and social activism, the uncanny parallel between the shooting of guns and the shooting of cameras became a discursive axis of the rhetoric of violence. For Fernando Solanas and Octavio Gettino in Argentina in 1971, the equation of gun and camera is crucial to a conception of "guerrilla cinema," a politicized "Third Cinema" in which both filmmaking and film viewing are modes of political praxis. Theirs is a metaphor of violence, perhaps, but one in which death is situated as the "other" of bourgeois/neocolonial representation.[57]

In Michael Powell's *Peeping Tom* (1960), on the other hand, the alignment of camera and weapon is erotically charged in their directionality and intentionality. The female body is overdetermined as the "other" of the patriarchal social, psychic, and cinematic apparatuses. The scopic and physical violation of women in *Peeping Tom* oversteps the limits of realist representation, and the phallic gaze is finally mortified.[58] The "mortifying gaze" of the rifle sights or the armed camera of *Peeping Tom* situates the perceived, the seen, the gazed at as being in one's discourse.[59] When the apparatus emerges as a discursive operation, a mere allegory of empowerment, the threatened violence becomes a violence of representation, and a potential political tool.

The fatal shooting and the mortifying gaze are points in cinema at which the "narratological converges with the grammatological," once the apparatus is taken to be the structure of filmic grammar. The spectacle of violence, in its combination of pleasure and pain, charges the phenomenological difference between viewer and spectacle with the power of discourse stripped to its most visible form. The otherness of the object seen and the otherness of the violated subject indicts the transcendental subject of vision within the causality of desire. The exclusion of the spectator is aligned with the exclusion of the dying person from the representable world. Violence draws one line between life and death and between spectator and spectacle, a line that is at once final and intangible, irreversible and fluid, a rhetoric of difference and sameness that is also the logic of desire.

During the 1960s and 1970s, as film studies developed as a field of study, "the apparatus" began to be sketched out as a mechanism of ideological control. At the same time, filmmakers began to articulate various forms of sexual and political desires within self-conscious forms of cinematic representation. Death figures as a key narrative event in many of these films, as an articulation of loss, despair, and failure. But at the same time it is the vehicle of an antiauthoritarian challenge to the discourses of control. And we shall see that this occurs as a function of representation as much as, and in concert with, narrative event. The mortification of the apparatus produces a spectator who is beside himself or herself, doubled as the constructed subject of narrative desire and the mortal, historical body outside the text.

Narrative mortality is a means of engaging with narrative closure in such a way that spectatorship is accounted for as a pluralist, active, and political activity. The art of "mortification" is a lesson learned from filmmakers working within specific sociohistorical contexts, with a range of different motives, interests, and concerns to articulate. The critical discourse on the New Wave cinemas has always stressed the Brechtian alienation effects, which encourage spectators to "participate," or at least formulate their own readings. More recent discourse about spectatorship in the cinema has tended to historicize and localize the plurality of readings that *any* text potentially inspires. If the cinema of the 1960s and 1970s paved the way for this crisis of meaning, it may also provide some clues as to the textual determinants of an "other" theory of spectatorship.

This book may be about a cinema of crisis, but it is not about apocalyptic historiography. The films have been chosen and analyzed in such a way as to understand "crisis" as a threshold of history: an articulation of change, transience, and transformation. By understanding the complexity of the relationship between mortality and narrativity, we may be able to transcend the mythology of loss implicit in the notion of crisis and be able to appreciate what is gained in terms of historiography and representation. The imminence of apocalypticism, the sense of impending catastrophe, takes on an immanence of historical import once narrativity recognizes itself as historical. In the New Wave cinemas, "the fiction of transition" is not a formalism but is embedded in social criticism. Although the New Wave core of this book consists only of Godard and Oshima, in the films of many of their international contemporaries (e.g., Pasolini, Rocha, Fassbinder, Shinoda, Truffaut) narrative mortality emerges as a politics of redemption and a desire for social transformation, articulated within the terms of specific cultural concerns.

The limits of the New Wave cinemas stretch deep into film history. If intertextuality is fundamental to these filmmakers' revisionist projects, many of their techniques can be traced to the cinema that preceded them. In Weimar cinema, in French poetic realism, and in the silent American "art" cinema (e.g., *Broken Blossoms* [1919] and *Greed* [1925]), one can see death becoming more than a form of narrative closure, but it is not until the emergence of independent cinema in the wake of film noir that it becomes legible as a politics of representation. It may be argued that, since *The Electrocution of an Elephant* (1903) and the *Execution of Mary Queen of Scots* (1895), real and enacted death have been a mainstay of cinematic language.

The work of Dreyer, Bresson, and Bergman provides further evidence of the pervasiveness of mortality as a cinematic discourse. These directors' preoccupation with death may have had a great influence on the New Wave, but mortality only becomes a discourse of history and representation once their existential and religious thematics have been exhausted. As Stanley Kubrick demonstrates in *Dr. Strangelove*, the pleasures of war were dangerously eroticized in cold war visual culture. After the Second World War, visual discourses of power and pleasure entered art cinema as allegories of mortality, having lost their "innocence" to the visual knowledge of war (e.g., John Houston's *Battle of San Pietro* [1945]).

Although the textual analyses in this book will not follow a historical chronology, it will become clear that the critical gesture of mortification becomes increasingly irrelevant over the twenty-five years it covers. The difference between *Beyond a Reasonable Doubt* in 1956 and *The State of Things* in 1982 is a difference between a cinema that is unable to articulate its anxieties other than "unconsciously" and one that incessantly and consciously performs its own mortification and therapy. Wenders in fact dramatizes the very theory of narrative mortality himself in *Lightning Over Water* and *The State of Things*. It may even be argued that he takes modernist cinema to a limit that he himself has been unable to go beyond in his subsequent work. Narrative mortality might therefore be periodized as a threshold of the postmodern, a transitional allegory that may date as far back as 1941 in *Citizen Kane* and that continues to be legible in a film such as Derek Jarman's *Edward II* (1991). Through the strategy of anachronism, Jarman deploys seventeenth-century dramatic technique in a melancholic elegy to AIDS in gay culture.

Between Lang and Wenders we find the Brechtian cinema of Godard and Oshima, as well as post-Vietnam American genre revision, both of which treat myth, fate, and narrativity as national and historical discourses. Violence figures in these cinemas as an apocalyptic allegory of history. If narrative mortality is the interpretation of this allegory, it may be perceived as being somewhat specific to the twenty-five years of this study. However, beyond the limits of the New Wave cinemas, in the "ultraviolence" of the 1980s and 1990s, narrative mortality has been intensified and concentrated in a very different mode of international independent cinema. In the conclusion, I will examine the more fully allegorical cinema of David Lynch and Peter Greenaway, for whom realism and violence are more radically separate. In the two serial-killer films that I will look at, *Henry: Portrait of a Serial Killer* (1986) and *Man Bites Dog* (1990), violence is more systematically stylized, and believability is no longer an issue of morality, politics, or representation. In this postmodern cinema, the threshold of narrative mortality virtually disappears.

At the other extreme, before 1956 one can find numerous Hollywood films that lend themselves to mortification. Douglas Sirk's melo-dramas, Anthony Mann's Westerns, films noirs, the films of Nicholas Ray and Sam Fuller—all may be read as allegories of narrative mor-tality, engaging in genres that are just on the edge of losing their credibility. Although *Beyond a Reasonable Doubt* cannot be con-strued as representative of this rich period of Hollywood history, it will be considered in the context of *Cahiers du Cinéma* film criti-cism and cold war America.

The most familiar signifier of narrative mortality may in fact be the invocation of "rosebud" at the end of *Citizen Kane* (Welles, 1941). Rosebud signifies Kane's identity by closing it, completing the circle of his life, and at the same time, rosebud is only a sign on a sled, a sign that fails to suture the wound of death, and fails to give mean-ing to either the life or the film. It merely signifies the attempt, coin-cident with the end.[60] *Citizen Kane* is neither the first nor the last film to represent such an ambivalence, although it is a tendency far more prevalent in postwar than prewar filmmaking. Among the many stylistic and narrative disruptions of Hollywood film of the forties[61] that are announced in *Citizen Kane,* we have to include an ambiva-lence about the security of the coincidence of death and closure. It may even be argued that such ambiguity formed the backbone of RKO production throughout the 1940s, right up until the studio's final production, *Beyond a Reasonable Doubt.*

The limits of the New Wave cinemas can be delineated through the theory of "ressentiment," the articulation of the modern in ethical terms, which enters cinema most emphatically after the Second World War and begins to be recognized as such in the mid-1950s. The loss of affirmative mythical structures unleashes a violence that was once contained. In the eradication of a fixed morality, violence acquires a new expressive capacity, as the *Cahiers du Cinéma* critics recognized in the mid-1950s. But even for the *Cahiers* critics, film noir involved a mise-en-scène of violence, a spectacular manifestation of social dis-solution, a revolution of the image:

> Violence has no other purpose, once the ruins of conventions
> are reduced to dust, than to establish a state of grace, a void,
> in the midst of which the heroes, completely unfettered by
> any arbitrary constraints, are free to pursue a process of self-
> interrogation, and to delve deep into their destiny.[62]

As their criticism was for the most part unconcerned with lived history, or any determinants beyond the text and its auteur, so also was their violence contained within the limits of the screen. It was resituated and made safe as the prerogative of authentic heroism and filmmaking. It remained authorized as destiny. Twenty-five years later, the secret desires of heroic and antiheroic identity may survive as allegorical discourses of social repression (e.g., *Boyz 'n the Hood* [Singleton, 1991], *Malcolm X* [Lee, 1992], *Menace II Society* [Hughes Brothers, 1993]), but the "natural history" informing genres of romance and destiny has long since been debased.

Godard may well be said to emerge as the focal point of this study for several reasons. The parallels between his project and Benjamin's—or, more precisely, Benjamin's Baudelaire—are striking. They serve to underline how Godard figures the end of cinematic modernism. His cynicism, however, on the brink of the postmodern, grasps the loss of cinematic "innocence" as the threshold of historical redemption. Although the obsession with Godard in film studies has by now fortunately waned, it is time to return more soberly to the politics of representation embedded in his early, genre-inflected films. An appreciation of the fakeness of violence and death in narrative film is one of the ways that Godard mortifies the auratic experience of classical Hollywood cinema. In Godard's films of the early 1960s, narrative mortality lies within the fissures between classical romance and a modernist contempt for symbolic, realist representation. The excessive violence of the American cinema of the late 1960s and early 1970s does not quite challenge the believability of the image, and thus limits belief to the visible. If narrative mortality is motivated by the belief in a different future, based in the memory of a different past, it is invoked in *Bonnie and Clyde* (1967), *The Wild Bunch* (1969) (both discussed in chapter 5), and *Nashville* without its radical potential being realized.

It is through Benjamin's diverse body of work that the method and the subject of this project come together. The theory of history as transience, the effect on culture of photographic representation, and Benjamin's hermeneutic method of criticism are all "theological" endeavors. Derived from Cabalist scholarship, his method searches "for hidden meanings that could not have been known at the time of their writing and rejects the historicist approach of interpreting texts in terms of authorial intent."[63] The relationship of this veritable archaeological method to photography is best characterized by his quotation of André Monglod:

> The past has left images of itself in literary texts that are comparable to those which light imprints on a photosensitive plate. Only the future possesses developers active enough to bring these plates out perfectly.[64]

In the allegory of narrative mortality, from the perspective of the last decade of the twentieth century, the past appears as a history of dead desires, attracting memory like a magnet to its fragmentary residues subsisting in film narrative. As a redemptive form of criticism, narrative mortality will be read as the "writing" of death in *a* history of cinematic representation. If death "itself" escapes representation, narrative mortality, like the apocryphal flashing of one's life before one's eyes ("like a film") at the moment of death, is the allegorical compensation for that lack. Once that lack is conceived as an allegory for other historical/moral/social/sexual "lacks," an allegorical vertigo ensues. Narrative mortality may be simply a rhetorical means of halting that vertigo with a name.

ONE

BEYOND PLEASURE
Lang and Mortification

● ————————————————————————

Our own death is indeed unimaginable, and whenever we make the
attempt to imagine it we can perceive that we really survive as
spectators. — SIGMUND FREUD[1]

Death has acquired a certain authority in narrative cinema as it endows film after film with a weighty burden of meaning. However, death can endow cinematic narrative with another kind of authority, one that extends beyond representation to the historical "real" of its production and reception. When Walter Benjamin refers to the authority of death for the storyteller, he makes a distinction between novelistic and storytelling narrative forms. In the "novelistic" mode, the individual reader warms his/her "shivering life with a death that he reads about."[2] For the storyteller, on the other hand, death is the sign of the transposition of history into narrative. It anchors the story in a reality that extends far beyond the time and place of its telling, and limits the narrator to the memory of others' deaths. Whereas the " 'meaning of life' is really the center about which the novel moves"

31

(p. 99), the storyteller's authority derives from the fact that a person's "real life" "first assumes transmissible form at the moment of death" (p. 94).

Benjamin's distinction may not be immediately applicable to cinematic representation, which always separates the story from its teller. However, it offers a model for the deconstruction of the binding process of mortality in cinematic narrative. Benjamin's "novelistic" evokes the closure of representation enacted by death, the closure of temporality, subjectivity, and ideology, the eternal present tense of the universal subject of narrative identity. Narrative mortality, on the other hand, like "storytelling," refers to the discursive rendering of death as a sign of historical transience, an undoing of the novelistic that takes place in texts themselves, but also in the reading of texts. Both death as closure and narrative mortality are "ideologies of form," the former in the service of the status quo, the latter in the interests of historical change and transformation.

This chapter will address the emergence of narrative mortality within the classical Hollywood style as the "cracking" of the authorities of closure and realism. It might be considered a transposition from the "novelistic" to "storytelling," which occurs as much by way of the film criticism of *Cahiers du Cinéma* as through an oppositional film practice. Fritz Lang's *Beyond a Reasonable Doubt,* a film that takes authority and death as its central figures, was described by Jacques Rivette in 1957 as "the antithesis of entertainment." Referring to Lang as a "storyteller" in a review entitled "The Hand," Rivette describes it as an antihumanist reduction of guilt and innocence to "mere appearances."[3] The analysis of *Beyond a Reasonable Doubt* will introduce the key themes of narrative mortality, situate them in relation to psychoanalytic apparatus theory, and illustrate their particular configuration within cold war American studio filmmaking.

Although one may find many of the techniques and effects of narrative mortality in films made before 1945, the allegory of narrative mortality is much more readable in the cinema after World War II. It emerges as a consequence of a great range of cultural transformations indirectly linked to international militarization and its global strategies of death and destruction. World War II constituted an overwhelming experience with death that caused many national cultures to reexamine some cherished principles and prejudices. Because of the institutionalized ideology of the Hollywood studio system, these shifts are writ larger in the American context, and ideological contradictions that surfaced all over the world may be most vivid within the American cinema.

The scope and scale of the war, and the diversity of its effects in different parts of the world and different social sectors, are large enough and heterogeneous enough to prevent mystifying World War II as a singular causal event. Fundamental changes to the economic structures of national film industries took place, along with developments in technologies of representation and communication (e.g., TV and lightweight cameras). Moreover, in the context of the shared experience of mourning and guilt over the European and Asian holocausts, film culture was "internationalized" in ways that exceeded the stereotyping of war films and the patriotism of national cinemas.

In addition to the emergence of several international film festivals, most notably Cannes, which was first held in 1946,[4] the discipline of film studies received an important boost in the work of André Bazin and *Cahiers du Cinéma*.[5] The extent to which these writers appreciated American and Italian film is well known, as is the role of their criticism in the subsequent Nouvelle Vague and radical European film praxis of the 1960s. What has not been recognized is the extent to which Bazin's film theory is based on a disavowal of mortality, on the one hand, or, on the other, the discourse of violence that the younger French critics and filmmakers appreciated in the films of their auteurist pantheons.

Bazin's theory of realism, which will be developed more extensively in chapter 2, is a theory of the preservation of subjectivity that he derives from Egyptian practices of mummification. Bazin's evolution of the history of the cinema is toward the fulfillment of the ancient desire to substitute the permanent image for the impermanent body.[6] The illusion of realist cinema on which his aesthetics are based, and to which his "great" directors aspire, is an illusion of immortality. Filmmakers such as Renoir, Welles, Rossellini, and Visconti preserve something of themselves, their vision and subjectivity, along with the objectivity of the photographed world, in the immortal permanence of celluloid. Bazin's writing on Italian neorealism, the key European film movement of the immediate postwar period, which he was largely responsible for critically endorsing and intellectually sponsoring outside of Italy, is informed by existentialist phenome-nology.[7] Read in conjunction with Bazin's essays on the ontology and history of the cinema, the Italian filmmakers' "art of lying" con-sists precisely in the substitution of an illusion of transcendence for the limitations of "authentic reality" and its mortal claims on subjectivity.[8]

Benjamin's conception of mortification offers us the repressed text of Bazin's historiography, and encourages us to grasp the disavowal of mortality for what it is: an ideological construction that holds his-tory prisoner in the grip of realism. Historiography as mortification proceeds by blasting open the myth of total cinema, but in such a way that the secret of historical difference hidden within Bazinian ontology might be released. Bazin's "sons" or successors at *Cahiers du Cinéma*,[9] the critics who were to become the French Nouvelle Vague and set off a flurry of highly innovative, politically and formally radical international filmmaking in the early 1960s, began the "blast-ing" process in their reevaluation of American and Italian cinema.

By the mid-1950s critics such as Eric Rohmer and Jacques Rivette had transformed Bazin's anxiety of mortality, the structuring absence of his film theory, into a discourse of mortality. Rivette, for example, in arguing that Rossellini's *Voyage in Italy* is a "metaphysical essay," an "incessant movement of seizure and pursuit," and a "conquest" of reality, notes also that the film involves "an intimate mortification of reality."[10] The mortifying potential of filmic discourse, once it becomes unmoored from an illusion of reality, is most explicit in the *Cahiers* writing on American film of the 1950s. The modernity of filmmakers such as Sam Fuller, Nicholas Ray, and Fritz Lang is consistently linked to the representation of violence. Rivette writes of these films that

> violence is never an end, but the most effective means of access, and those punches, weapons, dynamite explosions have no other purpose than to blast away the accumulated debris of habit, to create a breach—in brief, to open up the shortest roads.[11]

Throughout the *Cahiers* essays of the 1950s, violence is closely asso-ciated with a conception of "the modern" as something new and differ-ent. The fakeness of this violence, its departure from realist conven-tions, is not simply reflexive but points to the transience of Hollywood realism.

The modernity of American cinema for the *Cahiers* critics of the 1950s consisted in formal stylization and an excess of representation, which was a departure from the limited codification of Hollywood illusionism, but these formal traits were closely linked to narratives lacking a moral center. The famous *Cahiers* phrase, "Morality is a question of tracking shots,"[12] suggests that this discursive expressivity takes place within an unstable moral framework. Moullet, for example, says of Fuller:

> For many directors, movements of the camera are dependent on dramatic composition. Never so for Fuller, in whose work they are, fortunately, totally gratuitous.... At the end of *Steel Helmet,* for example, that slow tracking of the camera as, under the passionate bursts of machine-gun fire, the enemy soldiers sink to the ground in a rhythmic musical pattern.[13]

Violence remained linked to subjectivity for these critics—that of both the auteurs and the characters—but it was a freedom of expression that had its dangerous side: it existed in a void of conventions, both moral and discursive. Film noir, which emerged in the United States in the 1940s, was an especially rich terrain of discursive expressivity, excessive violence, and moral ambiguity in which anxiety-ridden male protagonists met their fates in shadow-torn environments of crime and dangerous women. But, as the example of *Beyond a Reasonable Doubt* should demonstrate, the very notion of fate demands some analysis in these films, which are strictly neither tragedies nor melodramas.

If the post-1968 *Cahiers du Cinéma* criticism is exemplified in the editorial essay on John Ford's *Young Mr. Lincoln,* violence remains a central critical category. Here it refers to the violence of representation—the excesses of textuality that belie the contradictions of idealized law and mythic historiography.[14] More recent criticism has returned to postwar American film as symptomatic of the contradictions that informed postwar American society. Genres such as the woman's film, the war film, and science fiction, along with film noir, Westerns, and family melodramas of the 1950s, display a certain amount of textual instability that points to the contradictions and nonconsensus of a society intent on denying its inner fragmentation. Dana Polan has described the films of the 1940s in terms of their discourses of power and paranoia, in which "power" refers to the unifying discourse of wartime unity, carried over into the homogenizing tendencies of consumer culture and mass media. The power of narrative closure and realist representation is, however, counterbalanced by an equally prominent anxiety provoked by the violence of war, cold war paranoia, the alienation of urbanization, the relative emancipation of women, and the difficulties of individualist expression within corporate capitalism and cold-war politics.[15]

Polan's historiography is indebted to Michel Foucault, for whom "power" is everywhere but originates nowhere except in the multiple discourses in which it is found. Power, in this theory, produces the possibility of its own resistance, its own misreading, which is how classical Hollywood cinema — once viewed as a repressive ideological state apparatus — can also be construed as the very writing on the wall of American hegemony. The failure of so many postwar Hollywood films to wrap things up, to completely close representation off from the vicissitudes of contingency, and their failure to contain their excesses, become legible as a resistance to the limitations and constrictions of the many codes that inform Hollywood cinema — codes of patriarchy, realism, and free enterprise as well as the generic myths of romance and destiny. "Narrative mortality" is, in this context, constitutive of the paranoia of postwar American film, produced within the terms of death as closure, the fatality that is the authority of death in narrative.

A Film That Does Not Believe in Itself

The textual and ideological contradictions of *Beyond a Reasonable Doubt* are, to some extent, grounded in the antagonism between Lang and RKO over the production of the film in 1956. Not only was it Lang's last American film, it was also the last film produced by RKO, and it represents well the aesthetic and moral exhaustion of some of the best studio filmmaking of the classical period. Lang himself says that he could not "make an audience love Dana Andrews for one hour and thirty-eight minutes[16] and then in the last two minutes reveal that he's really a son of a bitch and that the whole thing was just a joke. But thanks to my agent's mistake I was contractually bound to shoot the producer's original script."[17] Lang's solution to the contradictory script was, apparently, not to let us feel anything for Dana Andrews, who goes through the film like a somnambulist. Identification is made impossible and the viewer is forced not only to "read" the images, but to mortify the very idea of a hero, which is something quite different from a "loss of heroism."

Lang is an important figure for the *Cahiers du Cinéma* critics and New Wave filmmakers, and of course his émigré status partially explains his perspective on American social institutions. Authorship and auteurism, however, will be less important here than the analysis of the film's narrative structure and style. Although the film does not end with death (the final execution is not shown at all), nor include any remotely realist imagery of death, it "borrows its authority from death" by way of the conventions of the murder mystery, detective fiction, and film noir. Its treatment of the "issue" of capital punishment, moreover, aligns the absolute authority of the law with the authorization of images, resulting in a mutual mortification. It is crucial that this textual deconstruction takes place without ironic self-consciousness; its invalidation of transcendental ideals of justice and representation is constitutive of the historical context of its production.

The film becomes "a documentary of its time"[18] by relinquishing any claims to transparency, a conversion that takes place on several textual levels, of which the representation of death (and its repression) is central. Mortification, in Benjamin's *Origins of German Tragic Drama* (1928), refers most immediately to the conversion of symbol to allegory, the critical practice of distinguishing sign from signifier in such a way that the signifier is a ruin of the once unified sign.[19] For Benjamin, decay and transience are the emblems of a nonteleological sense of historical change. The impermanence of the present tense is registered in the failure of past, present, and future to be united in representation. It is a recognition of the historical differences embedded in representation. In his discussion of *Trauerspiel* (literally "Mourning Play" — the German title of Benjamin's book), Benjamin focuses on the memento mori and the theatrical tableaux of violent death. "In the very fall of man the unity of guilt and signifying emerges as an abstraction. The allegorical has its existence in abstractions; as an abstraction, as a faculty of the spirit of language itself, it is at home in the Fall."[20]

Benjamin's words can be applied to the imbrication of guilt and signification in the film noir mise-en-scène generally, but also to the "fall" implied in the "badness" of *Beyond a Reasonable Doubt,* its failure as entertainment. Benjamin's thought is particularly important to a critique of the mythologies of "loss" that tend to be linked to the representation of death. He enables the critic to read narrative mortality as a discourse of historical difference, transforming the loss of mythic forms of meaning into a more radical theory of historical temporality. Melancholia is, for Benjamin, an immersion in a historical situation in which transcendent ideals are invalidated. Narrative desire is frustrated, despite a textual linearity, and the "illusionist intention" is minimized to the point that "intrigue takes places like a change of scenery on the open stage."[21] With no irony or discursive distance attained by the text, the critic/historian has the privilege and obligation to read the text as the language of history.[22]

An example from early American cinema might illustrate the relevance of this theory to film history and representation. In *The Great Train Robbery* (Porter, 1903), the man who is dramatically thrown off the engine of a moving train is instantly transformed into a sack of sawdust. Although this representation of death may have been convincing to audiences of the time, it is much less so to today's audiences. The image is mortified and the film is no longer "good" but is the ruin of the realistic film it once was. (Of course, it may not have been convincing at all to 1903 audiences, who probably did not have the same expectations of realism. The image then registers the historical transience of signifying practices.) Whereas the skulls and bones of Benjamin's baroque emblematists registered the inadequacy of myths of transcendence, the representation of death in fiction film can become the emblem of performance and the inadequacy of narrative cinema to be reality because it is always the character and never the actor who dies in fiction film. Death becomes such an emblem from the perspective of historical difference, of which it is a potential sign, but also in the stylized performances and mise-en-scènes of film history.

Mortification is an allegorical discourse that is both found within texts and read into them. As a hermeneutic method, it is crucial to this book's method of textual analysis as a productive discourse in and of itself. Various critical terms, such as the "symptomatic text," "reading against the grain," "countercinema"—terms that cannot quite decide if the text at hand is "progressive" or not—might be subsumed by the notion of a text that is dead, ready to be redeemed by a different viewer. *Beyond a Reasonable Doubt* is precisely such a text, one that sacrifices itself, offering its images as the ruins of the classical Hollywood style of realism.

Implicit in the very notion of narrative mortality is that the meaning of a film is produced by an encounter of reader and text. This is not to relativize truth or locate it entirely with the ethnohistoricity of the viewer, or to render culture meaningless, but to mobilize the decentering of representation that reception theory has accomplished. Radical viewing, the reanimation of "dead" texts, reading against the grain, and so on are not necessarily privileged readings but empowered readings. Narrative mortality redeems the belief in representation as a belief in historical possibility.

The melancholy nature of *Beyond a Reasonable Doubt* is evident in the film's inability to believe in itself. It begins as a critique of capital punishment and ends with its protagonist, Tom Garrett (Dana Andrews), being sentenced to death for the murder of his estranged wife. The end matches the film's opening, which is a scene of an anonymous prisoner being led from his cell to the electric chair. Although Garrett, who witnesses this opening execution, is led off in the final shot of the film to his own execution, the "rhyming" of beginning and end is destabilized by the fact that he was supposed to have been the protagonist, the film's moral authority.

The opening critique of capital punishment, voiced by Garrett's prospective father-in-law, Austin Spencer (Sidney Blackmer), is epistemological, not moral, based in the relativity of circumstantial evidence. Garrett and Spencer test the believability of circumstantial evidence by planting false clues to indict Garrett for an unsolved murder, photographing their activities to prove (through a faith in the image) Garrett's innocence. Garrett reenacts the crime in order to be arrested, and is jailed and tried according to plan. But Lang strategically withholds Garrett's criminal activity and his history, setting him up for the viewer (and for the Spencer family) as a morally respectable and empathetic character, only to reveal in the second-to-last scene that he did in fact kill Patty Gray. The film sets out to denounce the subjection of a man's fate to "objects" (circumstantial evidence), but proceeds to objectify the protagonist himself and reduce him, by means of a panopticonic mise-en-scène, still photography, and a perversely restrained acting style, to one in a series of inert signs, a puppet with little control over either his destiny or his personality.

The final scenes of the film are especially saturated with a melancholia, which may become irony to the historian but, within the genre framework of studio production, are symptoms of an impossibility of closure. Although the guilty party is punished and a new heterosexual couple is formed (Susan [Joan Fontaine] and Lieutenant Kennedy [Edward Binns]), the restoration of law and order leaves something over, a "supplement" that is the cinematic and narrative apparatus. *Beyond a Reasonable Doubt* is marked by a series of bizarre narrative turns. The arbitrary elimination of Garrett's key witness, the miraculous discovery of Spencer's testimony (a letter that signifies in written language what we thought only existed in the destroyed images), and then the discovery that our hero, between scenes, murdered a wife of whose existence we were unaware renders the preceding narrative retrospectively meaningless, a pure process of specularity.[23] Although both realist representation and an ideal of social justice are mortified in *Beyond a Reasonable Doubt,* narrative mortality allows us to read this process not as a loss but as a gain, a movement beyond invalidated symbolic forms.

The particular melancholic attitude of *Beyond a Reasonable Doubt* concerns the cinema itself and the believability of its images. Immediately after witnessing the opening execution (the sight is withheld from the viewer), Spencer says to Garrett (they are in a witness box in the execution chamber), "After you've seen one . . ." and he is interrupted. The implication that an unequivocal indictment of capital punishment is only possible by seeing it makes its way into the film inadvertently, by the perverse concealment and strategic specularization of death. Garrett's death is necessitated by the narrative text, an authority that has cheated the viewer by concealing a key event: Patty Gray's murder. Moreover, the law that the narrative was to question is, in the end, upheld without question. The first duplicitous act singles out the authority behind the second, linking the techniques of narrative cinema with those of capital (death penalty) law in the regime of the visible.

Austin Spencer's accidental death midway through Garrett's trial is vivid and explosive, in contrast with the mainly flat, banal mise-en-scène of the rest of the film. Spencer removes the photographs, Garrett's alibi, from his wall safe as a radio announces that the jury's verdict will be announced that very morning. He places the photographs beside him when he gets into his car. As he backs out of his garage, a truck hits the car broadside. The only witnesses to Spencer's death are anonymous passers-by and a suddenly omniscient camera, which, waiting outside Spencer's garage, seems almost to have staged the accident. Lang uses a gamut of audio and visual techniques — screaming, music, rapid cutting, close-ups, a canted camera, and a flash of light. No corpse, but rather a car radio engulfed in flames, concludes the brief scene. The authoritative announcement of the continuation of the trial issues from the wreckage, marking the lost locus of patriarchal authority in this mid-narrative death at a crossroads.

Whether one wants to describe Lang's technique here as "expressionist" or "stylized" in the mode of film noir, the excess of violence underlines the narrative break of Spencer's arbitrary death. But it also displaces the character's mortality onto the film itself, which erupts in an attempt to signify this death. Just as the limits of the father function are suddenly revealed in the character's mortality, the film's limits are also suddenly exposed. The scene intimates that realist representation potentially breaks down with the representation of death, which it cannot fully represent.

Semiosis: The Discourse of Photography in Film

The most telling emblem of the failure of *Beyond a Reasonable Doubt* is the brief scene in which Susan Spencer and Lieutenant Kennedy examine the charred remains of the photographs that have been destroyed in Austin Spencer's car accident. Because they were taken with a Polaroid camera, there are no negatives. They are the ruins of Garrett's alibi that are enough to convince Susan of his innocence. However, as Kennedy points out, "they could be photos of anything." As photographic ruins, they mark the reduction of the image to an objective "creaturely" status: carbon garbage. Nowhere is the mortification of cinematic presence more vivid than in this scene, which, along with the awkward dialogue about "real evidence" and "belief" in Garrett, is truly melancholic.

The inclusion of still photographs within narrative film underlines the mortifying potential of photographic representation, jeopardizing a film's illusion of movement by acknowledging its status as still frames.[24] The photos in *Beyond a Reasonable Doubt* are not freeze-frames, but they flirt nonetheless with the masquerade of presence upon which the fiction of the narrative is predicated. They repeat the narrative action in imagistic form, and as fetishized objects they are intended to return (to be reproduced by Spencer) in order to absolve Garrett, but instead they seal another fate when they are destroyed in the car accident. Of the photographs in *Beyond a Reasonable Doubt,* Raymond Bellour says, "Both before and after the accident, they haunt the film, creating a sort of two-way mirror. The photo, shimmering in memory, plays with the truth of cinema."[25] They allow the viewer that time for reflection that the succession of film images normally denies—a time in which the viewer "adds" to the image. He or she adds precisely the knowledge of the image and its absent referent.

The referent in this case is doubly removed, or doubly duplicitous. Intended to establish Garrett's innocence, the photographs instead mask his guilt. The man in the pictures, Dana Andrews, is neither guilty nor innocent, but merely a man posing for a photograph. Lacking negatives, the Polaroid photographs are images without "depth," and they haunt the film as the elusory traces of the truth guaranteed by photography. The film, which relies on that guarantee for its narrative security, becomes in turn a free-floating ghost of a film.

Moreover, an identification is obliquely established between the authorization of images (outside the text) and the legal and patriarchal authorities (inside the film) insofar as all the photographs are either taken by Spencer or published in his newspaper. Spencer's death and the coextensive destruction of his photographs simply enact a transferral of narrative authority. Spencer has taken pains in his photographs to be absolutely accurate, including newspapers with dates and his own reflection within the frame, but when the photographs turn out to be an elaborate lie, Spencer's responsibility as enunciator is usurped by the enunciative strategy of the film itself.[26] Along with the prosecutor, all the viewer has left are the images of the film, images that have been designed, planned, to condemn Garrett.

It is precisely through this extensive use of photographs—which, as Bellour suggests, haunt the film with their absence, even when destroyed—that the film's systems partially break down. The strategic duplicity that the film enacts upon its spectator is at odds with the "supplement" that the photograph encourages the viewer to contribute. The instability of the narrative's final embrace of capital punishment is due to the extension of the questioning of "evidence" to the film's own evidence by virtue of the photograph, which cannot construct a spectator. Bellour's observation that "when film looks at itself, it never sees itself as it does in the photograph," points to the means by which narrative mortality in *Beyond a Reasonable Doubt* involves an uncanny recognition of the film's own fictional status.

The production of photographs within the text of *Beyond a Reasonable Doubt* is responsible for a very specific form of doubling, an uncanniness that is crucial to the film's narrative mortality. In the process of doubling, the repetition of images from film to photograph institutes a chain of signifiers in which none are originary. The anxiety of the uncanny is precisely the sense of loss implied in doubling. The transformation of the work of death in narrative film from authoritative "meaningfulness" to the radical work of textual praxis involves a recognition of the "ontology of the cinema"—its photographic basis—as a grasp on history. This "grasp" is, in a sense, the very possibility of mortification, which, even in Benjamin's writing, is closely linked to the mechanical reproduction of images.[27]

For Freud, although the double might have been originally conceived as a protection against death (by primitive societies), in the modern psyche it is also a "ghastly harbinger of death."[28] This, he says, is because of the "reminder" it contains of the "inner repetition-compulsion" that is the motivating principle of the death drive (p. 44). Freud further points to the effacing of the distinction between "imagination and reality," or "when a symbol takes over the full significance of the thing it symbolizes," as an example of the uncanny (p. 44). Film is uncanny in that it may preserve life in its indexicality, but at the same time it "murders" reality by mimicking it, repeating it, making it into an object.

The uncanny describes the effect of cinematic representation that fails to repress the reminder of the absent referent and the void that narrative realism sutures over. This effect is created in *Beyond a Reasonable Doubt* by way of the discourse of photography, but also, as we will see, by discourses of repetition and character doubling. These devices may not necessarily produce "fear" in the spectator, especially without the spectacular and iconographic conventions of the horror film, but they might well produce a split spectator, one who both believes and disbelieves in the film's moral and aesthetic ideals. Freud indulges in his own form of literary criticism when he chastises the writer who invokes the uncanny: "he deceives us into thinking that he is giving us the sober truth, and then after all oversteps the bounds of possibility" (p. 57). The uncanny is implicit in the themes of coincidence and fate in which the contingent real becomes subject to the powers of nature and narrative.

The uncanny "harbinger of death" offers a key tool for reading the mortality of representation. The term "semiosis" is a related means of theorizing the mortality of the body, and its transformation through decay, as a structure of representation. Although semiosis can refer to the physical transformation of the body,[29] for Charles Sanders Peirce, it is a human signifying activity, the means by which chains of referentiality ultimately lead back to an "*interpretant* and *ground* of representation."[30] The semiosis of narrative mortality is therefore the sign of history as decay within the cinematic signifier, which is to say the indexicality of time linking the image to history, if history is the singular (past) time in which the image was produced (shot). Mortification involves a violence against the referent of the film image, killing it and making it stop. Every film image and every filmed moment becomes a "ruin" of history and an allegory of the desire that once informed its present tense.

In *Beyond a Reasonable Doubt,* even the very ground of semiosis, the profilmic moment, is a fiction. And, of course, for Umberto Eco, semiosis refers to the infinite play of referentiality in which there is no "ground" that does not itself deconstruct or decompose.[31] The allegory produced here is one of a radical decentering and deflation of photocinematic authority. Garrett posing with a dated newspaper and a lighter he will subsequently toss into the bushes at the "scene of the crime"; Garrett holding a nylon stocking in the front seat of his car—these are moments that already stop the action of the film, repeating scenarios of desire in the presence of the father-in-law/ photographer/newspaper owner and editor, Austin Spencer. In the banality of these images, the narrative of desire is already in decay, subject to the mortifying gaze of the critic. The spectator of the film, offered the Polaroid snapshots as well as the newspaper photos and all the subsequent television images, sees a film that is always uncannily seeing its own fiction.

Death and Power

The historical analysis of *Beyond a Reasonable Doubt* as a "dead text" involves a mortification of its imagery and narrative desire, but also a recognition of its specific deployment of capital law. Lang's treatment of capital punishment in *Beyond a Reasonable Doubt,* as well as his mise-en-scène and narrative logic, are described by Rivette as a "proliferation of denials," of which the denial of the sight of death is emblematic. The repression of this image is balanced by an overdetermined representation of power: the imagery of the judicial system, paternalistic characters, and the power of (and over) photocinematic representation. The power of narrative itself is displayed as a violence against the spectator.[32] In Jacques Rivette's words, "We are plunged into a world of necessity, all the more apparent in that it coexists so harmoniously with the arbitrariness of the premises; Lang, as is well known, always seeks the truth beyond the reasonable, and here seeks it from the threshold of the unreasonable."[33] By enacting the denial that governs mortality in capital-ist discourse, the narrative apparatus "exposes" itself and its limits. If capitalism and capital punishment mutually reinforce each other in the context of cold war American policy, they become legible here as fictions of power and paranoia.

In Hollywood film of the 1950s, violence became a crucial means of transforming genre narratives into more complex historical documents. Ideological closure, whether through the successful solving of a crime or formation of a couple, or both, was in turn destabilized. *Beyond a Reasonable Doubt* is in this sense only one example of how, in the internal destruction of genre cinema that took place in the 1950s, death became a representation of doubt and anxiety. This is not simply a question of the imagery of violence, but is bound to the power of the representation of death. The ability to produce the spectacle of death is both a discourse of control and one of potential transgression. An uncanny conjunction of crisis and possibility, narrative mortality delineates the threshold of the representable.

The discourse of power is inscribed in the production history of *Beyond a Reasonable Doubt* in terms of censorship. The studio would not allow Lang to represent the opening execution "more realistically." Lang claims that he did shoot it "the way I myself had seen it: how they drag the man in, how he struggles and doesn't want to go,"[34] but he was prevented from including this scene in the final cut. The lack of "realistic" representations of death in 1950s Hollywood is due in part to censorship,[35] although it seems that death itself is censored from the original Hays Production Code, where only "the technique of murder," "brutal killings," and "revenge" are listed as taboo under the heading of "Crimes Against the Law," subsection "murder."[36] The one other proscription against representing death in the code is listed under "Repellent subjects": "1. Actual hangings or electrocutions as legal punishments for crime."

This partially explains why Lang was not allowed to make the opening execution "realistic," but it also indicates that the institutional guilt that is demonstrated in *Beyond a Reasonable Doubt* is shared by Hollywood. Implicit in this taboo is the realization that to see capital punishment is to condemn it. The capitulation to capital law must be at the expense of its visualization, and in *Beyond a Reasonable Doubt,* through the appropriation of authoritative discourses by patriarchal law, the optical apparatus of the cinema is perversely equated with "the chair."

Spectatorship, conceived as the chair in the cinematic apparatus, is a highly volatile element in the Langian system. Jean-Louis Comolli and François Géré have argued that Lang's films take the spectator on a "journey of mortification" in their systematic annihilation of secure ideological and scopic positioning. In *Beyond a Reasonable Doubt* this "journey" is a process of entrapment that effectively mortifies the moral/ideological pleasure of the viewing experience. This is especially evident in three short single-take scenes distributed through the second half of the film. In the first of these, immediately after

Spencer's death, Jonathan Wilson, Garrett's lawyer, visits Garrett in jail. The shot is framed in a fourth-wall composition, with the back wall comprised of bars, behind which a guard's face is fixed at the vanishing point of the image. Except for one imperceptible dolly back to reframe Garrett, the camera is static. The lack of an envisioning subject in a narrative so obsessed with looking is conspicuous, especially since the composition is repeated twice more. One might compare this minimal but tightly structured image to *Las Meninas*, insofar as the guard's distant face is, as Foucault says, "addressing itself to what is invisible both because of the picture's structure and because of its existence as painting."[37] Because the guard is fixed, like the spectator, "on the other side" of the image, he is like the mirror in *Las Meninas*, figuring the representational apparatus within the text[38] (figure 1).

The figurative place constructed for the spectator in the death-row shots is one of surveillance and control, not that of the imprisoned

Fig. 1. *Beyond a Reasonable Doubt.* In the panopticonic gaze at death row, Garrett (Dana Andrews), standing, is told by his lawyer that his execution is scheduled for the morning.

man. The camera placement identifies the gaze with the forces of empowerment that have imprisoned Garrett, and as such constitutes a cinematic version of the panopticon, in which the source of the gaze of power is itself invisible. Foucault describes the panopticonic structure of imprisonment, which was refined in the eighteenth century, as a mechanism comprised of "so many cages, so many small theatres, in which each actor is alone, perfectly individualized and constantly visible.... Visibility is a trap."[39] Not only does this perfectly describe Garrett's situation in *Beyond a Reasonable Doubt,* but if the major effect of the panopticon is to "assure the automatic functioning of power," Garrett is likewise entrapped in the drama of his indictment, the judicial mechanism that leads inexorably to his death. The very structure of the panopticonic apparatus, reproduced in these prison scenes of *Beyond a Reasonable Doubt* and in the cinematic apparatus itself, is organized around the containment of death.[40]

Capital law in *Beyond a Reasonable Doubt* is the abstract form of the apparatuses of execution and the cinema, equated in their techniques of witnessing, exclusion, and irreversibility. In *Beyond a Reasonable Doubt,* Garrett is subjected to a series of overlapping paternalistic, institutional, and representational discourses, from Spencer and Thompson the district attorney (who, along with Garrett's lawyer, Wilson, resemble each other), to the court and the state, represented by the judge and the governor (who also resemble each other, one generation older than the first set of fathers), to photographs, television screens, cameras, newspapers, and a huge microphone that is foregrounded in the shots of him on the witness stand.

The three panopticonic "death-row" scenes have serious ramifications for the spectator of *Beyond a Reasonable Doubt.* The guard returns the viewer's gaze passively, but fixes it nonetheless in a "transcendental," centrally privileged, spectatorial position—one that condemns Garrett to be the object of the gaze at the two moments of his self-realization of his death sentence. The spectator's place within the text is thus rendered highly contradictory. After Spencer's death, Garrett is the viewer's ideological or moral surrogate, but at the same time, point of view is structured around Garrett's condemnation. For Comolli and Géré, Lang's spectator is made to "pay for his place";[41] in *Beyond a Reasonable Doubt,* the viewer's ultimate

rejection from the text with "the end" is rendered scopically and ideologically from the moment of Spencer's death.

The prison scenes cast the spectator's impossible position as a
death-within-the-text, short-circuiting the momentum of desire in the
representation of a closed visual and ideological system. However, it
is not necessarily a positioning that takes place, as apparatus theory
might have it, because the assigned position of power is uncomfort-
able. The representation of so many witnesses, spectators, and juries
within the film suggests that the justice system is—as Foucault already
implies—more of a show, spectacle, and theater than a closed structure. The journey of mortification noted by Comolli and Géré is not
necessarily a dead end, but may open up a space for a redemptive
reading.

If the deus ex machina of Garrett's guilt retroactively casts the
film as a "fiction" produced by a disillusioned and cruel auteur, it is
an allegory of belief. Beyond a reasonable doubt, there is the state
and the law, which, like the allegory of resurrection, rob allegory of
"its arbitrary rule in the realm of the dead."[42] It is the necessity of the
law that produces the film's discourse of mortality, and because it
remains discursive (the sign of Garrett's indictment is the governor's
hand replacing a pen in its holder, with a blank "Pardon" document
in front of him), it remains readable as a discourse. By showing his
own hand with the deus ex machina and Spencer's freak accident,
Lang reveals this discourse of necessity to be entirely arbitrary. The
viewer's belief in Garrett's character, and in the film itself, is cast as a
desire to believe in representation; if the cinema is as unreliable as
circumstantial evidence, it is potentially freed from the tyranny of
the law. Beyond a reasonable doubt, there is also the blank space of
utopian ideation.

Narrative mortality in *Beyond a Reasonable Doubt* is a discourse
of power, in which incrimination can be read as a framing of individual destiny within the contours of state power and paternal authority.
Garrett's death sentence, which hangs over the film as both its goal
and its threat, might be regarded as symptomatic of the particular
historical juncture of the cold war. The executions of Julius and Ethel
Rosenberg in 1953 had brought the issues of capital punishment and
political transgression into public debate.[43] Capital punishment became

the deployment of absolute power in the name of democracy. It could only be demonstrated, however, with evidence of resistance: the circumstantial evidence marshaled against the Rosenbergs. Lang's story about capital law opens with the execution of an anonymous criminal, and eventually provides a subjective criminality that can only be produced within a discourse of resistance.

Garrett, it turns out, is playing the institutions of the press, the legal system, and the state off against one another, but in doing so he cannot be identified with any one of them. As an innocent man, he is narratively and literally framed by the disciplines that extend even to the "hand of fate" that kills Spencer. But the fact that he is actually guilty testifies to the means by which the power to punish produces the figure of the transgressor. Crime as social transgression, as nonnormative behavior, and the idea of a class of criminals are produced and maintained in the exclusionary apparatuses of power. If the judicial apparatus "always gets its man," the narrative of *Beyond a Reasonable Doubt* painfully produces that man, and it is not the spectator, or anyone with whom the spectator is inclined to identify. We may watch Garrett meet his destiny in the last scene with some sympathy, but it is of a highly intellectual order: that of the witness, not the lover.

The spectator who is framed here, forced into the witness box and denied the usual securities of narrative cinema, can be located historically. Foucault argues that the power to punish produces an illegality labeled delinquency, a term that, of course, enters common parlance in the 1950s, through a discourse of the family generated from popular Freudianism. Juvenile delinquency, in this context, is the naming of, and the attempt to accommodate into the "discipline" of the family, a segment of society that tended to fall through the ideological fissure between self-determination and "the aggressive expansion of corporate capitalism."[44] The delinquency that is so perversely produced in *Beyond a Reasonable Doubt* lacks the rebelliousness and resistance that characterizes some other contemporary films (e.g., *Rebel Without a Cause*), and remains a virtually abstract term of domestic deviance: the brutal murder of an invisible wife.

Within the historical context of cold war paranoia and the production of delinquency, narrative mortality may be read in the very stylistics and narrative instabilities of film noir, especially the "second

phase" of the genre, which for Paul Arthur corresponds to the sociopo-
litical isolation of communism "as the sole agent of domestic and international unrest."[45] The rise of Sen. Joseph McCarthy and the entry
into Korea in 1950 effectively institutionalize the shift from which
point "conflicts between personal and institutional demands and values" become central in the film noir text.[46] In this sense, *Beyond a
Reasonable Doubt* may not be as idiosyncratic as it appears, and its
allegory of narrative mortality might be more legible as a disbelief in
affirmative cultural institutions.

The tensions between individual and institution, paranoia and
power, subjective doubts and objective norms are frequently narrativized in film noir through the representation of death. Arthur suggests that the ambiguities of identity in film noir are typically registered in an experience of death of one kind or another:

> The objective status of death in film noir narratives is often
> convoluted, confusing, opaque. People don't just die; they can
> be understood as dead then suddenly return (*Laura*); they
> can, due to circumstances in which they *should* have died, be
> considered "resurrected" (*Kiss Me Deadly*); they can spend
> nearly the entire film with irreversible physical injury
> (*D.O.A.*). . . . Given the mutability of personal identity in film
> noir it is not surprising that there is a constant horizon of
> death — represented through explicit verbal reference,
> narrative action, and overall narrative structuring — and that
> this horizon is fraught with considerable ambiguity: who will
> die, and will that injunction be a final or a transitive state? No
> other group of films in Hollywood history treats this subject
> with such pervasive concern or with such emblematic
> uncertainty.[47]

The "death-row" shots of *Beyond a Reasonable Doubt* might, in
this respect, be regarded as typical of a purgatorial style of representation in which death becomes a discursive figure in American cinema. In this film it becomes particularly clear how the representation
of death potentially links the power of cinematic representation with
other forms of empowerment. Narrative mortality involves the realization of this process as potentially reversible, as predicated on social
and historical difference.

Beyond Pleasure

If narrative mortality is to be understood as an allegorical form of desire, a mortification of institutionalized desires, and an opening up of historical, utopian desires, it remains to situate this discourse in relation to psychoanalytic film theory. What has become known as apparatus theory may have been instrumental in deconstructing the logic of male desire that informs so much film narrative, but at the same time the phallocentrism of the theory itself limits its usefulness as a critical tool. Narrative mortality provides a means of decentering psychoanalytic film theory by emphasizing the difference of mortality over that of sexuality. The point is not to undermine the discourse of gender that informs a film like *Beyond a Reasonable Doubt,* but to amplify a feminist critique in such a way that a position of analysis and critique might be identified within the film's own discourse of desire.

Psychoanalytic film theory may be able to account for the film's panopticism and its oedipal trajectory, but it is notoriously unable to theorize a spectator who witnesses, reads, or maintains some kind of "difference" from the text at hand. A psychoanalytic analysis of *Beyond a Reasonable Doubt* would identify the constitution of male subjectivity as the film's logic of desire and difference. Certainly the three central women in the film are the terrain across which the protagonist's trajectory is traced. Insofar as Garrett is both "murderer" and "author" he encompasses a split between unconscious desire (transgression of the patriarchal law) and conscious repression (identification with the symbolic father). When Garrett says "Emma" instead of "Patty," he reveals his guilt by acknowledging his (sexual) history.[48] (Emma is Patty's real name, and it is because Garrett accidentally uses it that Susan deduces that he knew her and therefore killed her.) That he reveals his double identity with a slip of the tongue indicates the Freudian dimension of *Beyond a Reasonable Doubt.*

Susan Spencer, Garrett's fiancée, becomes the sign of the replacement of father by son, representing castration in her domineering, sophisticated behavior and attire, in her explicit threat to Garrett's work, and in her brief usurpation of her father's place at the office. Garrett's excessive concern to keep her at a distance is his "acceptance of the threat of castration from the father," the condition of entry into the symbolic order.[49] Garrett's encounters in the Club Zombie and its dressing rooms establish him as a desiring subject, but it is above all his relationship with Patty/Emma that constitutes his disavowal.

Unseen except for a single highly "contained" newspaper photo of her body, Patty's absence from the text is overdetermined when Lieutenant Kennedy shows her publicity photo to the barman in Miami, but it is *not* shown to us. Patty's punishment for eroticism is commensurate with her very (invisible) presence in *Beyond a Reasonable Doubt,* a variation or condensation of the woman's place in film noir: it is her "guilty secret" that the film is in quest of, and her punishment is extremely sadistic. The only image of her that appears is an abstract arrangement of body parts in a newspaper beside an empty landscape labeled "scene of crime" (figure 2). In a revealing interview, Lang describes Patty/Emma as an "unscrupulous black-mailer who is after [Garrett's] money with egotistical singlemindedness and without a moment's thought for the possibility that she is

Fig. 2. *Beyond a Reasonable Doubt*: The textual repetition of the imaginary, dead woman in Austin Spencer's newspaper.

ruining his whole career and his future life."[50] He has to supplement the absent character of Patty/Emma in order to defend Garrett; he has to amplify the femme fatale who lurks behind the film.

Between these two "symbolic" (Susan) and "imaginary" (Patty/Emma) women is Dolly, who stands in for Patty in Garrett's re-creation of the crime. As her name suggests, Dolly is a narrative fetish, representing both Garrett's desired relationship with women and a threat: she, like Susan, turns him in to the law. The film's misogyny underlines the contradictions of Garrett's oedipal trajectory, which is by definition a master plot that excludes women from subjectivity and desire. Without question, *Beyond a Reasonable Doubt* lends itself to a feminist critique of the logic of sexual difference in the film's system. Within the tenets of apparatus theory, though, the critique would have to locate spectatorship within that logic of desire and exclude female pleasure entirely.[51] Identification would rest entirely with male subjectivity. And yet there is surely a pleasure involved in the critique, in the reading itself, as well as a temptation to claim that the oedipal logic is subverted by the film's excesses of representation. Female subjectivity may not be entirely contained by a text that is so clearly troubled by it. The symptoms of textual instability may be the traces of a troubled culture, but it is difficult to reconcile such a reading with a psychoanalytic analysis. Narrative mortality may provide a means of transforming a symptomatic psychoanalytic reading into a redemptive reading.

The discourses of sexuality and mortality may be seen to coincide in *Beyond a Reasonable Doubt* in such a way that the family romance converges with the panopticism described earlier. The incoherency of the film's ending points to an excess of regulation and control that extends beyond imprisonment to the normative codification of postwar American society. If Garrett can be considered to be an oedipal protagonist, he is one who fails to successfully enter the symbolic order, represented as high society (Susan Spencer's world) and is cruelly excluded from it. The cruelty of the film, including Lang's duplicity against the spectator, marks the text as unpleasurable, as "beyond pleasure," arbitrarily cutting off the possibility, for Garrett, of social mobility and a normalizing marriage. For the spectator, it also curtails the desire for entry into this society built on power and repression. In the dissociation of the pleasure principle (Garrett's

desire and the spectator's desire) from closure (the invocation of capital law against Garrett), the text does indeed move beyond a certain
kind of pleasure: that which is inscribed in the oedipal master plot.

The mortification of desire is registered in the scopophilic gaze at
the female body, which is transformed into a melancholic gaze. In a
purely gratuitous scene in the Club Zombie dressing room, one of
the dancers (Terry, also a key witness) undresses behind a screen. A
mirror placed directly behind her, however, allows Garrett and the
film's viewer a voyeuristic glimpse of her in her underwear. This extremely crude mise-en-scène, along with several scenes of bad burlesque performances, circumvents pleasure with objectification as the
women are cruelly reduced to the status of "circumstantial evidence."
Patty's body is signified by "Foster's number nine body makeup"
(another piece of evidence) that once again overdetermines its absence. Lang's melancholia, therefore, may be the result of the lack of
scopophilic pleasure inscribed in his sexist gaze, and the film's redemptive potential is precisely in the deadness of this look.

In other words, a psychoanalytic reading may be called for by
this text in which socialization of the male subject is constituted in
and through language and female sexuality. However, it is a reading
in which the systemics of psychoanalytic theory are fractured through
the excessive strategies of regulation. It is not a desire for the Other
that motivates the narrative; nor is it simply a desire for closure, but
a desire for images and the representation of a crime. From the
lengthy trial scene, when Garrett is "fixed" physically and scopically,
the second half of *Beyond a Reasonable Doubt,* like the second half
of *Oedipus Rex,* abandons the proairetic code for the hermeneutic.[52]
Moreover, the conclusion of the investigation, which establishes that
Garrett himself is the criminal, is similar to that of Oedipus's recognition of his own guilt. But the more appropriate classical model for
Beyond a Reasonable Doubt may lie "beyond Oedipus": perhaps Garrett's trajectory, from the moment of Spencer's death, is no longer
that of Oedipus, but that of Oedipus at Colonus.

The continuation of Oedipus's story involves, above all, the retelling of the story of *Oedipus Rex.* Shoshana Felman writes, "*Oedipus
at Colonus* is about the transformation of Oedipus's story into history: it does not tell the drama, it is *about the telling* (and retelling)
of the drama. It is, in other words, about the *historization* of Oedipus'

destiny, through the *symbolization*—the transmutation into speech—
of the Oedipal desire."[53] Felman demonstrates that, for Lacan, *Beyond
the Pleasure Principle* "holds the key not just to history or to transference but, specifically, to the *textual functioning* of signification,"
which is "a *replaying* of the symbolic meaning of the *death* the subject has repeatedly experienced." For Lacan,

> Oedipus at Colonus, whose entire being resides in the speech
> formulated by his destiny, concretizes the conjunction
> between life and death. He lives a life which is made of death,
> that sort of death which is exactly there, beneath life's
> surface.[54]

In Lacan's discussion of *Hamlet,* we can find further clues as to the
function of death in narrative. "Something," says Lacan, "has changed
since classical antiquity in the relationship of the hero to his fate."[55]
This turns out to be knowledge, specifically, for Hamlet, that he
lives "in the hour of the Other," that he has "an appointment," which
is the hour of his destruction.[56]

The relationship between castration anxiety and the fear of death
was, for Freud, one of analogy, although the former was undoubtedly
the prior phenomenon in the psyche.[57] It has been argued that Freud in
fact tended to place death to the side, to subordinate it to matters of
sexuality, as is most evident in his treatment of Laius's murder in the
Oedipus myth, and in his neglect of Oedipus's own death in Sophocles'
Oedipus at Colonus.[58] Lacan's reading of Freud, however, accepts the
existential element of castration anxiety as fundamental. Stuart Schniederman suggests that the dead occupy that elusive category of the
real that subtends Lacan's conception of language and subjectivity:

> The dead also are real, not merely because death creates holes
> in the real. The gods and the dead are real because the only
> encounter we have with the real is based on the canceling of
> our perceptual conscious, of our sense of being alive: the real
> is real whether we experience it or not and regardless of how
> we experience it.... The concept of the real implies the
> annihilation of the subject.[59]

In applying psychoanalytic theory to narrative, one is in perpetual
danger of imposing the metaphors of patriarchy onto a text, a danger

epitomized in Lacan's reduction of all objects—including Ophelia—
into manifestations of the phallus.[60] "Hamlet," says Lacan, stakes "pre-
cious objects"—the paraphernalia of dueling (for Shakespeare), the
trace of the phallus (for Lacan)—"against death" (p. 30). However, by
noting the strategic occurrences of death in narrative, as indices of the
loss or lack of the real, against which the narrative is "staked," Lacanian theory might itself be read as an allegory of narrative mortality.

In *Beyond a Reasonable Doubt*, the story of Garrett's trajectory as
surrogate criminal is told first by Spencer and then by Lang, in images.
With Garrett's confession at the end, *another* story, hitherto buried,
is revealed. Significantly, this story constitutes the "truth" (the factuality, against which the film has been mere fiction) but remains untold,
either visually or verbally. "In the Langian system, the truth is what
kills, what condemns to death,"[61] but in this case at least, the slippery
signifier Patty/Emma reveals the truth as a void upon which the film
has concealed its fiction. Like the Oedipus story, *Beyond a Reasonable Doubt* is above all about father-son relations; in Laura Mulvey's
words, it is a "timeless stasis" of paternal authority that lies far beyond
pleasure. But it is also *about* this fiction of patriarchy, and about the
ways that it becomes myth (representation) insofar as sexual desire
is radically suppressed, relegated to a "riddling spirit of the Sphinx
[which] activates questions that open up the closures of repression."[62]

Patty/Emma, dead from the outset, belongs to the category of the
sphinx and the real—excluded from a narrative which nevertheless
flirts with her, and the real, as the elusive category of "truth." Possibly,
as a woman, she can be said to represent "the lack," that wound
which classical narrative is said to suture with its narrative operations.[63]
But she is also clearly identified with death: she is her death. The
film itself is revealed finally to be a series of false clues, mere signifiers, a narrative told selectively and seductively, only by virtue of a
lack, an ellipsis: the omission of the murder scene and Garrett's participation in it.

The viewer is left at the end of *Beyond a Reasonable Doubt* with
the disturbing feeling of wondering why this film has taken place.
What was it that Lang wished to show and tell? Despite the melodramatic turns of Susan's betrayal, the film is utterly lacking in moral
stakes; there is no sympathy generated for the protagonist/murderer,
or for his punishers. Garrett's death is "a decadent form of the Oedipal

situation"[64] insofar as his desire, organized around sexual difference (its recognition and acceptance as a symbolic order), is appropriated by another desire. A "metanarrative" subjectivity assumes his death, as he assumed Patty/Emma's, for its own practice. Garrett's ostensible goal—to marry Susan and construct an alibi—is replaced by that of Lang, to tell a story, a story that is not about death but thoroughly underscored by the death of the subject, in the film and of the film.

As the desire to narrate is reduced to its pure form (Lang, remember, did not wish to tell *this* story), mortality takes precedence over castration as the term of difference in signification. The film's ending not only agrees with the district attorney's stated objective, to "uphold the law of this state," but it also fulfills Spencer's comment early in the film that "Thompson [the district attorney] wants to reach the governor's chair over the bodies of executed men." Garrett's death is demanded simply by the desire of the logic of the text, which is left with his body as an extra term, a supplement to the restoration of the couple (Susan Spencer and Lieutenant Kennedy), a signifier that must be returned to the nothingness from whence it came.

What Rivette recognizes in his critique of *Beyond a Reasonable Doubt* is that this triumph of reasonableness is the production of a knowledge outside the film, an address to the spectator, indeed a quest for reason in an unreasonable world.[65] The object of mourning in *Beyond a Reasonable Doubt*—the trust in law and order, the belief in social justice—is potentially redeemed beyond the strict logic of the text, but it is so only as a nonrepressive form. The failed logic of desire that we have traced in terms of the Oedipus complex can also be described as an uncanny destabilization of the death drive, in which repetition and return become principles of redemption.

The Uncanniness of Repetition

If the key strategies of Thanatos in narrative representation are repetition and doubling, an important technique of narrative mortality in *Beyond a Reasonable Doubt* is the overdetermination of Thanatos. The extremes to which the techniques of repetition and doubling are taken in *Beyond a Reasonable Doubt* are the means by which desire takes on historical dimensions. The film's excess of control and regulation (e.g., the recurrence of father figures) finally separates fiction, doubt, and belief from truth, law, and knowledge. The inscription of Thanatos in *Beyond a Reasonable Doubt* is overdetermined by the abundance of verbal and visual repetition, working against the desire for the happy ending—the generic expectations of the solution of the crime and the winning of the girl. The "narrative impulse" of the death drive completely transcends the ostensible discourse of oedipal desire; what is attained (the legitimation of capital law) is not what was wanted (a critique of capital law). The film ends with a very literally unfulfilled desire for social transformation.

Freud's conception in *Beyond the Pleasure Principle* of a dynamic interplay between desire for difference and change (Eros) and desire for repetition and a return to "the same" (Thanatos), taken as a model for narrative process and limits, provides a theory of plot as "the internal discourse of mortality."[66] The Freudian notion of "repetition compulsion" as the manifestation of the death drive can be mapped onto strategies of repetition, rhyming, and binding that characterize narrative texts. The death drive is a dynamic of repetition and return that threatens the sovereignty of sexual desire in the Freudian psyche, and, for many theorists, "gives it form": the metaphoric counterpart to the metonymy of desire.

One might also argue, however, that Thanatos is never reconciled by Freud with the pleasure principle. In the *fort/da* game, it is the death drive that binds desire to representation, but it does so without necessarily ending, closing, or limiting representation to identity. Freud witnesses a child throwing and retrieving a toy, saying "*fort*" [gone] and "*da*" [there], a game that Freud interprets as an allegorical compensation for the mother's absence through a compulsively repetitive dialectic of loss and fulfillment (*Beyond the Pleasure Principle*, pp. 8–11). The open-endedness of the game, the play of presence and absence, may be fundamentally a structure of fantasy. Jean-François Lyotard observes that

> beyond the pleasure principle what Freud is surely trying to conceptualize is 'the eternal return of the same', as it manifests itself in the child's game, in the symptom, in the transference, but what he is trying to get at is not the *same,* but the *return.* What strikes him is not the *law* of repetition, but recurrence.[67]

In Lyotard's analysis of *Beyond the Pleasure Principle,* the death drive is a different desire than "the law of desire" that regulates sexuality and representation. It is a principle of "unbinding," which for D. N. Rodowick is an "uncanny recurrence of phantasy [which] always represents an attempt to restage the Oedipal drama of desire and identity, to rewrite it and to have it conclude differently."[68]

Rodowick points out that psychoanalytic film theory has conventionally assumed that pleasure in the classical cinema text is contained and closed by the principle of repetition. As long as the death drive is conceived as a binding force, limiting desire to the law of the symbolic order, spectatorship can only be conceived of as a completion of the text, an instrumental part of the closed system of the textual apparatus. If Thanatos is conceived of as a different dynamic that overwhelms the desire for closure, that grasps the absence of representation and ending as a threshold of the desirable, it is revealed as a discourse of fantasy and utopia. For Rodowick, this is crucial for a psychoanalytic theory of *critical* reading, which

> would watch and listen, with the floating attention of the analyst, for silences, equivocations, evasions, denials, and contradictions. It would understand the recurrences of form not as a desire fulfilled in signs, but as the dream of unfulfilled desire; repetition not as a drive toward ending, but towards new beginnings.[69]

Although the rhetoric of "gaps" and equivocations is a familiar film-critical paradigm, in *Beyond a Reasonable Doubt* the systemic form of such ambiguity is laid bare. In her critique of the "progressive text" argument, Barbara Klinger stresses that "the text, 'in practice', is an intersection at which multiple and 'extra-textual' practices of signification circulate."[70] Narrative mortality is precisely an attempt to stress the practice of the text, rather than its "true" political value or ideological position. The contingency of the "extra-textual" violently interrupts *Beyond a Reasonable Doubt,* not as a documentary materialism but in the disturbance of compulsive repetition. Narrative mortality yields a politics of representation in what might be described as a "regressive" text.

The film is indeed compulsive in its repetition. The plot itself is narrated by Spencer before being "acted out" by Garrett, whose observed behavior turns out to be itself a repetition of earlier (unseen) actions. The various pieces of evidence are each mentioned and imaged repeatedly in the trial and in the events that lead up to it: the murderer's hat, coat, and car seen by one of Patty's friends and acquired by Garrett; a bottle of body makeup and a stocking; a gold lighter given to Garrett by Susan. The scene of the crime is photographed and then returned to twice, once to photograph it and then to reenact the crime. The proliferation of photographs and headlines reduplicates narrative events. Many words and phrases, such as "reasonable doubt," "suspects," "dancers," "belief," "facts," and "fiction," recur again and again in the dialogue. In typically Langian fashion, these elements are used to link consecutive scenes and to establish rhyming patterns throughout the film. Photos held in the hand, newspaper headlines, and even the charred remnants of Spencer's photos are objects that as often as not open scenes (from dissolves), and from which the camera will always pull back to reveal who is seeing.[71]

These objects, images, and phrases enact a series of "correspondences" through the text, provoking a memory of details that are never insignificant. The necessity implied by the montage destabilizes the "normal functioning" of textual repetition, preventing these details from becoming mere "memory traces" that, in being repeated, might evoke the pleasure of quiescence and stability.[72] Instead, the obsessive repetition of *Beyond a Reasonable Doubt* instills a systematicity that deadens narrative desire, or seems to. In fact, the end is even more strongly desired. Peter Brooks observes that

> the paradox of the "dead desire" is of course that it continues very much to live, but in displaced and unrecognized form, as desire that cannot speak its right name ... yet for this very reason continues as a force in the present, driving the discourse of the subject forward in the word-to-word connections of metonymy, extending the desiring subject forward on those "rails" that figure the necessary dynamic of desire, a motor insisting — as narrative ever does — toward the unnamed meaning, the name that could be recaptured only in a recapitulative movement starting from the end.[73]

At the end of *Beyond a Reasonable Doubt,* with the closing of the trap, the spectator finds himself or herself "named" as the meaning of the text, as its dupe and its witness. The awareness of gaps, of that which was not revealed, stimulates one's memory to recapitulate and thus complete the text differently.

The repetitive details of *Beyond a Reasonable Doubt* that are eventually rallied as "evidence" in Garrett's trial are commodities: replaceable and infinitely repeatable. The coat, the hat, the car, the lighter, the body makeup, and the silk stocking are hardly used for their designated purposes, but are the stage properties that, as in Benjamin's *Trauerspiel,* propel Garrett toward his fate. A truly "objective" mise-en-scène, as Rivette puts it, co-opts memory as an inert series of signifiers: details that lack illustrative or decorative value. They are also exemplary of a certain automatism of the text, a force of repetition by which the trauma of "the real" is ironically alluded to. For Lacan, the *tuché* is "the real as encounter—the encounter in so far as it may be missed, in so far as it is essentially the missed encounter."[74] Whether this is the missing mother of the *fort/da* game, the trauma of castration, or, in *Beyond the Pleasure Principle,* the trauma of war experiences, repetition is the means by which this "reality" functions in discourse "automatically." In *Beyond a Reasonable Doubt,* the missing murder, as well as the viewer's own historicity (as the analyst in psychoanalytic transference), emerge as the determining traumas (*tuché* is borrowed by Lacan from Aristotle's "search for cause") of the textual automatism. "Repetition demands the new" for Lacan, insofar as it characterizes "the same" as lacking.

The physical similarities between the multiple father figures evoke another level of uncanny repetition, as does the figure of Garrett's double, Lieutenant Kennedy, who retraces Garrett's steps through the Spencer family and through the burlesque halls of Garrett's "other life." The hero function is split, finally, into the law-abiding romantic hero and the socially deviant criminal. The uncanny parallels between the two, however, point to the arbitrariness of the division. The sense of doubleness, recognition, and repetition implicit in the Freudian uncanny is precisely the momentary coincidence of the transience of self (mortality) and the fantasy of self (immortality): one's identification with the physical world of things coinciding with the quest for autonomous identity. Although Freud theorizes the uncanny by way of the doppelgänger of German literature, its "secularized" form in film noir retains the sense of fantasy linking criminal and cop.

A split identity (which is really no identity at all) is likewise un-cannily inscribed in the spectatorial address of *Beyond a Reasonable Doubt*. As in Lang's wartime propaganda films, the text at first assumes a spectator who is "humanist, democratic and liberal, and *necessarily* assumed so since it is on the basis of these ideological qualities that he is to be mobilized against [capital punishment or] Nazi bar-barism and inhumanity."[75] But this fantastic identity of the morally superior spectator who recognizes his or her humanist values in the film's opening address is taken away and replaced with the enforce-ment of law and order along with a discursive rendering of specta-torship ("the look rendered visible," in the words of Comolli and Géré). With the uncanny return of the criminal to the execution cham-ber, those humanist ideals are doubled with their representation. And as the spectator becomes a witness, he or she also becomes a nobody, excluded from representation, a voyeur.

Lacan speaks of "a trap for the gaze" in relation to Hans Holbein's *The Ambassadors,* in which the imagery of sixteenth-century mercan-tilism and *vanitas* is foregrounded by a perceptually distorted skull. In this picture, Lacan identifies the phallic ghost and annihilation of the subject with the disappearance of the gaze itself. By making the geometrical optics of anamorphosis visible in this painting, Lacan implies that Holbein produces a fascination with that which escapes the gaze. "One thinks it is a question of the geometral eye-point, whereas it is a question of a quite different eye—that which flies in the foreground of *The Ambassadors*."[76] A different perspective is likewise inscribed in *Beyond a Reasonable Doubt* through the very visibility of the laws of narrative, perception, and subjectivity at the vanishing point of their articulation, at their limits. The allegory of narrative mortality in this film is neither a subversion of a textual system nor a "misreading," but a different form of desire than that inscribed in apparatus theory. Its inscription is akin to Holbein's dis-torted skull. It is a desire for something other than the symbolic order, oedipal sexuality, and law of desire that govern this text with such vengeance.

But it is precisely this vengeance and the extreme violence of the plot itself that potentially redeem the text. The authority of death in this film is not the vise grips of destiny but the means of moving be-yond character to storytelling itself, an opening up of representation in a distinctively temporal mode. This is how Benjamin redeems the *Trauerspiel,* through the hindsight of a historiography that mortifies the past in order to redeem its unfulfilled desires. In a text as dead as *Beyond a Reasonable Doubt,* one may glimpse the raw structure of Hollywood's dream of closure: the solution to a crime, the constitution of a couple, and the restoration of law and order. The lack of pleasure achieved despite the necessity and rationality devoted to their ostensible accomplishment is indeed melancholic. In the absence of ironic self-awareness, however, critical spectatorship is invited to redeem the film as a discourse of history. As Benjamin says of the storyteller, it makes it possible to "see a new beauty in what is vanishing."[77]

Perhaps a similar redemption takes place in a film such as *Le Mépris,* in which, as we shall see, the latent melancholy of Lang's impossible dramas of destiny is recognized and drawn out by Godard. But in Benjamin's analysis of the inadequate *Trauerspiel,* death "frequently takes the form of a communal fate, as if summoning all the participants before the highest court ... in death the characters of the *Trauerspiel* lose only the name-bearing individuality, and not the vitality of their role" (p. 136). The theory of fate that emerges from his analysis is one of nonconfidence, of a destiny that is doubled with a defiance that is not yet aware of itself, which is precisely the kind of fate that unfolds in *Beyond a Reasonable Doubt.* "The German *Trauerspiel* was never able to inspire itself to new life; it was never able to awaken within itself the clear light of self-awareness" (p. 158)—and the same might be said of Hollywood in the 1950s.

Like many films, *Beyond a Reasonable Doubt* displays symptoms of instability, incoherence, and "perversity." And yet, to label it a "progressive text" is to attach a modernist aesthetic valorization onto a film that was neither produced nor received within such a context.[78] The problem is not so much one of authenticity (is it or is it not "art") as one of epistemology. The authority of the label "progressive text" and the dubious implications of "progress" betray a cultural criticism locked into a limited dualism of good and bad texts. "Mortifying" the text is a means of engaging with the transience of history as it is registered in cinematic representation. This is a film that demands that belief be suspended for historical rather than formal reasons.

Belief in the image depends on an ideologically invisible authority, not one who wields his power over viewers and characters with the audacity that Lang does in *Beyond a Reasonable Doubt*. Once in-visibility is understood as empowerment, cinematic authorship within the phenomenology of the apparatus can only be an act of mortifi-cation. The impossibility of authorizing images in Hollywood in the 1950s lies at the heart of Lang's modernist anxiety. Narrative mortal-ity is the means by which epistemological and moral belief systems are jointly ruined in postwar American culture. The moral vacuum of the film's ideological contradictions is specifically aligned with the unreliability, the virtually unreadable status of the film's own images. If it was "un-American" to disagree with the verdict reached in the Rosenberg trial in 1953, and if *Beyond a Reasonable Doubt* is read as a deconstruction of symbolic power structures that depend on exclu-sion, then the film's uncanniness can also be traced to the historical traumas of the period.

Lang's disappointment with American institutions of law and image production may have left him without anything to believe in in 1956,[79] but the redemptive counterpart of the mortification and melancholia of *Beyond a Reasonable Doubt* is already supplied by the *Cahiers* crit-ics. Resistance to the oppressive discourses of power and authority in *Beyond a Reasonable Doubt* does not take the form of paranoia, mad-ness, or unchecked desire. Instead it emerges as the void upon which the film's belief systems falter, an empty space waiting to be filled. It is precisely the discourse of Thanatos—repetition, doubling, and return—that takes the film beyond the pleasure of the police thriller or crime story and brings the exercise of capital law into uncanny alignment with the techniques of narrative cinema. The displacement of narrative desire, opened by the film's lack of self-confidence, is a space of mortification and redemption waiting to be realized by cre-ative spectatorship.

TWO

WIM WENDERS
Film as Death at Work

● ————————————————————————————

> Death is one of the rare events that justify the term "cinematic
> specificity." — ANDRÉ BAZIN[1]

Twenty-five years after Lang's last American film, Wim Wenders
crossed the ocean from Germany to make *Hammet* at Francis Ford
Coppola's Zoetrope studio in Los Angeles. Over the five years that
this $10-million film was in production, Wenders made four indepen-
dent films, among them the two features *Lightning Over Water* (1980)
and *The State of Things* (1982). Both films can be read as allegories
of narrative mortality, but the parameters are quite different from
those discussed in chapter 1. In this case, narrative mortality is produced
as an auteurist signature, an investment of subjectivity in cinematic
representation that is cognizant of the limits of that investment. Wenders will stand here as an exemplar of a realist cinematic aesthetic
that struggles with death as a narratological problem.

The fact that *Lightning Over Water* and *The State of Things* were
made *after* the other films that will be discussed refers to a certain

crisis of the European art cinema that developed in the 1980s. Emergent Third World cinemas, home video markets, and American independent filmmaking are a few of the factors contributing to the increasing commodification of art cinema. In critical discourse as well as distribution and festival practices, it began to be perceived as *a* mode of film practice among many others. Although this context will not itself be developed in this chapter, narrative mortality in *The State of Things* and *Lightning Over Water* engages, on different levels, with a variety of modes of film praxis, including documentary, experimental, Hollywood features, independent filmmaking, and video. Within a fragmented cultural landscape, narrative mortality allegorizes the mortality of a certain ideal of realist European art cinema.

It is significant that Wenders is working *after* Godard especially, because Wenders's narrative mortality is in part an allegory of the failure of the filmmaking promised by the French New Wave. The stylistic freedom of Godard's early filmmaking is honed by Wenders into heavily premeditated stylistic decisions and problems. My reading of these two films approaches them as theses or discursive essays on filmmaking in which the techniques and strategies of documentary realism are played off against narrative storytelling. The difference between the representation of death in documentary and fictional modes becomes a means of negotiating between documentary and fiction as aesthetic and economic practices.

Narrative mortality is the allegory of the dialectic of cinematic realism and narrativity, but it is also—in Wenders's cinema—an allegory of the identity of the male filmmaker who searches for himself in both the production of images and the telling of stories. Narrative mortality is produced in the futility of this search, and, depending on one's reading of this situation, the effect is either melancholic or redemptive. The conception of the auteur, which Wenders is bent on salvaging from the commercialization of "art cinema," is a mythic one. His attempt to resurrect those myths of subjectivity and cinematic representation (which we have seen to be already mortified in 1956) is articulated within the terms of cinematic representation. Redemption is inevitably allegorical for Wenders, and its failure is marked more strongly than its realization, but it nevertheless signifies a desire for a cinema with all the aura of Bazinian realism. For Wenders, narrative mortality is an allegory of the myth of total cinema, the ruin of its ideals.

The conjunction of documentary and narrative forms, and the conflict between them, which informs Wenders's version of narrative mortality, are specific to the contradictions of New German Cinema. The emphasis on documentary realism was necessary to a film movement intent on distinguishing itself from Hollywood illusionism for a more politicized approach to contemporary German society. The narrative impetus toward visual pleasure was also necessary, however, to compete with Hollywood for German audiences.[2] Questions of cinematic representation cannot be distinguished from economics, and narrative mortality is, for Wenders as much as for Lang, a function of the industrial constraints on feature filmmaking. The American colonization of postwar German culture, symbolized by the loss of Lang to Hollywood, is a pervasive theme in Wenders's work.[3]

Wenders's intense anxiety of influence vis-à-vis Hollywood involves an adherence to *la politique des auteurs*,[4] which remains for him, in 1980, an equation of vision and consciousness that survives the cruelties of the film industry. Moreover, he is at once attracted to and alienated from the classical mode of storytelling that Hollywood directors apparently achieve so effortlessly and guiltlessly. For his part, from his earliest films through *The State of Things* (1982), Wenders refined a restrained, descriptive narrative style born of such diverse influences as Peter Handke and Ozu Yasujiro; that is, Wenders employs an aesthetic of reality in which "nothing happens" to a greater or lesser extent in each of his films.

The event of death poses a narrative threat to such an aesthetic, a threat that is met head-on in *Lightning Over Water* and *The State of Things*. Both films were fairly spontaneously conceived with (relatively) lower budgets than *Hammet*. They are extremely self-conscious struggles with the act of filmmaking, the first with the more metaphysical aspects of the medium, the second with its institutions and economics. Intrinsic to the highly personal nature of *Lightning Over Water* and *The State of Things* is an exploration of mortality and narrativity as dual, defining characteristics of the medium.

It has been suggested that Wenders used directors to play the murderous gangsters in *The American Friend* because "gangsters and directors both manipulate others."[5] Wenders himself says that "the only men that conduct their lives like the mafia are directors. Samuel Fuller killed an actor and two stuntmen during a shoot because he had them do something that was too dangerous."[6] Wenders has given Fuller roles in three of his films. Like Godard, Wenders's auteurist pantheon is headed by the Lang-Fuller-Ray triumvirate, but Wenders also sees himself as the oedipal son of these Hollywood fathers. Mortality and the representation of death are thus a means of working out his different aesthetic of temporality, and, at the same time, his auteurist anxiety.

Beyond the parameters of intertextual homage, authorial anxiety, and cinematic bravado, Wenders's use of documentary engages several issues of cinematic representation of crucial importance to the notion of narrative mortality. Death can be represented in two ways on film: the actual documented death of films such as *Dying* (Michael Roemer, 1976), *Gimme Shelter* (David and Albert Maysles, 1970), *The Act of Seeing with One's Own Eyes* (Brakhage, 1972), and *Le Sang des bêtes* (Franju, 1949); or by an actor pretending to die. How does one know the difference, though? Death in film is constitutive of the epistemological relativity of phenomenological representation, marking the limits of visual knowledge and representation. It is impossible to document death, since it looks the same as life, and so death challenges representation with the invisibility of nonbeing; death presents an excess over visibility and representation.[7]

The inclusion of documented death in many fiction films constitutes another order of realism, which in some instances constitutes an intrusion of history into fictional narrative. The World War I footage in *Jules and Jim* (Truffaut, 1961), the holocaust footage in *Marianne and Juliane* (Von Trotta, 1981), the Sino-Japanese torture scenes in *The Last Emperor* (Bertolucci, 1987), although they have very different narrative functions, introduce an entirely different order of representation into the fiction. Like the killing of animals in film, this is an indexical order of signification in which the referent is historicized and given a "presence" that iconic and symbolic signification lack.

Paradoxically, performed or enacted death also has a certain authority in fiction film, enhancing the illusion of narrative realism. Hollywood, as an industry devoted to illusion, spends a good deal of its resources on the special effects that represent violence and death.[8]

Actors can do anything on film (although stuntmen often do it for them) except die. Although narrative may indeed tend to contain the "ferocity of death,"[9] it does so at the limits of representation. Violence in the cinema may not necessarily *fix* the spectator's belief, but it does set the limits of "disbelief," the boundary at which reality is displaced, because there can be no death in fiction. The "suspension of disbelief" is placed on trial in the representation of violent death, and the viewer is confronted with the double pleasure of complete loss of critical faculties and the appreciation of the simulation.

Wenders embraces this paradox as the site of a cinematic drama in *Lightning Over Water,* which poses a danger to the viewer in offering up the uncanny spectacle of death. In *The State of Things,* the paradox comes to stand for a kind of paralysis of film aesthetics and politics. Although all film images may well be ruins, signs of transience and decay (their photographic basis being a mortification of reality), the imagery of death is especially so. In the representation of actual death the body becomes the sign of difference and an other time, of which the cinematic signifier is merely a ruin. It underlines and potentially exposes the allegorical nature of cinematic representation, the disjunction between sign and referent, casting that disjunction as a historical displacement. Benjamin's claim that "allegory is in the realm of thought what ruins are in the realm of things"[10] is borne out by a dialectic of documentary and narrative cinematic representation that Wenders hinges on the representation of death.

We shall see that in Wenders's cinema mortality constitutes a certain threat to the eternal verities of identity and patriarchy. The potential of narrative mortality, the potential to open up a space for a different reading and a different kind of viewer, one who takes pleasure in the detachment of critical viewing, is not fully realized. The analyses of *Lightning* and *The State of Things* in this chapter are intended to demonstrate the grounds of this potential in the dialectic of documentary and fictional cinematic realisms.

Lightning Over Water: The Death of the Director

Nick Ray has a small part in *The American Friend,* as a painter who pretends to be dead in order to forge, or repaint, his old works for resale. This character resurfaces briefly in *Lightning Over Water* in

Ray's verbal proposal for the film.[11] Wenders rejects it, saying, "Why make the detour of turning him into a painter? . . . It's you, Nick. Why take the step away?" There is a sense in which *Lightning* is an elaborate exercise on Wenders's part in negotiating this detour, the inevitable "step away into representation."[12] In the literal rendering of the expression "film as death at work,"[13] the mortal temporality of the dying Nick Ray is almost aligned with narrative temporality, potentially closing the gap between the (documentary) Real and its narrative representation.

The gap is never closed because the film is not only a documentary about Nick Ray dying of cancer but also a story of Wim Wenders's consciousness of that process, of Ray, of himself, of the film project, and of the other people involved in the filming of death-at-work. This film is characterized by a Romantic dialectic of body and consciousness. The finite, mortal empiricism of the body is pitted against an eternal, or nontemporal, consciousness that might be preserved in the transcendent values of art and beauty. Moreover, this conception of subjectivity is played out over the two bodies of two directors. Wenders's "anxiety of influence"[14] in *Lightning* is not only concerned with the creative work of himself and Nick Ray, but also with physical presence, delineated through the parameters of performance.

The symptoms of Wenders's anxiety of influence can be read on the level of cinematic representation, as the death of the father is also a loss of transparency and of the "full" signification with which Ray worked in Hollywood. The struggle of the film to "represent" Nick Ray, to circumvent the act of presentation, is a struggle with the fear of death, the source of which is in Wenders far more than in Ray. This fear is precisely a fear of articulating temporal finitude (mortality), a fear of representing the "temporary" presence of Ray's dying body. In *Lightning,* the recovery of the transparent cinematic signifier cannot, ultimately, disguise its status as a disavowal of mortality.

Wenders's commitment to narrative is expressed in the use of confessional voice-over, the structuring of the film around his concern to make a film with/about Ray, the *découpage* in which scenes are invariably shot from two or more camera positions seamlessly edited together, and in the staging of performances within the film. From the opening shots there is a discrepancy between Wenders's claims to spontaneity through the vérité style of performance, and the shot setups that anticipate his arrival in Soho and in Ray's loft. The discrepancy is itself accounted for by the sounds and images of action outside the film takes that are recorded on Tom Farrell's videotape, which Wenders has liberally intercut with his own 35 mm images.

Given the cost and presence of the fifteen-odd member crew, which causes Wenders so much anxiety, there is a certain irony in the use of the video footage.[15] At one point, he says, "I was more and more under the pressure of making 'a movie,' and found myself stuck and preoccupied with the work itself and the sheer mechanics of setting up shots and deciding upon schedules, rather than being concerned with Nick." Especially in conjunction with Wenders's film images, the handheld, blown-up video image is "co-opted as the 'truth' or underside of filmmaking."[16] It is as if Wenders wants to document Ray and himself, their relationship, and Ray's dying, but must leave it to someone else, as he, like Ray, is committed to narrative. Farrell's video discourse supplies the sign of an "immediate" alternative to Wenders's far more mediated practice. Video is coded as "more real" than film in *Lightning.*

Farrell's videotapes include fragments of dialogue in which Ray asks Wenders, "Does it seem like acting, Wim?" Wenders answers, "Not at all," but later we "overhear" him directing Nick to "turn your head toward the camera...." On yet another level of representation, several theatrical interludes are explicit fictionalizations of characters' relationships to one another. In Wim's "dream sequence," he is lying on a hospital bed while Tom shoots him with his video camera and then strangles him, acting out their ostensible rivalry as two aesthetic heirs of Ray. Toward the end of the film, Ronnee Blakley and Ray play Cordelia and Lear intercut with lingering close-ups of Wenders and Susan (Nick's companion) observing the scene.

All of these trappings of fiction cannot efface the physical deterioration of Ray's body. The film, says Ray, is about "a man who wants to bring himself all together before he dies," but as he says this, his video image threatens to disappear in an underlit, unstable shot on a monitor. The fallacy of this quest, the impossibility of identity, is displaced in the split subjectivity of the film, Wenders's conscientiousness taking up where Ray's body fades out. Ray's implication that the cinema is up to the task of his unification is never in doubt, except that his spiritual survival is explicitly a filmic one. The blue-sailed

Chinese junk, which Ray conceived as a vessel to carry him to the cure for cancer, is the film's most powerful sign of transcendence. It sails out of New York harbor, shot from a transcendent, swooping helicopter, and displays on its deck a huge Mitchell camera and a moviola from which ribbons of filmstrip flutter. The funeral urn is prominent on the boat's cabin, from the credits that follow the "arrival" prologue to the final epilogue, indicating the postmortem exercise that the film really is.

Timothy Corrigan has deployed a Lacanian model to demonstrate the imbrication of auteurist anxiety and narrative mortality in *Lightning*. He describes the dialectic of mortality and consciousness in *Lightning* in terms of "narrative murders." If the work of narrative is a violence against reality, the "priority" of the father and "posteriority" of the narrating son, according to Corrigan, constitute a killing of the Symbolic in an attempt to recover the lost unity of the Imaginary. The son "narrates in the name of Death for the father's corpses"[17] insofar as narration is only made possible through the father's symbolic law of difference; the knowledge of the disavowal necessary for narrative presence and homogeneity takes the form of violence.

Because Corrigan collapses the terms father/son and reality/narrative, he can conclude that *Lightning* witnesses "a conversation which for once allows the son to speak for himself and to look directly at the physical reality of the father/auteur" (pp. 15–16). The killing of the father is the mythic (oedipal) strategy of recovering a unity with the mother. Indeed, *Lightning* ends with Wenders reading the words from Nick's diary, which are superimposed in Ray's handwriting over a long shot of the junk: "I looked into my face and what did I see? No granite rock of identity. Faded blue, drawn skin, and wrinkled lips. And sadness. And the wildest urge to recognize and accept the face of my mother."[18]

For Corrigan, any narrative is a murder designed to recover a loss, but the film noir trajectory from one (opening) murder to another (final one) is explicitly so. The killing of the father in the oedipal drama of *Beyond a Reasonable Doubt* might stand as a thematization of such a theory of representation. Bernardo Bertolucci observes that Wenders, in *Lightning,* resembles "a killer out of a thriller who would find out, by one of those poetic licenses only allowed to B films, that his client and his victim are one and the same person."[19] Corrigan suggests that Ray, the auteur/client, "escapes his role as the victim of his son's narrative which he has bequeathed and which always embodies his relationship to his son."[20] For Corrigan, whereas "innumerable" films are structured as narrative murders, the achievement of *Lightning* is its therapeutic stance vis-à-vis this strategy, transposing the theoretical into the physical, articulating a filmic unconscious. It is, for him, a "healthy" film, which suggests that the film's performances, as an acting out of personal and narratological relationships, are a form of therapy.

The notion of "narrative murders" offers a productive model for theorizing the relationship between auteurist anxiety and the function of death in *Lightning,* and yet Corrigan cannot account for the difficulty of representation that characterizes this film. Ray is far more than an "allegory for the entire film," and Corrigan's psychoanalytic framework has the same limitations as Wenders's medium in its inability to go beyond representation. How does Ray's cancer fit into a description of the film as narrative murder? If the film is a self-conscious act of murder, why is there no representation of death? How does Ray's natural death structure the antagonism between documentation and storytelling that so thoroughly pervades the film?

Wenders does not, after all, murder Nick, but watches him die—without, however, seeing the actual event. This absence is not simply a matter of discretion, but of explicit elision. Nick himself says "cut" to end the last shot of himself before the ensuing black leader and the epilogue, in which the film crew holds a wake on the junk. Nick finally utters the direction to cut after an extremely long take in which he displays his physical debilitation. His threat of sickness, of puking on Wim, on camera, is a displacement of his threat to die on camera, in sight. This, indeed, would be a narrative murder: Wenders allowing Nick to "pass away" while the film continues to roll.

Wenders's avoidance of representing actual death on film is a repressive gesture in recognition of the risk of an "ontological obscenity."[21] This is a term introduced by Bazin in an essay on *La Course de taureaux* in which he points out that death and the sexual act are distinguished from all other instants in that, when filmed, they are endowed with the potential for repetition, which, in life, they ontologically lack.[22] The "supreme cinematic perversion" is the reversed projection of an execution. "One cannot die twice. Photography hasn't this power of film, it can't represent the dying or the corpse, nor the imperceptible passage from one to the other."[23] Although the matador's death is a singular moment in time, "on the screen, the matador dies every afternoon." It is an ontological obscenity because of the contradiction between two temporalities: one that takes place *in time* (narrative and the mortal body) and another that *contains time* (the film object, capable of infinite repetition).

Real death in film is obscene for Bazin because of the grounding of his film theory in what has come to be known as "the mummy complex." Philip Rosen has pointed to the imagery of embalmment and preservation that underscores Bazin's key essays on the ontology and evolution of the cinema. He points out that Bazin's conception of realism is not only indexical but assumes a relationship between image and referent that is inevitably temporal.[24] Like the mummy that preserves the substance of a past life, the filmic image contains the trace of a past event to which it is indexically related:

Bazin's Egyptian mummies reveal a universal, unconscious human need which cultures must confront through ritual, religion, art or in some other way. This is the need for some fantastic defense against time. For any human subject, the passage of time is the approach of death, the ultimate material limitation on subjectivity. (p. 20)

In "Mort tous les après-midi," Bazin distinguishes between the subject of awareness and the objective time of things, between which death is a "frontier." As a singular instant, death belongs to the subjective pole, but as a representation "in the can" it would explode the basic, illusory premise on which the medium depends for its capacity as "defense strategy." The "creation of an ideal world in the likeness of the real, with its own temporal destiny,"[25] would crumble under the mortal sign of human temporality.

Bazin does not address the difference between real and enacted death on film, although in this particular essay he is indubitably concerned with *la mort réelle*. The enacted deaths in *Rome Open City* and *Paisà* do not appear to threaten the "factuality" of Rossellini's style for Bazin. What strikes him about the bullfighting film is the conjunction of spectacle/theater and death, which, when recorded on film, mars its status as an "objective replica of memory." The implication is that the suspension of disbelief necessary for cinematic illusionism is coextensive with a suspension of the knowledge of the spectator's own mortality. Actual death on film would therefore short-circuit the defense mechanism on which Bazin's ontology is based.

Rosen argues that Bazin's phenomenology is not simply a subject-object split but a subjective investment in the image in which temporality, rather than referentiality, defines the pole of representation: "Time passing, duration and change, are exactly what Bazin's ontological spectator is driven to disavow, for they raise the problem of death." For Bazin, "change mummified" is "the image of duration," so that realism, as subjective engagement with that sense of time, is "an act of heroism," a struggle against temporality as an irreversible, historical process.[26] "If 'no more cinema' is the goal of the myth of total cinema ... that slogan implies a subject no longer alienated and threatened by objectivity ('death') but rather in perfect communion with it" (p. 21).

Bazin's imbrication of phenomenology with romantic Catholicism situates subjectivity as perceptual self-definition (the artist as witness),[27] which is also an "irrational leap of faith."[28] Only by retaining many of the central categories of nineteenth-century thought can Bazin conceive of film as a "death mask." The filmed subject survives in the objective, material status of the film, a survival that depends on the repeatability of the profilmic instants, in which death cannot, ontologically, be included. Film does not conceal an absence, as post-structuralist thought (Barthes, Corrigan) would have it, but preserves a temporal relationship between image and referent. The guarantee of this relationship is the intentionality of consciousness and the myths and institutions of authorship as personal vision. Bazin is fully cognizant that the mechanical reproduction of images offers the lure of a triumph over time, while also taking place in time, registering its transience and objective difference from subjective consciousness. It is "obscene," however, to allow this difference to be perceived: it betrays a lack of faith in cinema's realist potential.

This dialectic of temporal difference and its disavowal is exemplified in a scene in *Lightning*, remarked on by most writers on the film, in which the sixty-seven-year-old, cancer-ridden Ray walks past a movie screen on which is projected an image of himself, approximately ten years younger, from his own film *We Can't Go Home Again* (figure 3). The man on the screen has a wild head of white hair, a plump red face, and an energy that the thin man shuffling to the bathroom lacks. This image might also be described as "change mummified," but it radically subverts Bazin's ontology of preservation, for it preserves two different times, situating "duration" as history. It foreshadows Ray's death, and does so at the expense of any temporal relation with the profilmic, for it is an other time, an other's time, that these images record. Realism as a subjective "obsession" with temporality is superseded here by an inscription of temporal difference.

Wenders's voice-over throughout the film itself constitutes a doubling of temporality by casting the whole image track onto a narrated past, marking the film as a post mortem exercise. The present tense of the image track, as a realist "preservation" of life, is constantly belied by that other present tense of reflection recorded on the sound track. Wenders's flirtation with the "ontological obscenity" of the representation of death reaches its apotheosis in the last long take of

Fig. 3. *Lightning Over Water*: Nick Ray watches his younger, healthier self in his film *We Can't Go Home Again.*

Nick in the hospital, in which Nick argues playfully but threateningly with Wenders about who should say "cut" and when. The medium close-up of Nick, held on-screen for almost five minutes, becomes an icon of the film itself; duration, or the representation of time, is specifically related to the irreversible temporality of history and mortality. Like Bazin, Wenders escapes the "truth of death" only by partaking in it.[29]

The extended duration of this shot of Nick has a destabilizing effect in its articulation of presence; Nick ceases to perform himself and "brings himself together" finally but briefly in a collapse of real and represented time. The identity of representation and event erupts in the performative order to "cut" in which the profilmic (Nick) acts upon the ordering and editing of images. (The performative is a device that, in written discourse, consists of words that act.) As Ivone Margulies puts it, "The reality of the profilmic acts upon the film's body" such that "the filmic body is for once dangerously and fascinatingly confused with the subject's image."[30]

And yet the film finally proposes "the elimination of the body as a troubling presence." The abrupt curtailment of Nick Ray's image with the directive to cut is "an eruption of performance" in the fiction of transparency.[31] In other words, the body is finally eliminated at one and the same time as the break between presentation (Nick's direct address) and representation (its position in the *découpage* of the film) is enunciated. The discrepancy between the unified self and the fragmentation of identity in language is thereby crystallized. Authorship is designated as the control embedded in the editing process, and despite the fact that it is Ray whose subjective presence is thus enunciated, Wenders emerges from the scene as enunciator. It is he who cuts to a long shot of the junk in New York harbor.

In his voice-over narration, Wenders expresses his anxiety regarding his representation of mortality: "Like a very precise instrument, the camera showed clearly and mercilessly that his time was running out. No, you couldn't really see it with your bare eyes, there was always hope. But not in the camera. I didn't know how to take it. I was terrified." Wenders's fear is not simply of Nick's death, but of his narrativization of that dying. Insofar as he is not photographing but filming, capturing the body's existence in time, the Bazinian paradox of "change mummified" is laid bare. The attempt at a unified representation of identity (a man bringing himself all together) is systematically challenged by the image of Ray's own body.

The tension between drama and document in *Lightning* is not only a question of realism, but more fundamentally one of performance. Narrative mortality is in this instance an allegory of the body of the film as it coincides with the body of the person/actor. The ontological obscenity toward which the film veers is, after all, produced by the conflict between the indexicality of the bodily presence of the man, Nick Ray, and the insertion of that body into narrative language. The tension evoked by Ray's performance involves the temporally finite body (biology) of the actor and the construction of the character of "self," a split that is constitutive of performance and is conventionally disavowed in the play of identity. Unlike most movies, the discourse of the body is enunciated in *Lightning,* and is articulated against the discourse of self.[32]

In this sense the filming of "death-at-work" is also a deconstruction of the precepts of method acting (in which the "self" is appropriated by the character), exhibited within the context of *Lightning* in the film clip of Robert Mitchum in Ray's *The Lusty Men*.[33] In this wordless sequence, Mitchum travels from an abandoned rodeo to an abandoned house where he finds a stash he presumably hid under the house as a child. This scene of return and recovery evokes very powerfully (as Wenders says to Ray) the sense of returning home. But the narrative containment extends to the performance style that is in such contradistinction to the film we are watching, in which self and body are in continual oscillation. Mitchum may not be the best example of a method actor, but in this particular sequence, in which he does not speak, he creates a character "realistically" through gesture, facial expression, and gait, completely collapsing biology (physical presence) and subjectivity. Ray's "genuine behavior" in *Lightning* shows up the "bad faith" of Mitchum's performance.

Mitchum's return home in *The Lusty Men* had already been evoked by Wenders in a scene in *Kings of the Road,* so the homage is also to himself as cinematic heir, for whom homelessness, identity, and return are intimately bound together. As Kathy Geist puts it, "*Lightning* implies that death is home for the homeless and at the same time the end, perhaps even the fulfillment of the search for identity, the quest for self-realization."[34] Ray's last film, the one that he walks past as it is screened in his loft in *Lightning,* is, of course, called *We Can't Go Home Again*. The question of performance in *Lightning,* construed as a question of temporality, is posed in terms of the narrative dynamics of repetition and desire. The film demonstrates the way in which return, repetition, and reproduction in the cinema are inevitably countered by the different temporality that marks the unfolding of narrative and life. Insofar as the desire for return is inevitably countered by the desire for difference, we cannot, in fact, go home again; subjectivity is always in transit. *Lightning* thus approximates the contradictions of *Beyond the Pleasure Principle* and the uncanny.

If the trajectory of *Lightning Over Water* toward Ray's death takes the form of storytelling, fiction, and performance, the "film surface" is a performance of time. But unlike most such narratives, "the strategies of completion that mask heterogeneity"[35] — containment and closure — fail. This performance is cruelly undermined by an impossibility of return; time is not "performed" but spent. The biological changes that we witness posit a unidirectional temporality that no amount of narrative repetition can completely "figure out" by making safe. This is precisely the danger posed by the film, a danger of a film that cannot fulfill its own goals.

Wenders's narrativization of Ray's death is ultimately signed in the richly colored imagery of the Chinese junk, its blue sails and red woodwork moving slowly across the glittering blue water, the camera swooping in from a bright sky. Opening and closing the film, these shots supply a visual image for the film's title, and become the mark of closure, a guarantee of narrativization through repetition, bound with the authority of "beauty." Images of the junk sailing across New York harbor are also intercut twice into the body of the film, photographed from various angles passing under bridges. The symbolism of river, boat, and bridge, together with the "transcendent" helicopter photography and "sublime" sense of space, coalesce in a discursive strategy very different from the confining close-ups of Nick Ray dying in the hospital.[36]

In the transition from Ray's debilitated body to the wake on the junk, in which crew members restore an identity to the man verbally, Wenders attempts to restore the transparent "preservative" ontology of the film image. The cut away from that excruciatingly long take of Ray's direct address hides the dead body, repressing its threatened visualization, and replaces it with a symbol of transcendence. The boat is charged with the poetic significance of Nick's immortality: a symbol of an endless trajectory through time, but also of his desire to go to China for a cure. If Bazin's phenomenology is marked by a Romantic gesture of transcendence, it remains a gesture (a "myth" of total cinema). The instability of the immortalizing, preservative sign— which is, for Bazin, the film image—is indicated precisely by his recognition of ontological obscenity. Wenders's substitution of the erotic illusion of transparency for the *difference* constituted by Nick's mortality is in keeping with Bazin's denial of death, not only in the desire for transcendence but in the allegorical, displaced status of its achievement (figure 4).

The presence of the camera, moreover, in the monumental Mitchell on the junk's deck, and the reflexive acknowledgment of the helicopter camera position link this transcendence to the artist or filmmaking auteur, a concept to which the film has, after all, been devoted. The fetish made of the cinematic apparatus is a means of reasserting the power of the image over the threat of mortality. But

Fig. 4. *Lightning Over Water*: The Chinese junk sailing out of New York harbor carrying Nick Ray's ashes.

again, it takes the form of allegory. The inclusion of the camera in the image defeats this power at the same time as it states the desire for a total cinema that might transcend the threat of mortality. An "aesthetic of reality," not reality itself, finally triumphs over the narrativization of mortality.

As the title *Lightning Over Water* suggests, the film adopts allegory as the work of mourning. The inability to "sum up" a man in a film, and the inability to know death any better by confronting it head-on, haunt the film as an evacuation of meaning, a loss of confidence in cinematic realism and technology. The apparatus comes to replace or stand in for the body, not to preserve it for eternity. For Freud, melancholia is the pathological form of mourning in which an identification takes place with the lost love-object. The lost object is normally a person, but Freud readily admits that it may also be "the loss of some abstraction which has taken the place of one [person], such as fatherland, liberty, an ideal, and so on."[37] At stake in *Lightning* is the secure place of the subject, not only on the level of Nick "bringing himself all together," but also for the subject of vision, who is first and foremost Wenders himself.

In Paul Virilio's words, "Today, directors (and politicians) have lost all prominence, and are swallowed up in technical effects, rather like Nicholas Ray in Wim Wenders' *Lightning Over Water*."[38] But Wenders himself is equally lost in the film's technologies of representation, and deliberately so. The work of the film is like the mechanism of melancholia, which consists of a libidinal cathexis of the ego with the lost loved object. In the Freudian scenario, the melancholic is unable to fully distinguish between self and other, and is in effect mourning a part of his or her self as lost. "After this regression of the libido the process can become conscious; it appears in consciousness as a conflict between one part of the ego and its self-criticizing faculty."[39] This conflict is indeed staged in Wenders's double role of performance and voice-over, in which he is both immediately "there" on-screen and removed into another time offscreen, often commenting on the loss of time figured in Nick's decaying body.

A similar split occurs in the spectator, who is at once bound to the "pleasure" of the text through its narrative and performance strategies and acutely aware of the "crime" of the film—its appropriation of finite (unrepeatable) time for this (repeatable) film object.

Wenders's spectator is lured into a Bazinian obsession for total cinema, but as the gap between reality and image is narrowed, that reality is at the same time dying, revealed as temporary. And yet the death of cinema, staged as the death of auteurism and the death of the "myth of total cinema," is perhaps more in the mode of a "mourning play" than Freudian psychoanalysis can fully accommodate. The allegorical mode of the baroque *Trauerspiel* (mourning play) was produced within a void of meaning, after the fall of language from the immediacy of speech to the doubleness of writing. Wenders's allegorical mode likewise mourns the death of a realist cinema with which he himself identifies closely.

Wenders's mortification of cinematic realism is staged among the ruins of modernism. Video fragments rupture the surface of the film, disfiguring its organicity, and may in themselves be interpreted as exemplary of a postmodern accumulation of the "ruins" of representation. One of the last video sections of *Lightning* is Wim and Nick's confessional conversation in the hospital (in which the announcement of John Wayne's death from cancer is heard on the radio), shot almost entirely in close-up. Wenders observes in this scene that "the film, whatever we did, looked very clean, pretty—like licked off. And I think that is a pure result of fear." And yet, shortly after this sequence, about three-quarters of the way through the film, the video disappears. It disappears because it inscribes a different temporality within the film, a discursive heterogeneity that threatens the possibility of transcendence, a desire that from this point will be challenged only by Ray's own filmed presence.

Wenders uses and exaggerates the difference between film and video, capitalizing on their different ontological properties.[40] The televisual referent does not necessarily belong to a different time; its indexicality does not necessarily embody a historical relationship because it has the alibi of "liveness" available to it. Video might be said to lack "aura" in Benjamin's sense, but in *Lightning* it also lacks that obsessive drive that governs Wenders's project, his anxiety of authorship and his obsession for a "total cinema" without mediation. Even if the liveness of the video discourse is only hypothetical in *Lightning,* it serves to highlight the complex mediation and subjective investment implied in Wenders's narrativization of Ray's last weeks. The graininess of the video image is the polar opposite of the transcendent "aesthetic of reality" of Wenders's final 35 mm shots of New York harbor. The video images offer a past tense to the eternal present of a film that finally tries to escape the claims of time by a recourse to beauty.

Farrell's ability to shoot everywhere all the time at close range gives his video discourse a spontaneity and intimacy unavailable to Wenders's authoritative structuring of Nick Ray's demise. Farrell's footage may be more "truthful" in its vérité style, but it is nevertheless *contained* by Wenders's dominant 35 mm discourse in an effort to repress its articulation of difference. Wenders's dismissive attitude toward video is expressed most blatantly in *Room 666* (1982), in which sixteen filmmakers attempt to answer the loaded question, "Is the cinema a language about to get lost, an art about to die?" in a hotel room with a television set behind their left shoulders. It is as if Wenders takes seriously Godard's analogy (in *Sauve qui peut*) between the film/video relationship and the Cain/Abel relationship. As Ray's competing sons, Wenders and Farrell confront each other in *Lightning* with the two tools of representation and their respective truth claims. Wenders's victory over Farrell is only at the cost of disavowal; the film's resolution in favor of full-fledged cinematic transparency, and its capacity for the preservation of life, are tinged with the ironic knowledge of the other ontology of video.

A cinematic ethic (the suppression of temporal difference) thus slides over a social ethic (the disavowal of death), transposing the difficult terms of "decency" into those of language. One critic of *Lightning,* Jon Jost (whose intentions may be less than objective as he too wanted to make a last film with Ray but was ousted by Wenders with his more solid financial backing), writes that "in his last months ... what Ray needed was love. Instead he got a crew who seemed to perceive life only through the mechanical devices of film. They rolled over him with a movie-making machine, and now they even choose to display the carnage."[41] Jost claims that the filmmaking activity hastened Ray's death, but even without such extratextual suspicions, the film does evoke a sense of horror for many viewers. Even before the titles roll, Wenders tackles the social taboos about death by confronting Nick with the subject of his own death as the subject of the film: "I wanted to talk to you Nick," to which Nick replies, "About what? Dying?"

Among the taboos against death in contemporary society, cancer has been described by Susan Sontag as being especially "obscene."[42] Wenders's aesthetic treatment of Nick's cancer has, perhaps, more affinities with the nineteenth-century mystification of tuberculosis than modern denial or clinical detachment. Sontag says that, "starting in the early nineteenth century, TB became a new reason for exile, for a life that was mainly traveling.... The Romantic view is that illness exacerbates consciousness."[43] Although the details of the work of the cancer within Ray's ravaged body are not withheld from the viewer of *Lightning,* this crude biology is finally eliminated with Ray's "last directorial assertion": to cut the long take. An act of consciousness, an aesthetic choice, thus sublimates the cancerous body. The cancer, however, affects the images themselves, which can only register the desire and not the achievement of such transcendence.

If, in *Lightning Over Water,* Nick Ray tries to "find himself" before he dies and Wenders's narrative is structured as an investigation into the filming of death-at-work, the film follows a familiar film noir course. Wenders's stay in New York with Ray is a form of passage in which death figures prominently as an ambivalence: is Nick already dead or is he dying in the course of the film? (Which is to say, is the film a document or a narrative?) Whereas, in the American noir texts of the 1950s, such a dead/not-dead ambivalence registered the duplicity and reversals of cold war politics, for Wenders it is closely related to the American/German-European dialectic that informs so many of his films. The noir protagonist's search for identity becomes, for Wenders, a quest for a self-image within an international cultural context.

Wenders's melancholia is directed everywhere except at post-Nazi Germany, and yet the persistent discourse of "home" as impossible narrative goal of his films is itself symptomatic of what Eric Santer has described as the "tasks of mourning" for the second and third generations in postwar Germany.[44] Although the German context of Wenders's cultural melancholia may be most overt in *Kings of the Road,* the traumatic memory of national history is no less pertinent to *Lightning* and *The State of Things.* The themes of exile and travel, and the abandoned child — which Elsaesser describes as "the key figure" of the New German Cinema[45] — are the signs of a generation struggling to be reconciled with its parents' history. "The dead souls of Germany" haunt Wenders's cinema both as a function of representation and as an oedipal nightmare in which Hollywood directors become surrogate father victims in fantasies of patricide.

The scrawled passage from Nick's diary, expressing a fear and desire to identify with his mother, as the last gesture of the film, finally exposes the limits of Wenders's narrative mortality. As in much of Wenders's work, women can only function as an idealized source of originary unity, and are thus equated with both home and death.[46] This particular passage is striking in its display of the symptoms of the film's oedipal anxieties, as the woman's body provokes that *Unheimlicheit* that Freud identifies as one source of the uncanny:

> Whenever a man dreams of a place or a country and says to himself, still in the dream, "this place is familiar to me, I have been there before," we may interpret the place as being his mother's genitals or her body. In this case, too, the *unheimlich* is what was once *heimlich,* home-like, familiar; the prefix "un" is the token of repression.[47]

After going through an exhaustive series of equivalents for the German word *heimlich,* the first and most familiar of which is "home," Freud notes that "*heimlich* is a word the meaning of which develops towards an ambivalence, until it finally coincides with its opposite, *Unheimlicheit*" (p. 30). The Bazinian "mummy complex" is itself a manifestation of the Freudian uncanny.[48] The narrative mortality of *Lightning* exploits this uncanniness as a melancholic allegory of cinematic realism and the myth of oedipal subjectivity harbored within its impossible realization.

Wenders's images of Nick Ray evoke his death in their depiction of temporal difference and the physical trajectory of mortality, but at the same time, that death is eluded. In the elision of actual death and the fetishization of the image and cinematic technology, Ray is finally immortalized in celluloid. Through the repression of the difference between image and referent, Wenders ultimately disavows that mortality which he has struggled to understand in the terms of cinematic specificity. Capitulation to an allegory of redemption in the celebratory imagery of cinema only barely masks the film's failure either to confront the ruins of the body of the director or to embrace the transformation of cinema beyond the "myth of total cinema."

In *The State of Things,* Wenders pursues these issues into the heart of the beast of Hollywood. Documentary and narrative realisms again collide in a mortifying relationship, but in this film, "storytelling" takes up where, in *Lightning*, "slick images" and preconceived sequences leave off. Again, narrativity is confronted with the mortifying challenge of its photographic basis in the historical real.

The State of Things: The Death of the Real

One of the last lines of dialogue that we "overhear" from the crew at Nick's wake at the end of *Lightning Over Water* is "Would you kill somebody for a great shot?" The conflation of the shooting of guns and shooting of cameras comprises the uncanny dimension of *The State of Things*. A relation of doubling exists between Wenders and the protagonist, Friedrich Munroe (Patrick Bauchau), a German director making a film in Portugal with American backing. When Fritz is suddenly killed by unseen, anonymous gangsters at the end of the film, an image shot by Fritz's super-8 camera survives him, suggesting, once again, an allegorical redemption of the auteur.

Although this film is as "international" as *Lightning* in its locations, casting, and financing, the "self" that is constructed—or rather, pursued—across this post-Godardian landscape is symptomatic of New German Cinema and its preoccupation with authorship and internationalism. Thomas Elsaesser argues that within the context of the wide range of cultural and economic funding measures that supported independent filmmaking in Germany in the 1970s, filmmakers were obliged to identify themselves as self-employed entrepreneurs as well as craftspeople and artists. "The author became a necessary ideological fiction," if for no other reason than to give a certain coherency to the diversity of film praxis that was to be subsumed under the nationalistic label of New German Cinema.[49]

Moreover, the difficulties of a national cinema in an international marketplace were epitomized in the New German Cinema and Wenders's place in it. Romanticism, from this perspective, becomes at once a nationalist trait and a militant discourse, in keeping with the political radicalism of the late 1960s and early 1970s, when the New German Cinema was struggling to define itself.[50] By 1982, when an "art cinema" could no longer be comfortably distinguished from commercial cinema, a Romantic conception of the visionary auteur informs *The State of Things* as a lost mythology, but also as the axis of difference between European and Hollywood filmmaking. For Wenders, this difference pertains to the role of authorship and the compromises demanded by larger audiences. It also pertains, in his cinema, to the different roles of mortality in the different forms of film narrative associated with commercial and "art" cinema. Narrative mortality in Wenders's films becomes the allegory of this difference, which cannot be convincingly sustained in the 1980s.

Wenders visited Chilean filmmaker Raoul Ruiz's set for *The Territory* on the coast of Portugal during a three-month hiatus in the shooting of *Hammett* in 1981. There he discovered the ingredients for the expression of his thoughts on the state of the art. Ruiz's production had temporarily halted because of lack of film stock and other supplies that had been cut off by his American financiers.[51] Wenders was thus supplied not only with cast, crew, and location, but also with the narrative premise for a film about filmmaking. Having more resources at his disposal than Ruiz, Wenders rounded up additional cast members and writers, film stock, and salaries, plus a distribution setup, and in under two weeks began shooting a film that had only the barest definition buried deep in the director's mind.

The State of Things was intended from the outset to be a process of discovery, a film that would make itself and be about its making, starting with even less of a script than *Lightning*.[52] Wenders and Robert Kramer generated scenes and dialogue night by night during the shoot. Interviews with the cast indicate a good deal of tension created by this spontaneous production method.[53] Wenders describes the project as "therapy," a "psychoanalysis of the cinema itself,"[54] a claim that is indicative of his personal stake in the state of the art. The film that emerges is a veritable thesis on time and narrative film, cinema, and storytelling, written across a double axis of cinematic realism and the economics of filmmaking. The thesis defended by the film (stated bluntly several times by Fritz himself) is that films need stories and stories need death. This necessity is not aesthetic so much as economic. Insofar as Fritz's American funding is conditional on it, death is posited at the nexus of film style and financing.

The necessity of death is, furthermore, a necessity of plot. The film comprises three very different narrative styles, beginning with a science-fiction film-within-the-film called *The Survivors*. This generic melodrama with a touch of epic is set in a postnuclear landscape, and is based partly on Ruiz's aborted film *The Territory*, and also on Alan Dwan's 1961 film *The Most Dangerous Man Alive*. After four or five minutes, a painted backdrop, then a director, then a crew are revealed by a sweeping camera movement that seems to answer the final shot of *Le Mépris*. Whereas Godard's film ends with a pan away from a film crew shooting Ulysses, out to a Mediterranean oceanscape, Wenders moves in from the restless Atlantic to a set similarly located on a cement, plateau-like structure beside the sea.

The bulk of *The State of Things* concerns the cast and crew of *The Survivors* waiting for film stock to arrive so they can complete the picture. Two actors, two actresses, two little girls, a director of photography, a scriptwriter, and the director Fritz and his wife mope around the deserted hotel without money, without motivation, and without any connective story line. This setting, as well as several particular shots in the hotel bar, recall Fassbinder's *Beware the Holy Whore* (1970), which ends in melodramatic death. Fritz periodically tries to telephone Gordon, his producer in Los Angeles, who has cut off the supply of film stock. Set in the Portuguese hotel and town of Sintra, this part of the film in which "nothing happens" aspires to the narrative minimalism of directors such as Antonioni, Akerman, Warhol, Ozu, and Wenders's own early films.

Finally, Fritz flies to Los Angeles, and finds Gordon driving around in a Winnebago, on the run from some mysterious gangsters to whom he owes money. Set mainly in vehicles, with references to film noir littering the dialogue, this section of the film acquires its relatively rapid pacing, to some extent, from Los Angeles itself (figure 5). (Wenders claims that the "imagery of L.A." was something that "happened to the film, like a capsule of speed.")[55] In the final sequence of the film, Gordon, the producer played by Allan Goorwitz, and the director Fritz make explicit the opposition between American and European filmmaking, the difference that the film has illustrated by way of sets, shooting styles, and narrative events. It is worth quoting this final dialogue, set in the back of Gordon's mobile home, the streets of Los Angeles moving past the windows like film screens:

Fig. 5. *The State of Things*: Fritz (Patrick Bauchau) is overwhelmed by the stylish photography of Los Angeles. Publicity still courtesy of Cinémathèque Québécoise.

GORDON: ... I tried to show dailies to these two loan sharks.... They thought it was a joke—what's the matter with the color? [laughs] In a funny way, those fuckin' sharks aren't crazy. We're the ones who're crazy.... They're not lookin' to kill me. They just wanted a fuckin' story. They had a hundred grand they were willing to shove out if I had a story. And I told them I had a story, it's about survival. We're all tryin' to survive, right? "The Survivors." If I'd 'a shot the same film with an American director and American cast, in color, I'd be sittin' on top of the world in six months.... Without a story you're dead. You can't build a movie without a story. Ever build a house without walls? It's the same. A movie's got to have walls....

FRITZ: Why walls? The space between the characters can carry the load.

GORDON: You're talkin' about reality. Fuck reality. Cinema is not about life going by. People don't want to see that.

FRITZ *and* GORDON *face the camera from the back bench of the van, Fritz leaning on film cans, the big window behind their heads like a screen; Gordon sings and Fritz talks at the same time.*

GORDON: Hollywood, Hollywood, people never had it so good.... What do you do with your days, my friend? What do you do with your nights, my friend? In Hollywood, in Hollywood. Never been a place where people had it so good. What do you do with your wife, my friend? What do you do with your life, my friend, in Hollywood? etc. What did they do with your head? When did you learn you were dead, my friend? In Hollywood, in Hollywood.

FRITZ: I made ten movies ... ten times, same story I was doing. In the beginning it was easy because I just went from shot to shot.
But now in the morning I'm scared. Now I know how to tell stories. Unrelentlessly. As the story comes in, life sneaks out. Life sneaks out ...
Everything gets pressured into images. Mechanism. Birth, as all stories can end, all stories are about death.

GORDON: Death, Fritz. It's what it's all about. It's the biggest story in the world. Second best only to love stories.

Exterior shots of mobile home, Fritz's car in parking lot, music up. GORDON *exits with small dog in his arms,* FRITZ *follows with super-8 camera; billboards, palm trees, and a huge cutout of a G.I. in background of parking lot.*

GORDON: Time for all good survivors to say good-bye, eh?

As they embrace GORDON *is shot in the back. Cut to a tilted, grainy image of* GORDON *falling to the ground.* FRITZ *holds his camera like a gun, rising slowly from a crouch by Gordon's body. Cut to the super-8 footage panning around the empty parking lot.* FRITZ, *turning with camera, is suddenly shot and falls. He props himself up on Gordon's body, still holding the camera in both hands. The super-8 image pans right to a truck.*

Close-up of Fritz's and Gordon's hands, the dog leash, and the camera. Cut to a canted fixed shot of the asphalt; a car pulls out and turns as the camera tilts down. Fade out.

The implication in this last scene of the film—that "films about the space between characters" are antithetical to storytelling—is more than a narrative opposition. It is also, and perhaps most crucially, a question of realism. Earlier in the film, Joe, the director of photography played by Sam Fuller, says that "life is in color, but black and white is more realistic." Indeed, Wenders's subtitle for the film is "Almost a Documentary."[56] The entire Portugal section involves actors passing the time in such quotidian ways as bathing, drinking, reading, playing music, painting, mainly by themselves in their hotel rooms. In the film's own terms, this is "more real" than either *The Survivors* or the Los Angeles ending, not because it is in black and white (the whole film is), but because of the unstructured nature of time. The demystification of the glamorous world of filmmaking involves a blurring of the boundaries between actors and characters in the performances of waiting.

Implicit in Fritz's death is a capitulation to storytelling. His revelation that "all stories have to end, so all stories are about death" is clearly Wenders's own discovery. Fritz's death situates the film finally in the realm of fiction because, with very few exceptions, it is always the character and never the actor who dies in the cinema. Death marks a boundary between fiction and documentary, at the limits of the claims that each makes to realism. If the documentation of actual death—such as that which is threatened in *Lightning Over Water*—cuts itself off from narrative fiction, the most convincing performance becomes just that in the representation of a character's death.

Perhaps it is not entirely fair to describe the ending of *The State of Things* as a capitulation to narrative, because there is a sense in which Wenders attempts to reconcile fact and fiction in the final shots. In interviews, Wenders has said that the film incorporates three kinds of images: one he calls "grammatical"—those that are necessary for the telling of a story, images that are not really new but have been seen before; second, there is a kind of image that precedes the shooting, "profound" images that Wenders stores at the back of his mind, such as those of the desolate hotel; and third, there is a category of "found images" discovered while shooting.[57] This third type is an impossible reconciliation of the first two, and lies at the heart of Wenders's filmmaking: the attempt to reconcile the contingent "found" image with narrativity. The representation of Fritz's death, in which he goes down filming, can thus be read precisely as such an attempt at reconciliation. As in *Lightning,* the desire to close the gap between film and reality is mystified through the narrativization of mortality. In this case, "storytelling" becomes an equally pressing desire, as the "grammatical images" are those of urban terrorism and film noir fatality.

Although Benjamin's distinction between story and novel cannot be mapped onto Wenders's distinction between story and real life, it exposes the irony implicit in Wenders's dilemma. For Benjamin, "The stuff that stories are made up of is real life," which the storyteller has experienced. "Death is the sanction of everything that the storyteller can tell," says Benjamin, insofar as "it is natural history to which his stories refer back."[58] A similar attitude can be detected in Wenders's privileging of the contingent, in his rhetorical embrace of a cinematic realism that lies outside psychological narrative. In Benjamin's larger project of reconciling aesthetic contingency with Marxist determinism, the historical forces that have overcome storytelling make it possible "to see a new beauty in what is vanishing."[59] The theory of the "found" image, which is always lost as soon as it is seen and photographed, may be the cinematic variation on this theme (which will be discussed again in chapter 4, on Godard).

Wenders's conception of "story" in *The State of Things* is something quite different than this, and is actually much closer to Benjamin's category of "the novelistic." His hero's experience, for example, approximates a tragic fall, as Fritz is brought down from his status as director to become an anonymous victim of urban crime. Wenders abandons his role as (Benjaminian) storyteller with the shift to Los Angeles and the isolation of Fritz from the ensemble of characters that carries the first three-quarters of the film. Wenders's conception of storytelling is laden with myths of heroism, "home," and teleological closure. Narrative mortality serves him as an allegorical means of reclaiming these myths without sacrificing the ideal of realist cinema free of narrative constraints.

A clue to Wenders's conception of storytelling, which he claims to have discovered in making *The State of Things,* might be found in his designation of the film as "a psychoanalysis of the cinema itself." His search for the cinematic repressed, the primal scene of film history, arrives finally at the violent death of his protagonist at the limits of fictional and documentary realism. Of all the intertexts laced through *The State of Things, The Searchers* is privileged as a means of investigating the truth of cinema. References to John Ford's film, as well as the book by Alan Le May from which it was adapted, occur throughout the film.[60] In *The Searchers,* Ethan, played by John Wayne, is a homeless Confederate veteran wandering in the desert, reading its signs, in the form of Indian messages, searching for values in the post-Civil War American West (and 1950s America). The dialectic between home and wilderness is overdetermined by Ford's mise-en-scène, in which the enclosed darkness of interior spaces is cut off from the bright white rectangles of desert glimpsed through cabin windows and cave openings. (The composition in the back of the mobile home described earlier is very similar.) The wilderness in *The Searchers* is already allegorically mortified, represented as a mythic space of desire.

  The Searchers therefore embodies a narrative of investigation that mimics both the cinematic apparatus and the psychoanalytic model of conscious and unconscious processes. The security of the home, which begins and ends the narrative, depends on an investigation of the realm of desire, of unharnessed drives, of the Indian and of the woman, and ultimately of the Western frontier. "Home" is the pole of consciousness, complete with its repressions and anxiety, and the wilderness is the unmapped region marked only by signs and symptoms, which must be read and interpreted for complete recovery of domestic stability. In the repeated use of the inside/outside composition, this duality is mapped onto the spectator's "safe" position in the dark, versus the open space of the screen. After the opening massacre of Ethan's family, a point-of-view shot from the dark space of the ravaged homestead is menacing because it is from the perspective of the dead (who only Ethan can see — the spectator, like Martin, Ethan's part-Indian nephew, is repeatedly refused the sight of corpses). The trajectory of the film is thus toward a recuperation of this grave to its original status as "home."

The intertext of *The Searchers* illuminates, above all, the discourse of survival in *The State of Things*. Gordon's last words are "It's time for all good survivors to say good-bye," but the only survivors are thousands of miles away, still stranded in Portugal. In Ford's version of *The Searchers,* a second family is formed and everyone survives except the Indians, who are massacred, their chief scalped by Ethan, who, after internalizing their savagery, returns alone to the desert, leaving the other characters safely embraced by the homestead. Like the hero of *The Searchers,* Wenders internalizes the savagery of the enemy in *The State of Things* by learning how to kill, but after shooting his protagonist/double, he will follow John Wayne back into the wilderness.

And here we must recall Wenders's ongoing experiences with Coppola and *Hammett.* His desire to make films in Hollywood was not simply financially motivated, but was an opportunity to exercise an auteurist anxiety: to indulge in the milieu of Dashiel Hammett and the men who adapted his work to the screen. The industrial structure and budgetary scope of Zoetrope studio, symptomatic of the Los Angeles mythos and Hollywood style, was hardly a surprise to Wenders, for whom American film is something of a personal wilderness.[61] From this perspective, the four films that he made during the production of *Hammett* (besides the two discussed here, Wenders also made *Reverse Angle* [1982, 17 min.] and *Room 666* [1982, 45 min.]) constitute a complex response to this foray into the unknown.

From Wenders's book of color photographs, *Written in the West,* collected while shooting locations for *Paris, Texas,* it is evident that the American West is for him a myth available only at one remove. The photographs represent a linguistic landscape of gas stations and motels, a West that has been thoroughly civilized but that is nevertheless big, beautiful, and flat, something very different from anything in Europe. In *The State of Things,* the wilderness, specifically the American West, is thus a metaphor for desire, untempered form, a myth that cannot be sustained by contemporary Los Angeles, where the narrative and the aesthetic ideals of the visionary filmmaker meet their end. In Los Angeles the image is at the service of the narrative demands of the film industry. The possibility of the filmmaker possessing his own images in Europe is, for Wenders, a lost ideal he seems determined to survive.

The discourse of survival is one of redemption, but it also implies a reactionary response to crisis, a perpetuation of subjectivity beyond the crises of postmodernism. Certainly the film's fatalism is an ironic recourse to a familiar narrative structure. In the equation of narrative realism with a teleological discourse of mortality, the death drive is the principle of repetition and return, binding narrative desire, the momentum of difference, to a point of stasis and closure. This seems to be the basis of the conception of narrative in *The State of Things*. Story is opposed to life; story is a force acting against life. The final death is another narrative murder, supplying an end to the film's search, defining the goal of that search.

In keeping with this model of narrative closure, Wenders also wants to understand death as closure as a "coming home" to the cinema of Lang, Fuller, and Ray, auteurs of classical Hollywood who are generally understood to have sustained some kind of integrity of vision within the constraints of the industry. (Fritz stops at Lang's "star" implanted in Hollywood Boulevard.) Thus the "unconscious" of *The State of Things* is comprised of two forces that might be called reality and fiction, which are translated into a dialectic of life and death. But this tension is overlaid with Wenders's own struggle with the commercial demands placed on the cinematic auteur. "Authorship" is effectively aligned with *documentary* realism as a visual pleasure principle of the auteur as witness. Insofar as the *fictional* demands of the industry are represented as inevitable and necessary, they are correspondingly aligned with the death drive.

Although "life" is characterized at the end of *The State of Things* as the survival of the economic demands and commercial compromise of filmmaking, in the Portugal section of the film, it is something quite different. "Life" there is synonymous with reality; actors playing actors with nothing to do places notions of performance, pretense, and fiction in question. Gordon is their producer, but he is also the only truly fictional character in the film, and Fritz's descent to his world, to Los Angeles and to his death, is also a movement by Patrick Bauchau from actor to character.

In his speech to the assembled cast and crew in the Sintra hotel, Fritz says, "Stories only exist in stories, whereas life goes by in the course of time without the need to turn out stories," a phrase that is referred back to by several of the actors in subsequent scenes.

Although Fritz endorses nonnarrative temporality as "life," a "life" that he subsequently tells Gordon "sneaks out" as the story comes in, within the extended Portugal section of the film life also "sneaks out" through a complex discourse on representation and time. In fact, Fritz's and Wenders's "lesson" involves the realization that representation *in* time (filmic representation) is necessarily a representation *of* time, and is in itself a mortifying process.

The scenes in and around the Sintra hotel that move apparently randomly from one character or couple to another, are marked by a range of comments on and representations of photography, painting, film, and video. The two little girls take Polaroids and shoot videotapes of the whole group in the hotel restaurant; Kate (Viva Auder) subsequently analyzes her child's photos in a tape-recorded letter to a friend; she also draws pictures of Fritz asleep, one of which she places on top of his prostrate body. Fritz's wall is covered with Polaroids. Anna is seen briefly in front of a trompe l'oeil of a Mediterranean villa; Joe/Fuller has a row of filmstrips hanging over his bed. The viewfinder of a still camera is reproduced several times over the image, targeting people's faces. Various conversations are virtually pedagogical analyses of painting, black-and-white film, and framing.

This discourse on representation reaches a kind of apotheosis in the reproduction of images from *The Survivors* generated on a computer by Dennis (Paul J. Getty III), the American screenwriter who, it is eventually revealed, has financed the extant shoot himself for his first screen credit. The final image that he prints out is a close-up of a hand, and it is this particular image that seems to provoke Fritz, finally, into traveling to Los Angeles to find Gordon. In many of these instances, the filmic representation in/of time is played off against the static images that freeze actions and bodies in time.

Furthermore, often in conjunction with this discourse on representation, "the passing of time" is repeatedly characterized as repetition. Julia's (Camila Mora) metronome, which she uses to practice her violin, continues to tick while she sleeps, and in one of her angry phone calls to an unidentified lover or family member, she says, "I just get stuck ... always the same taste in my mouth." To Mark (Jeffrey Kime), Anna says, "Nothing new can happen between us if it already starts with that feeling of déjà vu." Lying in bed smoking, Joe listens to an electronic voice issuing from his alarm clock speak the time every minute. The rhythm of Wenders's *découpage* of this part of the film, with many single-shot scenes, long takes, and fixed frames that move into slow-sequence shots, plus a repetitive, dirgelike sound track that punctuates many of the long shots of landscape, further characterizes the "passing of time" as uncanny in its repetitions and returns.

Under the graphic target of Mark's viewfinder, Anna says, "I'm glad the movie stopped. Now we have some time." This time, however, turns out not to be free of stories or death, for it is still a movie, and as representation, an uncanny doubling of life and image remains. Jerry, the Californian actor who tells a long and funny tale about his ugly childhood, tells Fritz, "Life without stories just isn't worth living." Fritz's "lesson" is that insofar as film takes place in time, it is going to be narrative, and unless one harnesses the death drive implicit in repetition and reproduction, the treasured "life" will inevitably become a discourse of mortality: the "passing of time" is also a passing *away* of life and time. Joe's wife's natural death (which Joe/Fuller hears about over the telephone) may be a fictional event, but in this context it underlines the implicit "harbinger of death" that lurks in this part of the film. The "waiting" element of de-dramatized performance is itself uncanny in terms of its temporal repetition and doubling of actors/characters.

Wenders's conception of "life" is further suggested by his emphasis on "found images," which, far more than sexuality, define the category of desire in the Portugal section of *The State of Things*.[62] Among the cast and crew of *The Survivors*, several amorous relationships exist, but they are all extremely ambiguous, to the characters themselves as well as for the audience. The individuals appear to be alienated and bored within their couplings. Moreover, the insomnia and masturbatory isolation of many of the characters create not only a desultory mood of pent-up frustration but also one of narcissistic self-absorption. Anna covers the mirror in her room in an attempt to circumvent it, but as a cliché of actors' personalities, Wenders draws on narcissism to further define the nonteleological, anti-"story" aesthetic of contingent realism. Observed in their hotel rooms by a camera that becomes explicitly voyeuristic in one high-angle shot of Julia naked on her bed, the characters perform their boredom.

If narcissism consists in "the subject's acquisition of an image of himself founded on the model furnished by the other person—this image being the ego itself"[63]—it is an internalization of desire not unlike that which takes place in melancholia. The treatment of one-self as an object, which Freud identifies in both the masochism of melancholia and narcissism,[64] also structures the uncanniness of the doppelgänger. Although the cathexis of the libido to an "other" under-scores the conventional narrativization of cinematic desire in fetishistic and scopophilic forms, Wenders articulates another kind of pleasure. The pleasure of contemplation, the appreciation of framing, is a structure of self-cathexis, a pleasure in the look itself, rather than in the image or an other's look. Indeed, the shot-reverse-shot structure of the cinematic suture occurs only occasionally in *The State of Things,* where "the look" is specifically attributed to the directors in and of the film. It is a gaze that is at once melancholic and narcissistic.

Although Wenders's photography of actresses Isabelle Wiengarten, Viva Auder, and Camila Mora involves an inordinate amount of nu-dity, the erotic potential is displaced onto the cutaways of carefully composed landscape, waves crashing on cement bulwarks, an aban-doned Volkswagen, long shots of the coast, and so on. Wenders's desire for *these* images is a desire for a certain kind of filmmaking. The women, objectified like landscape, are not only inaccessible, separated by the scopophilic mediation of the camera, but are also undesired. The erotic potential of the many bedroom shots is essen-tially killed by the accompanying discourse on photographic repre-sentation. No one really wants anything in *The State of Things* except to make a film; all other desires are turned inward. It is to this desire for image making that the final super-8 image of the film refers back. Even in *The Survivors,* the leader of the beleaguered, endangered group has a video camera with which he captures the desolate land-scape, the low-definition footage blown up to reproduce his vision. This discourse of vision is informed by a desire to be identified by one's look, by the images one possesses, and is in contradistinction to the desire for the Other. The images of abandoned cars, in both *The Survivors* and in Portugal, inscribe the sign of death in this desire to see what lies beyond the pleasure principle.

The category of "the real" is thus defined as the passing of time— in which life itself becomes a sign of death—on the one hand, and the valorization of the director's personal vision on the other.[65] This is perhaps the central contradiction of the film, which it is Wenders's project to confront and survive. Finally, instead of turning away from death in a nonviolent form of filmmaking, which is in fact thoroughly informed by mortality, Wenders embraces death in a redemptive return to fiction. What is repressed in the narrative structure of *The State of Things*'s capitulation to teleological narrative is the redemptive potential of that "dead" part of the film in Portugal. The image that survives Fritz's violent death is a sign of the subject of vision, the reverse shot of the look of a singular, dying protagonist; and it evokes, in its emptiness, the Portuguese part of the film.

The bullet that kills Fritz has no source (his assassins are Gordon's creditors, but insofar as they are never seen, they are also mythic inhabitants of the Los Angeles landscape), but the final super-8 shot is likewise unsutured. The lack of a cut back to Fritz's body or eye behind the camera signifies his death in its absence. As the camera keeps rolling, the frame drops down to the ground, suggesting that "found" images must be found by some*one* because they are not *just* images, but indices of vision, and must cease with Fritz's death. Insofar as there cannot be any "found images" independent of subjectivity, consciousness is thus privileged over empirical reality. And, moreover, the representation of the artist, Fritz, who not only suffers and dies but whose individuation is designated as the beginning and end of narrative (as the surrogate director of *The Survivors,* his vision also opens the film), situates Wenders's conception of story as that of Benjamin's novelistic, with temporality limited to the life of an individual.

Wenders's Romantic conception of the artist, transposed to studio filmmaking, is crucial to the final dispossessed image of the film. The canted super-8 shot of the Los Angeles parking lot survives the director, who is slain by economic forces, thereby linking the death of the author as subject with a vision of life freed from the structures of narrative, a recuperation of the real. The category of the real, of the space between characters, the found image, is redeemed by virtue of a transcendentally ironic gesture. The irony, of course, is that we are still in the realm of fiction, which, given the nature of the medium, no amount of "realism" can completely overcome. Both conventions of realism are effectively banished in this apocalyptic closure; neither narrative nor mortality can be completely eliminated from cinematic representation.

Wenders's psychoanalysis of film history is thus overlaid with his own repressed desire to be, perhaps, John Wayne. The "pleasure principle" against which narrative as death defines itself in *The State of Things* is scopophilic, but the death drive itself is characterized by Wenders as economic and technological. Gordon and Fritz are, after all, killed by the gangsters who lent Gordon money to finance Fritz's film, a film that did not guarantee anyone a return on their investment. The irony here is that *The State of Things* (in black and white — by the film's own logic, a sign of noncommercial viability — and denounced by most American critics as extremely boring) was not only financed, but the eight hundred thousand-dollar budget was underwritten very quickly, Wenders's name being enough of a guarantee for financiers. The value of Wenders's treatise on storytelling and cinema lies here, in the delineation of an economics of narrative that has determinants in the two spheres of representation and funding. His distinction between America and Europe may be a facile one and his self-conception as auteur may be a little overbearing, and yet his observation that the narrative structure organized by a "death drive" pays with the "found image" is an important one to retain.

The commercially produced film is made, as Stephen Heath has said, to be seen once and once only,[66] and is thus a "struggle against time." This teleology of the novelistic is what Wenders himself is concerned to survive. However, he can only do so by insisting on the status of the image as a subjective phenomenon, and the very substance of artistic vision. But when he eliminates (or at least reduces) teleology, "story" as a form of mortification remains in the mechanical reproduction of images. And it is not a Bazinian ontology of preservation that Wenders discovers in documentary realism, but an even closer proximity to death. His "found images" record the passing of time, and, like Benjamin's storyteller, Wenders's cinematic ideal remains authorized by mortality precisely because "everything is pressured into images."

The specter of Raul Ruiz and *The Territory*, which was completed once Ruiz got back his appropriated cast, crew, and location, shows up the limitations of Wenders's perspective. Ruiz's film, about cannibalism among vacationing campers, starts with death as the limit of the fictional, but evidently takes it beyond the marketable, as the film has virtually disappeared. *The State of Things,* on the other hand, won the Golden Lion at the 1982 Venice Film Festival, and has been released in the United States for home video, suggesting that Wenders has indeed "mastered" the art of storytelling. And although "Germany" figures in the film only as Fritz Munroe's nationality (overdetermined by the allusion to Murnau), the anxiety of authorship is clearly equated with cultural identity, both of which are tenuous myths in Wenders's vision of international filmmaking.

Both *The State of Things* and *Lightning Over Water* begin and end with the representation of death, and the nonnarratives between them are agonizing detours and discourses on their necessity. Fictional death is the apotheosis of the "grammatical image," and the contingency of the documentary ideal lies elsewhere, in another film, on another lost continent, which was Europe. In the narrative economics of the cinema, which can perhaps be described as its "unconscious," the representation of death has a price, which is the claim to represent something called real life. For Wenders, the image of violent death is the cinematic repressed — its primal scene, if you will — and the uncanny parallel between the shooting of film and the shooting of guns has the weight of truth.

In both *Lightning Over Water* and *The State of Things,* the allegory of narrative mortality refers to the mechanical reproduction of reality, or the relationship of film images to the profilmic referent. If mortification is the discourse of history in representation, in Wenders's films it involves a complex dialogue between documentary realism and narrative fiction. Whereas narrativity strives toward "home," meaningfulness, and a unified, coherent expression of identity, the documentary impulse inscribes a challenge of the contingent, mortal, and transient singularity of the historical profilmic. The perpetual displacement effected by this slippage may well be an expression of anxiety experienced by Wenders's generation. The desire to renew German culture while acknowledging German history can only occur as a form of mortification.

Eric Santer observes that postwar German cinema is preoccupied with "the constitution of the self" within the "psychic mechanisms beyond the pleasure principle" — those of mourning and melancholia.[67] Wenders's doubling of himself in both *Lightning* and *The State of Things* with directors-in-the-texts is constitutive of these films' narrative mortality. As Wenders's representative within the film, Fritz's desire is much like Nick's in *Lightning*, to "bring himself together" through a film. Moreover, the only real reference to German culture in *The State of Things* is Fritz's fictional filmography, which comes up on the computer screen.[68] Its parallels with Wenders's own filmography suggest the allegorical nature of Fritz's character, and the impossibility of his assuming an identity of his own.

In *Lightning Over Water* the body of the film flirts with the body of its auteur-subject, only to be irrevocably and irreversibly separated from it. Closure can only be achieved ironically, and Wenders is unable in either film to close the gap, finally, between the eternal film image and the historically limited referent. Narrative mortality is, for Wenders, a negotiation of loss. The unities of self, of art, of a German cinema defined in opposition to Hollywood, are mythic categories available in the 1980s only as allegories of desire. Wenders's mortification of these myths takes the form of a melancholia in which the dead objects are not completely relinquished.

Wenders's cinema is not in ruins despite the fact that he exemplifies Benjamin's observation that "the only pleasure the melancholic permits himself, and it is a powerful one, is allegory."[69] History in *Lightning Over Water* and *The State of Things* is stranded in the present tense, as the loss of an unspeakable past does not give rise to a history of the future. Wenders may not return to the Nazi period as so many of his contemporaries have done, but the difficulty of history nevertheless informs his filmmaking as a form of narrative mortality. Utopia remains bound to the fetishes of home and maternal origins, and "survival" pertains not to the barren landscape of *The Survivors* but to the ability to reproduce oneself in images. For the radical potential of narrative mortality, we must turn to Wenders's predecessors in the 1960s, and a generation of auteurs that is significantly repressed in his personal history of the cinema.

THREE

OSHIMA NAGISA
The Limits of Nationhood

●

> We know that once we are conscious of it, we have to react to the
> desire ingrained in us to overstep the limits. We want to overstep them,
> and the horror we feel shows to what excesses we shall be brought,
> excesses which, without the initial horror, would be unthinkable.
> — GEORGES BATAILLE[1]

One of Oshima's best-known films, *Death by Hanging* (1968), might be considered the repressed text of *Beyond a Reasonable Doubt*, laying bare all the contradictions of the two institutions of cinema and capital punishment, analogizing them and mutually indicting them. The space of the imaginary is opened up by exploiting that very doubt in the believability of the image that causes so much anxiety in Lang's film. As in *Beyond a Reasonable Doubt,* the body of the "guinea pig" is at first that of an automaton, and, like Garrett's, it is *given* memory, history, crime, and guilt, under the threat of execution. For Oshima, however, narrative mortality involves the deliberate production of transgressive desire within the very specific cultural and historical terms of Japanese cinema.

105

Oshima claims that every filmmaker secretly craves "to record on film someone actually dying."[2] His fascination with this transgression is manifest in his representation of death, his narrative deployment of it, and his conception of mortality as a limit to be overcome. What makes Oshima's work especially pertinent to the present study is the sociohistorical determinants of these limits in his work. The Japanese New Wave, a radical moment in a highly distinctive national cinema, deployed violence and sexuality for overtly political ends. In Oshima's films, the representation of death is stylistically and narratively linked to a historical conception of nationhood: the desire for a new Japan.

In his writing on cinema, Oshima insists on subjective expression as a stylistic strategy of challenging traditional Japanese cinema. The different configuration of aesthetics and politics in Japanese culture also involves a different valorization of subjectivity; narrative mortality functions as a means to this end. In a 1960 essay, Oshima chastises Japanese directors for their lack of any inscription of self in their films, and he cites Godard's *Breathless* as a model to emulate.[3] In another essay, he introduces a term of "active involvement," which, he says, can only be realized by the negation of those "hidden methods of self-restraint" that have "penetrated" Japanese filmmakers themselves.[4] The politics of desire that inform narrative mortality in Oshima's 1960s films must be understood within this framework and distinguished from the discourse of individualism in Japanese cinema of the 1950s (e.g., Kurosawa's bourgeois humanism), and also from the paranoia and anxiety of American melodramas of the period.

Oshima's subjective intervention ultimately takes the form of mortifying the dynamics of Japanese melodrama, marking the historical thresholds beyond which they might be rearticulated. The ideological task was to define a radical Japanese subject position that would be neither the universal humanism of the 1950s nor the imperialist/conformist passivity of traditionalist ideology. This process is accomplished by way of two techniques: a documentary sociological realism, and a revision of Japanese narrative conventions, especially their codes of mortality. These two strategies, along with a highly stylized representation of death, come together in Oshima's allegory of narrative mortality.

Oshima's fictions are consistently articulated through a "reality principle" of historical specificity, which is inscribed in his films by three
principal means. The first is through the use of the Japanese flag,
onto which the body is mapped in many different ways. The round,
red sun becomes circumscriptive, circular and closed, and the body
is inscribed within its singular dimension, a strategy that is most explicit in the mapping of the child's round head onto the round sun
of the flag in *Shonen* (*Boy*) (1969). Allegorical sunsets figure prominently in *Death by Hanging* (1968) and *The Sun's Burial* (1960); and
flags drape the sets of many of the films. In the last scenes of *Cruel
Story of Youth* (1960) Mako wears a bright red dress with white suns
on it, and dies wearing this dress.

Second, Oshima's narrative material is consistently derived from
popular news stories, coextensively representing two levels of reality: historically specific events, and the tabloid journalism that they
spawned. At the end of *In the Realm of the Senses* (1976), for example, Oshima's final voice-over notes the popular support that Abé
Sada (the prostitute who killed and castrated her lover) received
from the Japanese people, who largely sympathized with her, suggesting that her expression of desire, violently linked to the body,
does ultimately have some significance to the body politic. Third, a
stylistic documentary impetus exists either in a vérité-style technique,
location shooting, or direct address, often in Oshima's own voice at
the beginning or end of the narrative, as in *Death by Hanging, In
the Realm of the Senses,* and *Boy.*

The iconography of Japanese nationalism is so central to all of
these films that the problem of the subject is perpetually that of the
Japanese subject. The designation of historical limits and their transgression occurs within Oshima's characters, but also within the address
to the spectator, who is not necessarily assumed to be Japanese. In a
1975 interview, Oshima said that "our generation cannot rely on the
congeniality of our all being Japanese to communicate,"[5] a critique
of ethnographic essentialism that is thoroughly carried out in his
films. His challenge to consensus society produces an international
audience (indeed, Oshima's films may be more widely known outside
Japan), and yet his formal and narrative strategies, despite their Brechtian influence, are not easily abstracted from the Japanese context.

Although Oshima's spectator may be transnational, plural, and crucially divided in both cultural and psychic ways, the *represented* subject is very much a unity, anchored in the body. Alongside the thematic and visual imbrication of body and flag, the body, in Oshima's films, is used in continually innovative ways as a means of survival. Especially in *Cruel Story of Youth* (1960), *The Sun's Burial* (1960), and *Boy* (1969), it is sacrificed, drained, and battered by and for economic ends. Characters existing on the margins of industrial capitalism have only one asset—their bodies—and it is a political, historical reality in which the bodies of these protagonists circulate. Prostitution, as a grand metaphor for the interpellation of the personal into the political in Japanese society, as Oshima represents it, extends to the mortality of the body.[6]

Social attitudes toward death in Japan, from the heroics of hara-kiri (seppuku) to the romance of double suicide, are an extreme instance of an ideological discourse of death. In keeping with Marcuse's theorization, the bodily, biological fact of death tends to be suppressed (as "pollution" in Shinto doctrine) in favor of the social significance of death. The samurai or *yakuza* (gangster) dies with his lord or master; lovers express a socially unacceptable love in their joint deaths. Ian Buruma notes the inherent contradictions in these practices: "Death is a release from the dictatorship of the group, while at the same time preserving it.... death, in other words, may be the ultimate freedom and the pinnacle of purity, but it is also the final and most important debt to pay."[7]

Certain parallels exist between Oshima's filmmaking and Marcuse's social philosophy, both generated in the late 1950s and early 1960s. In *Eros and Civilization,* Marcuse claims that the "performance principle" of human civilization, "the prevailing historical form of the reality principle," has been appropriated by Thanatos, and that a utopian vision involves precisely a championing of Eros over Thanatos. The development of a *new* reality principle free of the delimiting repression implicit in the priorization of mortality involves a liberated sexuality, as well as a liberation from the "instinctual goal" of death.[8] Two of Marcuse's emphases—the appropriation of the death instinct by the Nirvana principle in a repressive static society, and the primordial (Freudian) role of the father—make his thesis particularly apt to a discussion of Japan. The rituals of double suicide and *bushido* (the code of the samurai), as well as the emperor system, are key components of the sociological reality principle in Japanese ideology.

Marcuse notes that "the relegation of real possibilities to the no-man's land of utopia is itself an essential element of the ideology of the performance principle."[9] In Oshima's films, utopia is only occasionally depicted as a fleeting moment in the context of apocalypse. The imagery is parodic in *Cruel Story of Youth* (Mako and Kiyoshi on a beach, complete with sunglasses and designer swimwear) and allegorical in *The Sun's Burial* (the surviving heroine finally runs from the burning slum, through a huge archway into a magnificent sunset). The limits beyond which a utopia is possible are, however, systematically represented in and through the image of and desire for death. Often it is an eroticized image, linked to the characters' sexuality. In this way the melodrama of desire that Marcuse articulates is transformed into the writing of an allegory of desire, which is, for Oshima, the ability to imagine a new and different Japan. Whereas Marcuse implies a "release" of Eros from Thanatos, Oshima's politics of representation involve a rewriting of Thanatos as Eros, a discursive rendering of the desire to die (e.g., sacrifice) as the desire for a radical alteration of reality.

If hara-kiri and double suicide are particularly Japanese ways of dying, it is imperative that "Japaneseness" be recognized as an ideological construction. Western criticism has tended to misrecognize Japanese formalism as "progressive" modernism, and "Japaneseness" has tended to mean "otherness" vis-à-vis Western bourgeois realism.[10] Given the nonillusionist tradition of bourgeois aesthetics in Japan, the Brechtian strategies adopted by Godard and his European contemporaries in the 1960s did not, in themselves, provide radical representational tools for Japanese filmmakers. The formal task of the Japanese New Wave involved a conversion of presentational aesthetics into a "theatrical sign"[11] or a move through realist representation to the other side, to "ruin" both Japanese ideals of cultural authenticity *and* Western aesthetic ideals.

Narrative mortality emerges as a crucial deconstructive strategy for the Japanese New Wave in its imbrication of formal and thematic conventions. If the "theatrical sign" is not simply Brechtian, it is because it is deployed in narratives that are anchored intertextually in Japanese cultural history and the imagery of nationalism. Narrative mortality is also a crucial critical tool for non-Japanese film criticism if it is to move beyond formal analysis and into the domain of ethnography. It enables a mortification of exotic "otherness" and a recognition of the nationalist character of Japanese ethnography and aesthetics. The degree to which social practices are institutionalized in cultural forms is made explicit in the forms death assumes in Japan.

The absence or lack that resides at the core of Western anxiety and is figured in death as in castration has a slightly different status in Japan, where a proximity between the living and the dead is maintained in various ways. In both Zen Buddhism and Shintoism, the two dominant (and nonexclusive) belief systems in Japan, the "boundary" between life and death is perceived as fluid. The role of ghosts in Japanese literature, and especially in the Noh drama (in which the living and the dead mix freely), is indicative of the extension of community to the realm of the dead. Zen Buddhism, with its ideals of asceticism and aesthetics, involves a sense of "oneness" with the world, an experience of undifferentiation or continuity with nature achieved through satori, or enlightened selflessness by means of contemplation and/or meditation. The Nirvana principle as the goal of life thus institutionalizes death as the fulfillment of such a practice. The sign for *mu,* or emptiness, engraved on grave stones, designates mortality as "nothing": neither transcendence of "this world" nor even departure, but participation in the continuity of being. The lack or absence upon which Western representational strategies of disavowal are based is also the foundation of Japanese aesthetics—not as something to be disavowed, however, but as a desired state of being. Disavowal presupposes difference, and it is this presupposition that Oshima's dialectics in *Boy* and *Death by Hanging* redeem by discovering ego on the verge of its extinction.

Nonillusionist, presentational stylistics are incorporated into Oshima's films, but the disjunction between signifier and signified refers in his work to the gap between subject and object. If vision in Zen aesthetics is a means of identifying self with other/object in the pursuit of satori or enlightenment, its subversion must be a splitting of the subject and object of vision. The separation of subject from object, the gap that is fetishized for the voyeur, has a radical orientation in Japanese culture. Stephen Heath claims that Oshima's representation of "seeing" is "a disphasure of look and sight,"[12] but the

Japanese spectator can be described as having always been "divided," confronted with many-voiced discursive operations.[13] Oshima's discovery of the Japanese subject is a politicization of the body of the person, mortally limited and disjunct from the realm of eternal nature and objects.

Death and Desire in Double Suicide

Two films of Oshima's stand out because of the intertextual relation to the specific ways that "tradition" has been accommodated into cinematic representation by Mizoguchi Kenji and Ozu Yasujiro. Death is a central trope of both of these directors' narrative modes and is crucial to their nationalist appeal, as well as to their melodramatic strategies. In *Cruel Story of Youth*, Oshima goes so far as to allude to the Christian thematics of transcendence that inform Mizoguchi's films. In *Boy*, his shooting style changes dramatically to mimic the formal stasis of Ozu's family dramas. In both cases, the stylistic and thematic imitation is developed into a complex revisionism in which familiar narrative strategies are mortified in order to redeem the desires that inform their narrativity.

Cruel Story of Youth was the centerpiece of what was promoted as the Japanese New Wave in 1960. The trilogy of which it is part might also be seen as a three-part response to Kurosawa's 1946 film *No Regrets for Our Youth*. Despite the promise that Oshima represented to Shochiku studio of a revitalized film culture (ostensibly modeled on that blossoming in France), the films were bitter expressions of political impotence in the face of the renewed security treaty of 1960 and the continued military alliance of Japan with cold war America.[14] *Cruel Story* is about a teenage couple who support themselves by extortion and pimping, living a life of back alleys, bars, hitchhiking, motorcycles, and prison. Their cruelty extends to each other, their families, and their aborted child, and yet, in true melodramatic fashion, they are the victims of a fragmented, unforgiving society that finally drives them to their deaths (figure 6).

The discontinuities of the final scenes of *Cruel Story* are as dramatic as those of *Beyond a Reasonable Doubt*, but where they lead fatalistically in the latter film to an inevitable death, here they build to a kind of narrative exhaustion. After their release from jail, Mako

Fig. 6. *Cruel Story of Youth*: Kiyoshi (Yusuke Kawazu) and Mako (Miyuki Kuwano) seeking violence and sexual freedom on the road to a new Japan. Publicity still courtesy of New Yorker Films.

and Kiyoshi literally cannot escape from the social forces that inhibit their relationship. Kiyoshi finds himself economically bound to his mistress and pursued by jealous thugs. He is bound to the underworld as tightly as Mako is to her moralizing family. After their failure to escape from Kiyoshi's mistress, the couple walk along a crowded street. On extreme screen right they walk into a shakily backtracking camera while people swarm around them on the crowded sidewalk and traffic roars beside them. The unsteady camera and the characters' lack of ideas (they say they have "nowhere to go") threaten a lack of closure, suggesting that they will simply be swallowed by the city and the image will disintegrate, the film having nothing left to show.

In their final dialogue, Kiyoshi says that both men and women are mere "tools of society" and he cannot take responsibility for himself, much less for Mako too. He suggests that they "call it quits," and when Mako asks him what he means, the convention of double suicide, which would be called for by Mizoguchi or Chikamatsu Monzaemon at this point, is underlined. But Oshima refuses them this possibility of transcendence, and after Kiyoshi exits right he cuts to Mako walking alone, at extreme screen right in relief against the unfocused red, white, and blue neon background. The stylization of costume and mise-en-scène that the film has incorporated throughout is finally divorced from narrative content. Mako's echoing footsteps are all that can be heard; her isolation against the diffused representation of the city and the iconography of her red-and-white dress introduce the allegorical level on which the film will close.

The double suicide motif alluded to in the dialogue is reinforced in the representation of the actual deaths. The ambiguity of Mako's accidental fall from a moving car, her telepathically triggered response to Kiyoshi's death, the car in Kiyoshi's alley (which may or may not be the same car that Mako falls from), the rapid crosscutting between the two events, and the final split-screen composition are all means by which the specifics of these two individual deaths suggest a nonmaterial connection between them. Mako's sudden sensing of Kiyoshi's death invokes the mystical ontology of double suicide, that a socially impossible love could be realized on a different plane of existence, outside of history.

As if it were tacked on arbitrarily to the end of the narrative, the final death sequence is of a different discursive order than the rest of the film. The melodramatic mode gives way to the allegorical through a strategic refinement of the narrative stylistics that characterize the film. The *zengakuren* demonstration,[15] which Mako and Kiyoshi watch in the second scene of the film, follows an insertion of black-and-white newsreel footage of a student demonstration in Korea:[16] a historical mimesis is translated into cinematic terms. To Mako and Kiyoshi, joining such a militaristic, highly organized demonstration is only another form of conformism, against which their desires are explicitly cast in relief, beginning with their dialogue about sex on the sidelines of the demonstration. Instead of joining the students, they rent a speedboat, go out to a logjam where Kiyoshi rapes Mako, and then fall in love. The last few shots of the *zengakuren* are not only very short, fragmenting the mass of people into close-ups, but shaky, taken by an obviously handheld camera. Similarly, the final sequence of *Cruel Story,* in which the mise-en-scène is again predominantly red and white, opens with a repetition of this exaggerated handheld technique (the image moves up and down, rather than being simply unsteady). Mako and Kiyoshi, emerging from Kiyoshi's room, begin their *michiyuki,* or lovers' walk to death.

The *michiyuki* is a vital convention of double-suicide plays, usually covering a succession of bridges, and it is signaled most overtly here by the melodramatically ominous soundtrack.[17] The repetition of the shaky handheld camera work in the *michiyuki* is, on the one hand, a crude realization of Oshima's desire to represent his own volition in the image, and, on the other, a transposition of the unrest of the *zengakuren* onto Mako and Kiyoshi. Since the couple remains to the end of the film very much outside the political sphere, this is a crucial means of situating their deaths in a historical-political register. The *michiyuki* itself and the final split-screen composition of the film, in which Mako's and Kiyoshi's lifeless faces are placed side by side, are equally explicit interventions of Oshima onto the narrative.

The crosscutting between the two scenes of Mako's and Kiyoshi's deaths is Oshima's penultimate intervention. He manages to take control of the fatalism of double suicide and exploit that discourse of control—the subservience of characters to narrative—for a politics of desire. More than a deromanticization or demystification, narrative mortality operates here as a deconstruction of the closure of love-and-death, and an opening up of sex and violence as different discourses of desire. It is a transposition from "natural" to "cultural" forces, and a transposition from melodrama to allegory.

In terms of both style and narrative, *Cruel Story* evokes the melodramatic cinema of Mizoguchi. The film is constructed as a series of tableau-like scenes, each with a strong sense of unity achieved in part by the extensive use of long takes and by the sometimes awkward ellipses between them. Moreover, the emphasis on Mako as a heroine whose oppression is represented by way of rape also recalls Mizoguchi. Mako's fall from a moving car echoes a similar incident in *Sisters of the Gion* (1936), in which a woman is violently thrown from a moving car and breaks her leg. Mako's march into the camera near the end of the film recalls the way that Ayako, the heroine of Mizoguchi's *Osaka Elegy* (1936), suddenly walks into a close-up at the end of that film. Mizoguchi abruptly cuts off the long-awaited emergence of Ayako's subjectivity, and, while it is as brief in *Cruel Story,* this subjective presence is finally killed by men *in* the film, lifting Mako's desire onto an allegorical plane.

In stark contrast with Mizoguchi's *feminisuto* "worship," or idealization of female sacrifice,[18] for Oshima and his contemporaries, feminine sexuality is in itself an allegorical discourse of political desires.[19] The sadomasochistic form of sexual relations in the film speaks of the contradictions implicit in a political discourse that appropriates female desire without politicizing female subjectivity. Rape stands as a sign of the weakness of Oshima's male characters, and its annihilation of female desire remains repressed in many of his films as well as his writing.[20] The contradiction is certainly symptomatic of Japanese culture, and can perhaps be read in the film's abrupt shift from melodrama (in which Mako's repressed desire is written boldly) to allegory (in which her desire becomes that of the nongendered historical subject). The failure of romance is also a failure of sexual relations in the film, and both Kiyoshi's aggression and Mako's passivity are signs of this failure.

Oshima's revision of Mizoguchi is accomplished by what seems to be an appropriation of the Hollywood melodramatic style of the 1950s.[21] Certainly the use of Eastmancolor Cinemascope in itself constitutes a radical gesture in the conservative production system of Shochiku-Ofuna.[22] The use of color in costumes and sets and the expressive use of objects and locations are strategies of displacement, the means by which "the unspeakable" is represented in the text. Peter Brooks's description of melodramatic resistance would seem to be eminently applicable. Desire emerges as

> a victory over repression. We could conceive this repression as
> simultaneously social, psychological, historical, and
> conventional.... The melodramatic utterance breaks through
> everything that constitutes the "reality principle," all its
> censorships, accommodations, tonings-down. Desire cries
> aloud its language in identification with full states of being.[23]

The "manifest material" of the mise-en-scène of *Cruel Story* includes such things as liquor burning in glasses, brightly colored telephones, close-ups of shoes, orange-and-blue mise-en-scènes, close-ups of burning cigarettes, and construction sites. This rich plethora of "modern,"

"Western" signifiers far surpasses the linguistic content of the film and supplies a dynamic level that is utterly lacking from the performances.

The bright colors and loud noises of sexuality, violence, thrill seeking, and dancing are means of expression to be substituted for empty political rhetoric. This is particularly true of Mako. The inexpressive performance of Kuwano Miyuki is betrayed by her flamboyant (brightly colored, full-skirted) dresses and her tinted and teased hairstyle.[24] Her introduction to sexuality is channeled into strategic social deviance, as the couple make their living by amateur extortion, prostitution, and pimping. The expressionistic "triumph of desire" is actually realized in the brief beach scene in which Mako and Kiyoshi, wearing bright colors and sunglasses, reconcile their differences. But this image of consumerist utopia is parodic; in the second shot of the scene, Mako is wearing the red dress with white suns on it that she will wear to the end of the film and eventually die in. The brief glimpse of a romantic setting sun is immediately followed by their arrest upon returning home. Closure is deferred.

Although melodrama seems to be the dominant construction of death in Japanese film, and informs this national cinema as a metagenre to the same extent that it does Hollywood film, a number of significant differences between Japanese and Western melodrama need to be addressed.[25] Western melodrama, as it has been theorized by Peter Brooks and Thomas Elsaesser, is an expression of latency and interiority, an eruption that takes place on the surface of discourse and points in its very excessiveness to something that escapes representation.[26] Roland Barthes observes that Westerners cannot understand Japanese puppet theater (*bunraku*) because, for us, "to attack meaning is to hide or invert it but never to 'absent' it.... What is expelled from the [Japanese] stage is hysteria." In the presence of the puppet manipulators on stage, "work is substituted for inwardness ... the *inside* no longer commands the *outside*."[27] He claims that "excess is given only within the very code of excess ... the signifier cunningly does nothing but turn itself inside out, like a glove."[28]

In Chikamatsu Monzaemon's *bunraku* plays of double suicide, the couple is generally doomed from the outset, their love proscribed by their social commitments, and the narrative is simply an elaborate detour toward their desired goal.[29] The Japanese "moral occult"[30] is played out through the dual concepts of *giri* and *ninjo,* terms that embody a range of polarities, but refer most immediately to the contradiction between obligations to society—including one's family, village, class, trade, or business (*giri*)—and individual, "authentic" human feelings (*ninjo*). Interdependent, symbiotic moral principles of exteriority and interiority, *giri* and *ninjo,* sometimes interpreted as restraint and emotion, are forever at war within the Japanese melodramatic psyche, and only in death can the struggle be overcome.[31] A lovers' suicide is unquestionably a performance, a display of *giri,* obligations to each other, and *ninjo,* rejection of the social forces (class, especially) that conspire to keep the lovers apart, suspended in perfect harmonious balance.

Often the decision to die, in both samurai films and melodramas, is an expression of *ninjo,* the realm of "emotion" described by many commentators as being incomprehensible to the non-Japanese.[32] In Ian Buruma's popular ethnography, "every Japanese is equipped with a non-verbal emotional transmitter which functions only with other Japanese,"[33] and the silence of death is the ultimate expression of such nationalist communication. *Ninjo,* for Mizoguchi, is closely tied to woman's desire, but it is neither suppressed by nor triumphant over *giri.* A perfect balance between *giri* and *ninjo* is what is desired and often attained, with the effect of emptying the violence of melodramatic death of its potentiality. The "struggle" that informs Western melodrama is eradicated in Japanese melodrama by the laws of nature and divine providence; the pleasure of suffering is the pleasure of fulfillment in death.

Ninjo remains "incomprehensible" to non-Japanese, according to ethnographic film criticism (e.g., Sato, Buruma), in the same way that Japanese melodrama is for Barthes. It becomes a means of protecting the "meaninglessness" of the nonrealist traditional forms, which are virtually impossible to maintain intact within narrative realism: it endows them with the "meaning" of Japaneseness. The theatrical styles and narratives that inform classical Japanese film melodrama are built upon a "moral occult" that has no hidden meanings or Manichean struggles between desire and repression. Emotion is produced not by the unseen, but by the visibility of forms: the beauty of balance, the poverty of means, the perfection of technique, and other categories of Japanese aesthetics. Transposed to the cinematic medium of presence and absence, representation and invisibility, tradition itself is produced as the "unspeakable" that cannot be articulated within the realism of a photographic medium.

A central strategy of the Japanese New Wave of the 1960s was a recasting of melodramatic desire so that the principle of *ninjo* becomes a discourse of resistance, while *giri* is recast as social oppression. That this involved a recourse to Western melodramatic forms does not necessarily belittle the project. In *Cruel Story of Youth* (and other films, including Shinoda's *Double Suicide* [1969]), Western and Japanese melodramatic forms come together to produce an allegorical mode of representation in which "stylization" becomes a writing of historical desire.

The formal and narrative engagement with traditional Japanese melodrama situates the narrative desire for death on an allegorical plane. *Cruel Story of Youth* exhibits an indulgence in the excesses of cinematic representation in order to go beyond the realism on which traditional melodrama falters. The signifier is no longer an empty glove but an empty glass, waiting to be filled by the realism that is just beyond its grasp. Hysteria returns, not to characters but to discourse itself. In this way, Oshima's Japanese melodrama does not become its "opposite"—Barthes's psychological Western melodrama—but it becomes allegory. Moreover, the national allegory implicit in classical Japanese film melodrama is brought to the "surface" of the text as a discursive production of Japanese subjectivity.

Suicide in Japanese history and culture is a central trope in the construction of national allegory, but it would be a mistake to believe that it always referred to the same constellation of ideas. Indeed, the famous suicides of the twentieth century—from General Nogi (1912) to novelist Dazai Osamu (1948) to Mishima Yukio (1970)—are a history of shifting nationalist desires. Despite the notoriety outside Japan of Mishima's "theatrical suicide," it elicited a great deal of contempt and consternation within Japan, a great change from the respect that was generated by Nogi's patriotism and loyalty to the dead Emperor Meiji fifty-eight years earlier. Alan Wolfe compares Mishima's seppuku to Dazai's "schizophrenic" *jisatsu* (self-destruction, murder of the self, to be distinguished from the codified militarist act of seppuku), accomplished only after several failed attempts:

Whereas Dazai represents a "fragmented, schizoid" subjectivity, and his suicide a prototypically modern alienated variety, Mishima's seppuku stands for an effort to revive a "coherent" premodern notion of the individual subject, one connected with the romantic notion of a "nobility of failure" extending back to Japan's protohistoric age. As a metaphor, then, Mishima's seppuku projects a desire for control, whereas Dazai's *jisatsu* infers an inability to master the modern situation.[34]

None of Oshima's characters actually commit suicide, but many of the deaths are desired in the schizophrenic style of Dazai. When characters die at the hands of others (e.g., Kichi in *Realm of the Senses*), the terms are significantly expanded beyond the limits of Dazai's existentially alienated subjectivity. Melodrama provides the vehicle for an expansion of the narrow terms of *jisatsu* onto the terrain of the family and society. Psychology, fetishized in the literary tradition of the Japanese "I"-novel,[35] gives way to national-historical allegory written in its own terms, not those of the suicidal self. As national allegory, literary and historical suicides tend to evoke "some sense of a need for a spirituality thought to be lacking in the contemporaneous era,"[36] and in this sense they are fundamentally melodramatic, pointing to that which is lacking. Narrative mortality in Japan involves grasping the desire implicit in the allegorical act of suicide as historical, rather than spiritual, possibility.

From the *michiyuki* on, *Cruel Story* is allegorical in the sense of its status as writing, in the different discursive level that the text quite suddenly acquires. Unlike melodramatic representation in which excess of expression makes up for the limitations imposed on language and symbolic systems, in allegory that excess is rendered as language itself. Walter Benjamin points to the mode of address in allegorical representation and its fundamental relation to mortality:

> If the object becomes allegorical under the gaze of
> melancholy, if melancholy causes life to flow out of it and it
> remains behind dead, but eternally secure, then it is exposed
> to the allegorist, it is unconditionally in his power. That is to
> say it is now quite incapable of emanating any meaning or
> significance of its own; such significance as it has, it acquires
> from the allegorist.[37]

The emblem is the model of allegory for Benjamin, because in it "the essence of what is depicted" is "dragged out before the image, in writing, as a caption" (p. 185). "At one and the same time [it is] a fixed image and a fixing sign" (p. 184). This is partly accomplished in the final scene of *Cruel Story* by way of the sudden burst of music that accompanies the split-screen display of the two bodies, but the stylization of the entire coda and its formal disjunction from the narrative point to the role of the allegorist.

Maureen Turim has noted that Oshima's images are emblematic in their "presentation of themselves as signs."[38] His use of the sun in the 1960–61 trilogy and the Japanese flag itself (as we will see in *Boy*) is perhaps exemplary of this strategy, and in the scene in question, Mako's dress with white suns on red is an instance of what Audie Bock describes as Oshima's "dead flag fantasies."[39] Where the expressionism of melodrama diffuses the signified into a realm of excess, allegory directs signification into a specific schema. At the allegorical end of *Cruel Story*, the flip side of transcendence is realized: the material or biological pole of death that melodramatic representation ordinarily displaces onto spiritual or sexual desire.

The seventeen-second static shot of Kiyoshi in medium close-up on the ground with blood and multicolored ooze coming out of his mouth—shot in a rich orange light—especially places the emphasis on the biological fact of death. And yet the lovers' deaths take on a historical significance which may be described as the inverse of punishment or moral allegory. Mako and Kiyoshi become martyrs for social criticism, their deaths emblematic of exclusion and the failure of a renewed Japan. At the same time, Oshima's use of these images, his intervention and control of them (film as "camera-stylo"), establishes his subjectivity outside the closed circle of melodramatic pathos, outside the object, not contemplating but repulsed.

Benjamin insists that "the body comes into its own" in death no less than the spirit does, and the baroque dramatists' emphasis on the "physis" was not only "a question of reflection about the end of their lives" but an obsession with the body and its signifying properties (pp. 217–18). The corpse is the "pre-eminent emblematic property" because allegory fills out and denies "the void in which its objects are represented" (p. 233). Melodramatic death, such as Miyagi's in *Ugestu Monogatari* or Plato's in *Rebel Without a Cause*, avoids the sight of the corpse and allows for a thematic reconciliation of the surviving characters, precisely through allegories of resurrection, something that Sirk succinctly ironizes in *Imitation of Life*. Melodramatic death creates a void that, when filled, effects closure. Allegorical death is cruel because the void remains empty.

The representation of the body itself, drained of life, is a privileged signifier for the allegorist. Like the death's head, or skull, in baroque culture, the bruised and bleeding body is, for Oshima, the site of writing, a writing that places demands on the reader or viewer. Where the allegory of the crucifixion (and likewise double suicide and seppuku/ hara-kiri) sublimates the body into the symbol, the allegory of hell displays itself "as allegory" and the body is separated from its meaning. The allegory of damnation signifies transitoriness and, for Benjamin, the subjection of humanity to nature—not to God.[40]

Since, in the Japanese tradition, "god" *is* nature, and transitoriness *is* redemption, there is not the same legacy of allegory as in the West. Benjamin describes allegorical expression as an "oriental rhetoric" that only becomes "profound" when combined with the Western "doctrine of the fall of the creature, which brought down nature with it" (p. 224). The redemption in nature of the Japanese body, the continuity of the self in the natural world (as ashes rather than as a corpse), mystifies transitoriness as repetition and return. The subjection of humanity to nature does not imply decay, transformation, and "mortality" in Japanese eschatology, but the rule of divine fate. The allegorical emblem is not a "ruin" in traditional Japanese aesthetics, because it lacks that sense of loss that Benjamin identifies in the splitting of representation from meaning. Oshima's strategic use of this Western form in *Cruel Story*, at the specific juncture of 1960, signifies the subjection of humanity to itself, rather than to nature or divine fate. The transitoriness of the subject as a historical subject is portrayed as cruel, arbitrary, and therefore changeable.

There is no question that Kurosawa preceded Oshima in the strategic representation of violence in the Japanese cinema (e.g., *Throne of Blood* and *The Lower Depths,* both 1957), but Oshima's exploitation of the corpse as political allegory was a crucial means of employing discontinuous signification for Brechtian purposes. The discourse of melodrama in the body of the text of *Cruel Story* specifies this signified content as subjective, inward, as "desire," but the abrupt transition to allegory embodies the subject as mortal and therefore vulnerable to violence and to the repressive, familial forces that society represents to the individual.

The New Wave movement had pretty well exhausted itself by the time of Oshima's *In the Realm of the Senses* (1976), a film that marks the limits of the political duality of desire and repression. It encapsulates the futility of desire in narrative as radical praxis by mortifying the very limit of the End, beyond which desire must go to be realized. Sada and Kichi move from one windowless boudoir to another, making love throughout the entire film, and while flags and soldiers are omnipresent in their brief excursions outside, the action of the film is explicitly set off from the 1930s militarism in which the narrative is set, or set off from. Desire as resistance becomes simply escapism and an impotent political force. Insofar as Kichi's death is achieved as a heightened form of sexuality, it is an overwhelmingly literal rendering of the mortal erotics of narrative. The final high-angle shot of Kichi's body, inscribed with bloody characters saying "Sada and Kichi forever," is another abrupt shift into an allegorical mode of representation. Sada, moreover, after castrating her dead lover, wanders around Tokyo "carrying what she had cut off." The convention of double suicide is again subverted, and Sada is not "liberated" by her transgression but returned to the historical "real," the newspaper stories from which the story came.

For Stephen Heath, *In the Realm of the Senses* "comes near the limit of the historical function of the subject" because repetition does not lead *back* in this text, but perpetually forward to a terminal point of death. A key to the rearticulation of desire and mortality in *In the Realm of the Senses* and *Death by Hanging* is a redirection of repetition *away* from the sameness of death and toward the difference of historical time. Dana Polan points out that "the possibility of a new form of repetition" is predicated on "the divided inclusion of the spectator."[41] Oshima's Brechtian approach involves a harnessing of a politicized alienation effect to produce a theatrical sign that allegorizes Japanese "tradition." Rituals, including execution and intercourse, are repeated in Oshima's narratives so as to preclude the possibility of return. Oshima's desire to film an actual death, like Sada's murder of her lover, is a desire to leave things permanently unfinished. The ontological obscenity of filming death and thus repeating the unrepeat-able, is cast here as a politics of representing desire in and through mortality.

The Boy and the Flag

Oshima's films have often been described by Western critics as an illus-tration of an inside/outside conflict, usually referring to the relation-ship between the personal and the political, the individual and soci-ety.[42] However, the articulation of difference in Oshima's films can only be fully appreciated within the context of the conventions of differ-ence in Japanese culture. An inside/outside dialectic has traditionally distinguished between the authentically Japanese and the foreign.[43] If the interiority of *ninjo* corresponds to the essential Japaneseness of the Japanese character, unknowable to the outsider, *ninjo* and *giri* do, in fact, correspond to an inside/outside relationship, but it is not a self/other distinction so much as one between homogeneity and heterogeneity.

The relationship between the individual body and institutions of power is the obverse side of what Foucault calls "bio-power."[44] The deployment of death as one of the main techniques of biopower in Japan is made explicit in *Boy*. For this film, based on an incident that generated widespread sympathy in Japan, Oshima borrowed the actual newspaper headlines about a family of *atariyas,* or traffic-accident extortionists. The family's occupation in *Boy* is a continual flirtation with death, and the father who orders his wife and child to jump in front of moving cars says that he's "died once already in the war," bringing into play the ideology of sacrifice that underwrote Japan's military endeavors in the Pacific war. This leads the boy to say that he "doesn't know how to die."

The absolute lack of pathos in Oshima's treatment of the story is due in part to a critical distance maintained, again, through a tableau structure with multiple ellipses and minimal point-of-view editing. But this time Oshima's use of traditional forms is very de-liberate, and is bolstered by the fact that *Boy* partakes of a genre in which Ozu worked extensively, that of the tendency film or con-temporary family melodrama. Oshima uses it to further implicate the

exploitation of the body into the Japanese ethic of *giri* or duty, obligation, and loyalty.

Perhaps the most remarkable feature of this film is that almost
every shot of the wide-screen mise-en-scène of *Boy* is designed as a
metaphor for the Japanese flag. In much of the narrative, the mother's
red sweater or her hair, which she dyes red halfway through the film,
is center-screen. Oshima does the same thing with Ozu's "painterly"
use of red in the interior decor and exterior environments, repeatedly placing a small area of red lacquer, plastic, cloth, or building
center-screen. The analogy of this composition to the flag is encouraged by the omnipresence of Japanese flags throughout the film, literally drenching the boy's environment and often placed center-screen
themselves. Every shot, therefore, is allegorical: each scene is an allegory of Japan, and each shot is a signifier, its composition a form of
writing, obliquely cut off from "full" realist representation.

The boy's round head is established in the film's first two shots as
itself isomorphic with the round sun of the flag, suggesting that the
boy's manipulation and oppression by his parents are a metaphor for
the more general construction of the Japanese subject. Thus the unnamed boy protagonist of this film is literally inscribed as a sign in a
narrative constructed as a series of signs. In other words, subjectivity
is "contained" and closed off on two levels: as the boy is to the family, psychoanalytically and ideologically, so the individual is to Japan.
But the third level, the relation of the subject to the narrative, remains
unsutured until the final shots of the film. Again, it is the limit of these
relationships that the film ultimately delineates by aligning death with
a "reality principle" outside of representation and leaving the boy
precisely at the point of its transcendence.

The ideological critique of death is accomplished in *Boy* by a narrative that splits apart the two principles of process and unity, metonymic change and static repetition. Because the family is continually on the move, there is no repetition of place; every scene is in a
new location. Interiors of inns and restaurants may be similar, but they
are never the same; the roadways, parks, fields, and trains are never
returned to. We see the family eating again and again, but never in
the same place. Likewise, the boy and the mother repeat their little
drama many times, but never in the same place with the same car. The

only repetitive visual constant is the flag and its analogues in the mise-en-scène (figure 7).

"Home" thus becomes a crucial locus of desire for the boy, figured in a folk song from Koichi, where his father comes from and where he was presumably born. But when the boy runs away alone to visit his grandparents, he can only afford to take the train to a town with the same name as theirs, where he enacts an imaginary reunion by himself. Toward the end of the film, when the boy, his little brother, and their mother are finally enjoying the first domestic scene of the film, the police break in and arrest the father as he enters the house.

The boy's occupation of throwing himself in front of cars is the means by which a "death wish" is substituted for the comfort of home. Oshima translates the masochism of this found story into a narrative propelled by a conception of death that is at once heroic and escapist. Although the only "returns" in *Boy* are to the rehearsal of dying and to the omnipresent design of the flag, there are two levels of memory operative in the film. One consists of stills and freeze-frames of

Fig. 7. *Boy*: The boy (Abe Tetsuo) with his parents (Koyama Akiko and Watanabe Fumio) and younger brother surrounded by flags. The mother's sweater in this shot is red. Publicity shot courtesy of Museum of Modern Art Film Stills Archive.

images from inside and outside the diegesis inserted at two strategic points in the narrative; the other consists of the boy's voice-over and a short series of flashbacks in which he recalls a death that he witnessed. Each of these configurations of memory consists of a principle of "return," by which the film redefines mortality in terms of a politicized subjectivity.

The first series of stills occurs about halfway through the film, commensurate with the second instance of the boy's voice-over.[45] None of these stills are repetitions of images from the film, although several are of the boy himself, and the black-and-white ones are clearly from an entirely different order of representation. A shot of the boy in his underwear lying on a white sheet is inserted into the series as he says, "Since it really hurts now, I don't have to lie to the doctor. Even an ordinary child can say that it hurts." His skin is very pink and he looks into the camera silently, lying on his side.

In this sequence, the stasis of the cognate photo (the still that fills the frame completely) is particularly important because of the tension created between the photographs and the shot of the body on the bed. The latter is equally unrelated to the preceding and succeeding scenes, is equally unsynchronized with the sound track, and is equally static. The boy does not move, but blinks, indicating that the image, the film, is moving. Time passes in a "present tense," whereas the black-and-white photos relate to a past, even if it is a time outside, between the scenes, of the film we are watching.

The tight framing of the boy's exposed body, together with his first admission of pain, is the first intimation in the film of his mortality. The color stills of him lying on the street could be of his imagined future death, or they could be single frames of his masquerade of injury. But like the black-and-white stills, they stop the film and mark its illusion of presence; surrounding the shots of the boy on the bed, they threaten movement with stasis. As the film has internalized the relentless traveling, the unceasing motion is threatened graphically by the photograph at the same time as the threat to the boy's body is made explicit. His mortality is thus analogized with the movement of the film.

Another cognate photograph is included toward the end of *Boy* following a series of newspaper headlines that read "Shakedown ring ... Couple used child; Suspected couple indicted; Discovered through photographic I.D." The black-and-white photograph is of the family on the street in a location where we saw them previously enact one of their crimes and where they were photographed by journalists. As the image is held on the screen, a man's (Oshima's) voice-over reports journalistically the details of the family and their activity. In the final scene on the train, the family sits with plain-clothes policemen. The image is suddenly frozen and the voice-over gives us a detailed biography of the father, under which seven stills in black and white and color, taken from the film itself, are presented. After another still shot of the family, seven more stills of the mother accompany a similarly detailed biography of her.

Although this series of stills provides the film with a memory, uni-fying its discrete moments by way of repetition, it is not a subjective flashback. The memory, rather, pertains to a history outside the film. Although the images of the mother and father are obviously enacted, the biographies, as they are authoritatively enunciated by Oshima, have the weight of documentary truth. The death of the film, the end of the narrative, is thus taken up by a return to a lived history in the mode of Benjamin's storyteller, whose "wisdom" is derived from experience.[46]

But this is not the end of the film. It is followed by a short sequence in which the boy finally emerges as a subject of discourse. Whereas the trajectory of the film has been linked to the boy's mortality through the still images and the static mise-en-scène, in the last shots the boy's memory, vision, and desire are represented through the con-trasting metaphor of a moving train. Until this point, the boy's only conception of transcendence, of a different reality, is through a cul-tural co-optation of his imagination by fantasy narratives. When the police interrogate the boy, they show him a photograph of himself. He says, "That's a man from outer space."

However, in the very last shots of the film, when a policeman asks the boy whether he likes the sea and whether he liked being on a plane, the boy, who has until now denied being an *atariya,* defending his mother and father by refusing to indict their criminal activity, finally says, "Yes. I went to Hokkaido" (the northernmost part of Japan), an admission that constitutes a confession. Before he answers, a shot of the train tracks from the front of the moving train is followed by a close-up of the boy, a reverse shot of his look out the train window, another close-up of him, and four flashback images that comprise the second level of memory mentioned earlier, this time an explicitly subjective one.

The four images that the boy perceives in flashback on the train are of a girl's lifeless face with bright red blood on her forehead (from two different angles) and a red boot in the snow (the second time as a snowman's nose). Connected by dissolves, the series goes girl, boot, girl, boot. These images all derive from earlier scenes set in Hokkaido. When the family travels to this northern snow-covered island by plane toward the end of the film, they have traversed all of Japan. The boy looks across the sea in a blizzard to a distant horizon that is "not-Japan." On a snowy road, a family fight is followed by a freak accident shot in black and white. The boy's little brother runs from the father's violence and a jeep swerves to avoid hitting him. While the mother, father, and baby flee, the boy remains watching while the driver and the young girl in the jeep, who have been killed by the abrupt stop, are taken away by ambulances.

The girl's boot falls off and the boy takes it home. He subsequently uses the red boot as a nose for his snowman, which he violently demolishes. The composition of that mise-en-scène, in which the bright red L-shape of the boot is set against the homogeneous white landscape, indicates the semiotic reading that the narrative demands. Insofar as the red-and-white mise-en-scène matches the design of the flag, the shape of the boot points simply to otherness, to the not-Japan that the boy has pointed to on the boat.

Although a number of interpretations of these scenes and the memory they produce have been offered by critics,[47] the boy's possible sense of responsibility for the death — his psychological response to it — is less important than the pure phenomenology of seeing death. He does say to his parents, "Maybe I killed her," but the freak accident is never referred to again or explained. Because the girl is the first female of his own age that he has encountered, his fascination with her image is a fascination with the other sex as much as it is with her death and a vision of not-life. These indices of otherness mark for the boy the limits of his social construction, barriers he transcends in his final confession. Instead of the death that he has desired, Oshima leaves the boy on the verge of identifying himself as something more real than "a man from outer space." Through the image of another's death, inserted arbitrarily as a completely fictional event in this "true story," the boy attains a sense of himself as a person independent of his parents, free of his masochistic dependency.

In the boy's flashback images of death, a number of narrative tropes coalesce to give the film a retrospective, retroactive structure that allows the boy to overcome his desire for death. These images of the girl's face and the boot are, like the previous shots of the boy's naked body, static but filmed: representations of stasis. Furthermore, they are repetitions of earlier images and, on another level, repetitions of the red-centered mise-en-scène, emblematic of Japanese nationalism. Like the series of stills accompanying the parents' biographies (the "dossier of the film itself in stills"),[48] this short series of remembered images fills the convention of narrative binding or unifying, but the effect of the repetition is not one of closure.

The four shots differ from the Oshima-narrated stills in their crucial relation to the boy's memory, finally producing a discourse of subjectivity. They supply a visual counterpart to the three instances of the boy's voice-over, a subjective register of vision that has been previously designated as a locus of antagonism. The boy's memory of the accident is bound to his point of view although the accident scene itself is shot in the "objective," distanced style of most of the film, with no reaction shots or eyeline matches. Not even the cutaways to the girl's face or the boot in the snow are sutured by the boy's look. There are only four instances in *Boy* in which the boy's point of view is represented, all of them overdetermined, and in two of them he is punished for looking.[49]

The inscription of point of view and coextensive identification of a subject of vision is finally established by the glance out the train window, a *moving* point-of-view shot. Finally, a dialectic of metaphor and metonymy that has been entirely lacking in the preceding scenes is realized. The boy "disappears" into the field of the other, becomes the "Absent One" of Oudart's suture theory, not to reach the limit of his historical construction — his death — but to go beyond it by way of his vision and memory of death. At the same time, the boy's admission that he went to Hokkaido is motivated by an identification with specific symbols of otherness. His difference from his parents, his opposition to them, is predicated on the sign of difference: the not-circular, the not-male, the not-living, and the not-Japanese.

Boy is perhaps the ultimate expression of Oshima's "dead flag fantasies." The stasis that is rendered in *Boy* explicitly conjoins the ideological stagnation of the child's inability to criticize or renounce his parents with Japanese aesthetic formalism. The repetition of the red-centered composition, as a self-imposed aesthetic structure, mimics this formalism, specifying both its nationalistic and its static character.

Moreover, the implication of Ozu in Oshima's revisionist formalism, referenced specifically by the family drama and the use of red, can be extended to the status of Ozu's films as chains of signifiers. Ozu's frontal symmetrical compositions and virtual disregard for continuity editing emphasize the presentational character of each of his short shots.[50] In *Boy*, Ozu's style, with all its traditional connotations, is subjected to implicit criticism by analogy to the repressive nationalistic and patriarchal conditions in which the boy is situated. Oshima's use of Ozu's "presentational" film aesthetics involves a flattening of the image; he drains it of its illusionist potential of full signification and makes it an emblem of death.

The image of the girl's face on the white snow with bright red blood on her forehead is an "excessive" gesture, narratively gratuitous but crucial to the film's representational politics: it aligns the lack of life with the inertness of signification. The flag itself becomes an emblem of mortality, as do the rituals of family life that Oshima has theatricalized to the point of excess. The girl's death is, in a sense, a sacrificial gesture that enables the boy and the spectator to transcend the limits of the knowable, rational world. If, for Bataille, sacrifice "reveals what normally escapes notice," namely, "the continuity of existence" beyond individual "discontinuity,"[51] the Japanese context reverses the terms. The heterogeneity of individual mortality is revealed beyond the national allegory of homogeneous duty-bound dying. Nevertheless, Bataille's main point, that sex and death share an erotic component in the dialectical equation of sameness and difference, remains a fundamental tenet of Oshima's deployment of narrative mortality.

The case of the "*atariyas* who used their child" was not an isolated incident of traffic-accident extortion, but it was unusual, Oshima says, because of the role of the family unit and the fact that they traveled all over Japan. He was attracted to the story because of its "tourist" aspect as well as the "theatricality" of the crime.[52] And indeed, as important as the travel undertaken by the characters is the ethnographic quality of Oshima's observation of his actors, especially the "nonprofessional" orphan, Abe Tetsuo. Nationhood in Japan has been historically founded on an ethnographic conception of the Japanese character, a "nativism" that also informs the privileged content of melodramatic *ninjo*. Narrative mortality in *Boy* can be read across Japanese nativism or indigenous ethnography, particularly since this discourse informs the specificity of Ozu's stylistics. In his essay on *Boy,* Oshima even quotes from the ethnologist Yanagita Kunio: "Reality is infinitely more profound than the world we have access to in reading books or listening to stories."[53]

The interdisciplinary Japanese study of Japanese identity, which in Japan is called *nihonjinron,* has been traced by many commentators to Kunio's early twentieth-century ethnography. *Nihonjinron* is basically a decadent form of *kokugaku,* or the discourse of Japanese nativism that began to be written in the Tokugawa period (1600–1867). Emerging with the rise of the bourgeoisie, it was originally a radical narrative, challenging "the entrenched domination of Chinese culture in Japanese life," which the ruling Edo oligarchy manipulated as an instrument of power. According to H. D. Harootunian, *Kokugaku* involved the "elimination of culture itself as a category," and the terms of being Japanese were derived from experience, work, and worship:

> Nativism, in its Tokugawa incarnation, rescued daily life, custom, and "household duties"—the alterity of an official discourse that privileged mental over manual labor—and converted them into the content of discursive knowledge. This move made the center equivalent with what hitherto had been alterity and removed the [cultural] center to the place of the Other.... this new form of knowledge presupposed closing all distances between subject and object.... No difference was supposed to intervene between what humans did and made and what they could possibly know; practice and hermeneutics became the same thing.[54]

The political strategy of *kokugaku* effectively backfired with modernization, as cultural praxis, far from being banished, came to supersede political praxis in the formation of a hegemonic order of cultural identity. Harootunian argues that when the identity of "the ordinary and abiding people" became the privileged subject of *kokugaku* (through the ethnography of Yanagita Kunio), the zen of daily life became linked to nationhood (p. 417). The elimination of phenomenological difference went hand in hand with a dissolution of "historically determinate classes into the larger category of a folk unmediated by history." This effectively "identified the Subject with the Other in order to repress otherness as the heterogeneous place of language and desire" (p. 437). Moreover, in the context of a rapidly industrializing and urbanizing Japan, the signified content of the ahistorical "folk" is inevitably absent and the discourse becomes one of "incurable nostalgia."

The radical project of *Boy* is a redemption of the Japanese subject within the language of desire. Narrative mortality operates here as a mortification of the aesthetics of Ozu, the cinematic exemplar of *nihonjinron*. The performances and the mise-en-scènes of Ozu's narratives arguably involve a rigorous aestheticization and politicization of daily life. They are indeed melodramas in which the absent signified refers to an egolessness of Japanese history, the privileged content of *nihonjinron*. Especially in Ozu's postwar work—family melodramas of arranged marriages, generational differences, and dying patriarchs—the perfect balance of *giri* and *ninjo* that is achieved contains an attitude of melancholy toward a changing Japan.

Interiority in twentieth-century Japan has tended toward a category of insularity and of loss, and "otherness" belongs specifically to history and "the repressed alterity of a more authentic life."[55] The melodramatic structure of Japanese nationalism is one in which authentic emotions are inexpressible because they belong to the past, but also because they belong to experience, not representation. Closure in Ozu's narratives is always resignation to the death of desire and to the impossibility of Japanese subjectivity after the "fall" of Meiji,[56] resignation not only to Westernization and modernization, but to realist representation as well.

Oshima's narrative mortality involves a recovery of the Japanese subject from his or her nationalization, and the emphasis on experience in the form of historical materialism may be perceived as a dialectical return to *kokugaku*. The immediacy of documentary style in *Boy* functions as a "corrective" to the fictional escape from daily life. The narrative is anchored in "experience" through ethnographic impetus and journalistic authority. By leaving the boy unnamed in the film, the distinction between actor and character breaks down. It is Tetsuo's mortality (the boy who plays the boy) rather than the fictional events he performs that the spectator is finally alerted to.[57] A similar confusion takes place in Ozu's casting of Ryu Chishu and Hara Setsuko in similar roles throughout their careers, which is perhaps the strongest discourse of nativist representation in his work, and in contrast to *Boy,* it constitutes a mystified ethnography.

In *Boy* the allegorical potential of death is exploited in order to designate, once again, another space beyond the film, beyond representation, beyond the "historical limit of the subject." Death in this film is at once the emblem of ideological and representational stasis, and of otherness. The boy's transcendence in the final shots of the film is most simply a transcendence of the conception of death as the goal of life; in this sense it is a redemption of subjectivity. The narrative does not stop arbitrarily "in the banal," or even in the "documentary" of the family. It stops at the point at which the boy Abe Tetsuo becomes a subject of vision and memory, a point that is conventionally located at the point of death. Again, through strategic mixing of Japanese and Western representational styles, Oshima deploys narrative mortality for a politics of the existential individual.

The film demonstrates that, within the specific cultural and historical dynamics within which Oshima was working, the disavowal of death can become a progressive political strategy. This is in keeping with Marcuse's politics of mortality, but it also takes place within a politics of representation. The difference between the Real (history, including the presence of the spectator) and the representations of the subject gives rise to an imaginary space beyond narrative, after the knowable end. Through the discovery that death is an excess of the Real, a point beyond history, and his own existence, the boy is freed from the constricting bonds of the family. Death is situated as a sign masking a void, its repetitions leading nowhere, but its emblems everywhere in Oshima's Japan of the late 1960s. Radical praxis consists in imagining that space as a history of the future.

In Oshima's films, narrative mortality is a key means by which the nostalgia endemic to *nihonjinron* is transformed into a more radical historical discourse. American styles of narrative, costume, and individualism in *Cruel Story of Youth* and *Boy* are deployed in the Japanese context not to signify a "loss" of traditional modes but to show up the stagnation of Japanese traditionalism. Oshima's politics are no less "nationalist," but the representation of the nation is constructed on the ruins of *nihonjinron*. Narrative mortality involves a redemption of the Japanese subject in representation, on the other side of his or her melodramatic exemption from discourse. Desire comes into play not simply as a discourse of sexuality and individualism, but as a utopian thrust beyond the limits of representation, narrative, and history. Narrative mortality may be once again described as a politics of spectatorship, as Oshima addresses a historical viewer outside representation.

The address of the spectator, *anata mo,* is the culmination of an extensive splitting of representation.[58] Harootunian suggests that the institutionalization of Zen aesthetics, and its collapse of representation in bourgeois culture, nullified the radical potential of nativism:

> The unification of subject and object not only reaffirmed the centrality of culture as a privileged category of perceiving the world, but the process annexed politics to its authority. The ensuing arrangement made it increasingly difficult to imagine politics as a semi-autonomous space for pursuing forms of plural or diverse interests.[59]

If the "separation of a knowing subject from the object of knowledge" became necessary for political activity, narrative mortality becomes an important wedge to pry them apart. The distinction between addresser and addressed pertains to a division between reality and imagination, history and subjectivity, that originates on the site of the body. In the Japanese New Wave cinema, difference is resurrected in forms of spectatorship, gender, and mortality for a radical politics of otherness in the context of 1960s Japan.

The representation of death — its allegorical potential and its designation of a threshold — is exploited by Oshima as a radical alternative to the totalizing closure of Japanese "traditionalism." His intertextuality ensures that this is not simply a capitulation to "Western" representational practices, but a complex rewriting of Japanese ide-ologemes. The interiority of *nihonjinron* is transformed into individ-ual expression so that the lost secret of Tokugawa nativism (*koku-gaku*)—that lived experience is itself aesthetic and political—is recovered on the other side of its cinematic representation, beyond narrative.

The Japanese New Wave embarked on a crucial project of allego-rizing indigenous representational strategies, of politicizing them for a discovery of history and difference, and defining spectatorship as a dialectical rather than contemplative category. As Takeo Doi points out, "For the Japanese, freedom in practice existed only in death, which was why praise of death and incitements towards death could occur so often."[60] In Oshima's films "the desire for the freedom of Japan" is given concrete forms of expression that necessarily engage with the desire for death in a radical way. What is often carelessly described as "nihilism" in the Japanese New Wave is in fact an allegorization, a mode of writing in which the spectator is offered a place outside the closed circuits of ritual and repetition to understand "freedom" as historical difference, as material change, and as otherness.

In his conclusion to *Eros Plus Massacre,* David Desser analyzes three films that mark the decline of the movement: *The Inferno of First Love* (Hani, 1968), *Eros Plus Massacre* (Yoshida, 1969), and Oshi-ma's *The Man Who Left His Will on Film* (1970). In all three, he notes, "the deaths of filmmaking protagonists is the death of cinema, the death at least, of a politically radical cinema.... That there is nothing to film, that the will to film leads to the death of film, is a function of fading political aspirations."[61] In 1969, *Boy* anticipates this demoral-ization through its oppressive stasis and excessive containment. The leap of imagination needed to break out of cultural homogenization, conformism, and nationalist ideologies of sacrifice is truly heroic. Even in *Cruel Story of Youth,* the recourse to allegory is produced within a framework of resignation. The Japanese subject in Oshima's films cannot be renewed without a struggle. By the time of *In the Realm of the Senses* in 1976, that struggle has been mortified. In its ruins, sexual desire is channeled strictly into sex, producing one of the most futile deaths in film history.

FOUR

JEAN-LUC GODARD
Allegory of the Body

● ──────────────────────────────────────

The greater the significance, the greater the subjection to death,
because death digs most deeply the jagged line of demarcation between
physical nature and significance. —WALTER BENJAMIN[1]

In a 1965 interview, when asked about all the blood in *Pierrot le fou,*
Godard responded, "Not blood. Red."[2]—indicating that for him, as
for Oshima, the representation of death is a form of writing in the cinema. This treatment of death allows for a carnivalesque, ironic attitude toward mortality in which the bonds of pathos are broken with
laughter. At the same time, though, in the throes of his ongoing critique of film language in the 1960s, Godard maintains an attitude of
melancholy in the face of the loss of illusionism. The representation
of death is always and inevitably allegorical in his films, oscillating
between these two contradictory impulses toward discovery and loss.
Because *Le Mépris* (1963) and *Pierrot le fou* (1965) demonstrate most
clearly Godard's tendencies toward the melancholic and the carnivalesque, respectively, analyses of these two films will form the
substance of this chapter. It should be stressed, though, that the two

137

attitudes are dialectically engaged in a singular project of thresholding between the modern and the postmodern, and between resignation and expectation.

Certain real parallels exist between the projects of Godard and Wenders, for whom, as we have seen, narrative mortality also involves a melancholy attitude toward cinematic representation. For both directors, a pantheon of Hollywood auteurs is a crucial locus of the lost possibilities of the cinema, possibilities remote from their own helplessly self-conscious engagements with representation. For Godard, however, the representation of death belongs to a discourse of materialism, a historical project that is absent from Wenders's more subjective endeavors. Narrative mortality is produced as an allegory of consumer society grounded in the transience of the cinematic signifier — that very transience which Wenders disavows.

The analysis of narrative mortality in *Le Mépris* and *Pierrot le fou* will demonstrate the role of death and closure at a crucial moment in film history and criticism. In the mid-1960s, as *Cahiers du Cinéma* was moving from auteurist cinephilia to a critique of representation, Godard was working with Hollywood genres, but moving toward a more politicized mode of filmmaking. Narrative mortality provided a strategy of mortifying a classical cinematic heritage while redeeming the utopian character of generic romance and adventure. Narrative mortality takes the form here of an "allegory of the body" in which actors and actresses perform as documentary subjects, and thus as indices of a lived, experiential history that intersects with the mortifying discourse of cinema. The bodies of actors — most famously Jane Fonda, but, as we shall see, Bardot, Karina, and Belmondo as well — animate representation and at the same time expose its limits.

Compared to his Maoist-inflected films of 1967–72, "politics" in the early part of Godard's career is downplayed; there is, nevertheless, a politics of representation that is closely linked to the contemporary discourses of Marxism and existentialism. The intellectual climate in France in the 1950s and early 1960s was one in which Marxists disillusioned with Stalinism, and existentialists (such as Sartre) seeking to reconcile phenomenology with social commitment, found themselves on common ground. Historical materialism became a discourse of the quotidian in Henri Lefebvre's revisionist Marxism, and at the same time accommodated the priority of "existence" (over essence) in existentialist discourse. Mark Poster's succinct description of the basic affinities between Marxism and existentialism is that "both accepted Hegel's early attempt to define reality as unfolding in time, as an essentially temporal phenomenon. Consequently, Marxism and existentialism posit the primacy of life over thought."[3]

The existentialist slogan "Existence precedes essence" finds form in Godard's idiosyncratic conception of "life," a faith in the documentary verities of image production, derived from neorealism and Bazin's film aesthetics. "Life" comes to refer to the representation of historicity and experience, in which psychological characterization and "meaning" take second place. "Death" becomes the ironic authentication of this discourse of "life." Godard's improvisational method of filmmaking flows, as Jean Collet has remarked, "from the will to express the instant." Collet's monograph on Godard, first published in 1963 (and updated in 1968), highlights the existentialist dimension of Godard's early filmmaking, and the related role of mortality: "An instant of life acquires its particular value when one is conscious of death. For Godard, to capture life is, more precisely, to capture death.... One must therefore work quickly. Filming is a pursuit. All of Godard's work takes place under the sign of speed."[4] Indeed, it is the car accident that becomes the emblem of death in Godard's films.

Death in the early films tends to be highly stylized, never realistic or psychological. It tends to happen quickly, violently, and inevitably, at the end of the film. Of his scripting-while-shooting method in 1962, after *Vivre sa vie,* Godard admitted, "What caused me a lot of trouble was the end. Should the hero die?... Finally I decided that as my avowed ambition was to make an ordinary gangster film, I had no business deliberately contradicting the genre: he must die."[5] Deaths at the end of the films that precede *Le Mépris* and *Pierrot le fou* tend to separate (at the last moment) the means of representation (*discours*) from the narrative plot (*histoire*). Generic conventions are thereby foregrounded, but neither completely discarded nor respected. The two main strategies by which this is accomplished are through stylized performance and displacement onto the sound track. Susan Sontag describes the effect of these techniques: "There can indeed be no internally necessary end to a Godard film, as there is to a Bresson film. Every film must either seem broken off abruptly or else ended arbitrarily — often by the violent death in the last reel of one or more of the main characters."[6]

In *A bout de souffle,* Belmondo's stylized death scene underlines the generic necessity of his demise, which is above all a performance for the American girlfriend. Arthur (Claude Brasseur) likewise undergoes protracted death throes at the end of *Bande à part,* flailing and stumbling far beyond the calls of genre, only to emphasize the role of genre and narrative convention as the very cause of death. Arthur's death is offset by the happy ending of his partners in crime, Odile and Franz, who romantically sail off to Brazil for equally generic reasons. The tragedy of *Bande à part* is not death, but the limited choice of generic endings. Although Godard uses them both, the "happy" and the "unhappy," both are empty of consolation and closure. In *Vivre sa vie,* despite Nana's independence and autonomy she becomes a victim of urban crime; the world "chooses" her partly because, despite Godard's freewheeling film praxis, stories still have to end.

In Godard's genre revisionism, the representation of death contributes to a mortification of genre and its mythic dimensions. In the case of *Le Mépris,* this involves an emptying out of the symbolic assumptions of genre and a retention of its structure of desire. To be told of a central character's death, but not to see it (which happens at the end of *Le Petit Soldat, Les Carabiniers,* and *Masculin/Féminin*), is to be cheated of that pleasure of closure that even the most tragic narratives offer. As with the stylized deaths, Godard might be said to have his cake (maintain his reflexive, modernist style) and eat it too (end with death). Even before Godard introduces "red" ("not blood") and car accidents into his films, the representation of death is instrumental to his deconstruction of cinematic representation and narrative.

The phenomenology of death in these films places in question its visibility, and also its relation to subjectivity. The Godardian character who dies spectacularly, discursively, and intertextually is a subjectivity constructed purely from signifiers and refers finally to the Godardian subject who "cannot return to the world," who cannot represent a "self" as a meaningful totality, because subjectivity continually evades him in the status of the image. In Mikhail Bakhtin's remarks on death

in Dostoyevski (which, he says, is usually violent and, unlike Tol-
stoy, often unnaturally caused by murder and suicide), he makes the
following distinction:

> Death from within, that is, one's own death consciously
> perceived, does not exist for anyone: not for the dying person,
> nor for others; it does not exist at all. Precisely this
> consciousness for its own sake, which neither knows nor has
> the ultimate word, is the object of depiction in Dostoevsky's
> world. This is why death-from-within cannot enter this world;
> such death is alien to its internal logic. Death in Dostoevsky's
> world is always an objective fact for other consciousnesses.[7]

The point of view of the dying person is completely alien to Godard's allegories, in which death, as a mode of writing, is a form of
communication from which the dying person is excluded.[8] Death
takes on the objective form of the spectacle. This is a phenomenology of death that recalls not Sartre so much as Maurice Merleau-
Ponty. In "The Film and the New Psychology," Merleau-Ponty says
that "the movies are peculiarly suited to make manifest the union of
mind and body, mind and world, and the expression of one in the
other."[9] The antithesis between being and consciousness that underscores Sartre's philosophy was bridged by Merleau-Ponty in order to
describe social reality in terms of perception. For him, subjectivity is
a conjunction of self-perception and perception of the self by others;
thus behavior, worldly existence, cannot be separated from consciousness. As Poster puts it, "Merleau-Ponty held up the body as fulcrum
of being-in-the-world, facilitating a reconciliation with Marx's concept
of the 'sensuousness' of human action."[10] Although Merleau-Ponty
included no critique of representation in his program for the cinema,
for Godard the problem of representation was a given, and he placed
the problem of the body as subject at the center of his work.

Thus we will find in the discussions of *Le Mépris* and *Pierrot le
fou* that the two sides of Godard's deployment of narrative mortality,
the melancholic and the carnivalesque, are linked through a discursive self-consciousness that recognizes that "all is discourse," but
also that this is not a dead end for political desires. Within discourse
are desires that might be animated "on the other side," if you will, of

the alienation produced by discursive reflexivity after the "fall" of representation, within the historicity of the profilmic. The phenomenology of spectacle and photographic reproduction that radically separates objective and subjective veracities is balanced by a narrativity that struggles to reconcile them through the conventions of closure, romance, and destiny.

If utopian truth-values are dependent on the believability of the future, in Godard's narratives the essence of the image, its intimate inscription of life, its vérité, is in a continual process of being lost and found. Mortification and the disjunctions of allegorical representation are the means by which this duality is inscribed. Whereas in *Pierrot le fou* it takes the form of irony, and death is the discursive sign of thresholds and temporality, in *Le Mépris* allegory is limited to the ruins of classicism. The myth of fate is painfully deconstructed in this film only to reveal the naked fragments of the believability of cinematic representation.

Le Mépris: The Myth of Fate

The chief intertexts of *Le Mépris* are Homer's *Odyssey* and Alberto Moravia's *Il Disprezzo* (*A Ghost at Noon*), a novel about interpreting *The Odyssey* that Godard took for the basis of his screenplay. Fritz Lang plays himself in *Le Mépris* as the director of a film of *The Odyssey,* and the narrative revolves around the attempt to make this film. Paul Javal (Michel Piccoli) is a reluctant screenwriter, on the job only for the money, and is vaguely analogous (less vaguely in Moravia's text) to Ulysses. His wife Camille (Brigitte Bardot), for whom he is trying to earn money, is likewise related to Penelope. The first half of the film, set in interiors in Rome, deals largely with their marital troubles, their lack of communication, and their encounter with Prokosch (Jack Palance), the pretentious American producer of *The Odyssey,* who identifies quite explicitly with "the gods." The second half of *Le Mépris,* set in the vast exteriors of Capri, is an indulgence on Godard's part in wide-screen color film, but the rift between husband and wife is deepened (figure 8). Paul allows Camille to be seduced by Prokosch, and while he sleeps they are killed in a car accident. The film ends with Lang and Paul (and Godard, as Lang's assistant) shooting Ulysses' return to his Mediterranean homeland.[11]

Fig. 8. *Le Mépris*: Paul (Michel Piccoli) and Camille (Brigitte Bardot) carry on their "boudoir drama" in the epic setting of the Mediterranean. Publicity still courtesy of Photofest.

The car accident is rendered with a mythic and tragic resonance, but, at the same time, it is merely discursive and allegorical. It thereby emblematizes the film's two themes of classicism and language. Classicism is invoked through the Greek intertext, but it is also linked to the classicism of Hollywood cinema through the role of Fritz Lang. Language in *Le Mépris* is consistently cast as arbitrary, limited, and quite distinct from the fullness of classical representation; Francesca

(Giorgia Moll), Prokosch's interpreter, has to constantly help the other characters negotiate the abysses between Italian, French, German, and English. The limited primary colors of the characters' clothing and the interior decor are likewise distinguished from the rich natural tones of the Mediterranean landscape.

The invocation of Greek epic poetry and tragic drama reveals some striking parallels with Walter Benjamin's diverse writing on modernity and representation. Benjamin wrote *The Origins of German Tragic Drama* (where the theory of allegory was first broached) in Capri in 1924, and the conception of nature and history in that work is indebted to the Mediterranean landscape and its mythic status in Occidental thought. Benjamin's theory of "auratic" experience, allegory, and historiography is grounded not only in the early modernism of Baudelaire's mid-nineteenth century but in the experience of the rise of fascism in the 1930s. This is why it is important to distinguish the promise of history from the aestheticization of politics. As the "Work of Art" essay concludes:

> Mankind, which in Homer's time was an object of
> contemplation for the Olympian gods, now is one for itself. Its
> self-alienation has reached such a degree that it can
> experience its own destruction as an aesthetic pleasure of the
> first order. This is the situation of politics which Fascism is
> rendering aesthetic. Communism responds by politicizing art.[12]

The aestheticizing potential of totalizing narrative is crucial to the production pressures of *Le Mépris,* pressures that Godard himself experienced from his producers, Joe Levine and Carlo Ponti.[13] The spectacular version of *The Odyssey* envisioned by Prokosch is cut off from history precisely by its gesture of realism, its pretentious mimeticism. *Le Mépris* produces its politics within the ruins of the mortified aesthetic realm of Greek epic poetry, and Benjamin's ideas are key to the reading of this allegory. In fact, I hope to show that the film illustrates the pertinence of those ideas to narrative mortality in the cinema in a broader sense. For this reason, a short detour through some of Benjamin's ideas is in order.

Benjamin's two theories of storytelling and allegory might be seen to be related to the notion of myth (although it would be a mistake to assume a totalizing coherence to Benjamin's thought, which evolved over two decades). Just as storytelling is defined by Benjamin in opposition to the novel, allegory is defined in opposition to the symbol. The "fatedness" of the novel, as well as the unified totality of the symbol, are mythic entities that are no longer viable in modernity. Corrupted by capitalism, they possess an "aura" that is still desirable for its relationship to belief and collectivity. Story and allegory acquire their historiographic significance by pointing to that which is lost. Likewise in the cinema; although mechanical reproduction has eclipsed "aura" (itself a myth),[14] the illusion of reality contains a hint of lost aura: "the sight of immediate reality has become the 'blue flower' in the land of technology."[15] Death figures in Benjamin's thought as the sign of historical difference—the sign in narrative of the eclipse of closed circuits of repetition, myth, ritual, and fate—but at the same time holds within it the possibility of a recovery of the mythic.

Allegory breaks apart mythic structures by virtue of its different temporal form, which is "progression in a series of moments,"[16] as opposed to the mythic eternal recurrence of the same. The mythic characteristic of eternal recurrence is, for Benjamin, "an attempt to link two antinomic principles of happiness with each other: namely that of eternity and that of the yet once again."[17] The breaking apart of myth is therefore a question of realizing the threshold between repetition and discovery, a threshold crystallized in death as a singular event that is nevertheless inevitable. In the Greek epic, he identifies a privileged site of divergence between myth and tragedy: "the tragic hero enters upon the threshold of a new time," in which the laws of destiny and fate are not so much transcended as rendered visible.[18] If this evokes Godard's narrativity, Benjamin also stresses the role of the body in this process: "It is the achievement of his *physis* alone, not of language, if he [the tragic hero] is able to hold fast to his cause, and he must therefore do so in death."[19]

The distinction between story and novel, moreover, extends to a theory of memory, which is best expressed in the following brief discussion of *The Odyssey*:

> The perpetuating remembrance of the novelist [is] contrasted with the short-lived reminiscences of the storyteller. The first is dedicated to *one* hero, *one* odyssey, *one* battle; the second, to *many* diffuse occurrences. It is, in other words, *remembrance* which, as the Muse-derived element of the novel, is added to

reminiscence, the corresponding element of the story, the unity of their origin having disappeared with the decline of the epic.[20]

These two kinds of memory are further defined by way of Proust: remembrance is "voluntary"—infused with consciousness, or intentional—and reminiscence is "involuntary"—stimulated by images and correspondences that embody experience (*Erfahrung*). "Only what has not been experienced explicitly and consciously, what has not happened to the subject as an experience, can become a component of the *mémoire involontaire*."[21] Where the former (*mémoire volontaire*) is "mythic" and therefore inert, the latter has access to "aura." In Benjamin's Arcades project, he derives an "accidental" theory of historical materialism from this contingent notion of memory, a sense of inevitability that is different in kind from the immanency of teleology and destiny: "this project—as in the method of smashing an atom—releases the enormous energy of history that lies bound in the 'once upon a time' of classical historical narrative."[22]

The link between Proust's *mémoire involontaire* (the taste of a madeleine that takes one back to a corresponding point in history) and the shock of montage that provides film with its revolutionary potential is the idea of "the dialectical image." Waking as the telos of dream, the moment wrenched from the continuum, and the utopian vision articulated as memory are all thresholds on repetition and discovery, and are likewise analogues of death as the sign of both inevitability and difference. As Winfried Menninghaus puts it,

> Benjamin's theory of myth seeks a blasting apart of myth but at the same time does not want to relinquish the whole potential of its forms of experience. These forms include, even more than language, the *image,* and that is why the theory of dialectical images, too, bears witness to the field of tension in Benjamin's reflections on myth. The dialectical image, on the one hand, tends to break up the mythical power of images … and, on the other hand, it implies that the genuine form of knowledge itself is, at least in part, based on images and thereby on myth.[23]

Benjamin's notion of "aura" is intimately connected with his mimetic theory of language.[24] The experience of modernity involves, for Benjamin, a fall of signification from an identification between word and thing, a "non-sensuous correspondence" or an indexical relationship, to a pervasive splitting of signifier from signified:

> The direction of this change seems definable as the increasing decay of the mimetic faculty. For clearly the observable world of modern man contains only minimal residues of the magical correspondences and analogies that were familiar to ancient peoples. The question is whether we are concerned with the decay of this faculty or with its transformation.[25]

The "blue flower" of the cinematic illusion is thus, for Benjamin, an example of the transformation of the ancient identification of language and reality, available in modernity only as "second nature," or allegory. Miriam Hansen has described Benjamin as being "less interested in a critique of ideology than in redeeming the reified images of mass culture and modernity for a theory and politics of experience."[26] The same might be said of Godard's early films, with their emphasis on spontaneity, location shooting, and intertextuality within the context of generic narrative forms. Both Benjamin and Godard derive from Brecht a critique of catharsis; they are also both concerned with representing an experience of modernity, a conception of "life" in historical-materialist terms.

Le Mépris articulates a fall of the cinema from myth to allegory, from image to language, from the unquestioned mimeticism of Hollywood and neorealism to the discursive self-consciousness of the French New Wave. In the light of Godard's cinephiliac film criticism of the late 1950s, Le Mépris can be read as a treatise on the disappointing discovery that illusionism is such an elaborate deception. The aura of Hollywood is alluded to as a mimetic naïveté that is ostensibly outside the limits of genre, commodification, and ideology: a certain belief in representation that the self-conscious, "modern" filmmaker is alienated from. Godard can only refer to it allegorically.

Narrative mortality emerges as an allegorical means of glimpsing an immediacy of representation within the ruins of classicism. At stake for Godard is not simply the forms of representation, but a mimetic simplicity prior to film language. On one hand, this involves the Marxist-existentialist nexus of "life" and contingency, a discourse that is perhaps more relevant to *Pierrot le fou*. On the other, it involves the utopian promise of genre, the unquestioned teleology of genre film-making toward romantic transparency, fulfillment, and transcendence.

Voyage in Italy (1953), the film that Paul sees "for inspiration" in *Le Mépris*, is also set partly in Capri and engages fairly directly with ancient history. The moment in *Voyage in Italy* when the plaster casts of the couple buried under the ruins of Pompeii (a man and a woman who "found death together") are uncovered is perhaps an example of a dialectical image in which history is suddenly crystallized. In the context of Rossellini's narrative, the redemptive potential of the image is channeled into the romantic reconciliation of the couple (Ingrid Bergman and George Sanders). As an intertext of *Le Mépris*, it points at once to the role of genre in the truth-value of the cinema and to the intrinsic relationship between historiography, as an ability to relate experientially with the past, and communication. Neither is possible for Godard's characters, and so accidental death replaces Rossellini's miraculous recovery of love.

In *Le Mépris* itself, two myths are mortified—destroyed under the auspices of melancholy. The first is that of marriage and its concomitant objectification and fetishization of female sexuality; this is the discourse of Bardot. The second is that of Fritz Lang and the myth of the auteur. Crucial to Benjamin's theory of myth is the distinction between the content of myth and the function or status of myth itself, and it would be hard to claim any redemptive potential in the resurrection of either of these myths of patriarchy or authorship. They are both "emptied out" in the fatal car accident, with the hope of recovering the mythic status of the image in the final shot of the film, a pan out to sea. By analyzing the two symbols of Bardot and Lang as they function as mythic discourses in *Le Mépris*, a third myth that informs the film will emerge: that of narrative closure attained through reconciliation (love) and fate. It is this that is finally mortified in the tragic car accident of the ill-fated couple.

Godard appreciates Bardot as a tabula rasa: "She is all of a piece and must be taken as such." Comparing her to Anna Karina, he says, "With Anna I could have shown that the character believes something other than what we actually see. With Bardot, that wasn't possible. She has another truth to her."[27] In Godard's earliest films there is a consistent, if ironic, attempt to "get inside" the actor or actress, especially Karina, to reach the soul through the image,[28] while his subsequent highly critical analyses of Jane Fonda in *Tout va bien* and *Letter to Jane* (both 1972) recognize the very coded nature of film performance.[29] Bardot in *Le Mépris* remains precariously balanced between these two conceptions of female performance. Despite the equation of vision and love in the opening scene ("I see all of you, therefore I love all of you" are the film's opening words), the character, Camille, cannot be penetrated to reveal any essence of Bardot. She dissolves only into "fashion model" or "movie star." The real Bardot is inaccessible precisely because, like Jane Fonda (the two were both promoted as sex kittens by Roger Vadim), she has already been taken up into culture; she is already "written" and therefore cut off from experience.

The famous opening scope-size shot of Bardot's naked body may parody the producers' demand that Godard include Bardot nude, but the scene becomes, retrospectively, the locus of a full or complete ideal of representation. The subsequent breakdown in communication is already ironically alluded to by the mediating use of colored filters. This breakdown is itself conveyed as an inability to "possess," or to "know," Bardot (on either Paul's part or Godard's). A series of images is inserted into the film that censors Camille and Paul making love on the sofa. These images separate the image of Bardot's body from the narrative role it ostensibly fills. The images making up this sequence are both diegetic and nondiegetic, and are from no coherent spatial or ideological point of view. Compared to the opening shot of Bardot, the nude and fashion images register a loss of "aura," while the other shots — outtakes, flash-forwards, and flashbacks — are of the order of a *mémoire involontaire* (and *not* a "dossier of the film itself in stills"). Bardot's look directed at the camera, which silently accompanies her voice-over, echoes Benjamin's observation that eyes that have "lost their ability to look"[30] are an allegory, or loss, of "aura." This gaze is reduplicated in the painted eyes of the statues of gods in Lang's film of *The Odyssey*. "To perceive the aura of an object we look at," says Benjamin, "means to invest it with the ability to look at us in return." And yet, "Baudelaire describes eyes of which one is inclined to say that they have lost their ability to look."[31]

The female body is, for Baudelaire as for Godard, the object of the melancholy gaze (which of course belongs to the poet, critic, or filmmaker) and the locus of the blank stare. Miriam Hansen notes that Benjamin's conception of experience and memory "hovers over and around the body of the mother," fetishizing the uncanny idea of "home" as the imaginary memory of the womb.[32] Baudelaire's women, who fail to return the poet's look, are, for Benjamin, analogous to the photograph and the cinematic apparatus itself, in which the distance between spectator and screen is also a temporal, historical distance between the profilmic past and the viewer's present:

> In so far as art aims at the beautiful and, on however modest a
> scale, 'reproduces it', it conjures it up (as Faust does Helen)
> out of the womb of time. This no longer happens in the case
> of technical reproduction.... What was felt to be inhuman,
> one might even say deadly, in daguerreotypy was the
> (prolonged) looking into the camera, since the camera records
> our likeness without returning our gaze.[33]

Bardot's unseeing eyes overdetermine her commodification and short-circuit any claims to beauty or truthfulness that either Paul or Godard might want to make via her body.

The outtakes, flash-forwards, and flashbacks of Bardot, on the other hand, break up the fixity of narrative, the mythic time of desire, and point to a more radical role of the image. They provide a passage *through* time, dialectically relating past, present, and future instants, not through the subjectivity of flashback, but through the allegorical gaze that wrenches *discours* from *histoire*. Bardot in these shots becomes Bardot acting as Camille, isolated at several of the instants of the shooting of *Le Mépris,* a time outside the historicism of narrative. She may be no less fetishized, but she is briefly freed from the structures of classical narrative film that have been designed to contain the threat of the feminine.[34]

If Baudelaire, according to Benjamin, saw a detachment of *sexus* from *eros* in the unseeing eyes of his would-be lovers, Godard sees the promise of romance eclipsed by pornography and the fetishization of femininity. At one point in *Le Mépris* Paul notes that naked women only appear in the movies. Paul can no more possess Camille than the spectator can the image, but what should be emphasized here is not Godard's particular brand of feminism,[35] but the allegorical stance toward femininity and its consequences for closure. Temporality and historicity become functions of "distance" in the look at the woman, who remains only a token of desire under the melancholy gaze of allegory; and it is a distance that cannot be closed in narrative.

A similar deflation of scopophilic pleasure was noted in the discussion of *Beyond a Reasonable Doubt*. Godard's melancholia is more self-conscious, taking into account the commodity fetish that Bardot represents within a star system that precedes Godard's use of her. Lang's more formalist inscription of gender within the apparatus of the cinematic gaze is more rhetorical than ironic. Neither Godard nor Lang is concerned with challenging or deconstructing the objectification of women in film narrative. For each, narrative mortality is a means of redoubling misogyny. The feminine serves as a symbol of romantic, utopian desires ("a cinema in accordance with our desires," as Godard quotes Bazin at the opening of *Le Mépris*), but a symbol that has "fallen" in cinematic representation to the sign of that possibility. Neither offers a critique of the representation of women, although their melancholia may open a space for such a reading.

Godard does extend his mortification of voyeuristic scopophilia one step further than Lang (and several steps further than Wenders, in retrospect) in linking the desire to possess with the desire to represent, and situating his own narrative discourse at one remove from the realization of these desires. It is only insofar as this is a historical difference that Godard's narrative mortality can be conceived as a radical praxis. The desire to possess women through representation is mortified with the necessity of historical decay. The mediated gaze of exploitation is still present in the film, but it is a commodified gaze, aligned with the dead classicism of the film's imagery. In its ruins one can glimpse the "shock of the new" in the brief outtakes of Bardot in that "other time" of the shooting of the film. The character of the "other woman" Francesca/Giorgia Moll, who may be said to evade commodification through her knowledge of language and through Godard's more oblique treatment of her, is also associated with the historical specificity of the production of the film in the opening shots of her with cameraman Raoul Coutard.

The redoubling of discourse attached to the representation of Bardot also applies to the figure of Fritz Lang in *Le Mépris*. He represents both the full symbolic possibilities of classical Hollywood cinema and the allegorical, written modernism of his Weimar heritage. He combines, for Godard, the mythic qualities of narrative film, grounding them in a history that goes beyond Hollywood, and a vision of their ideological limitations and utopian possibilities. If Benjamin's theory of allegory was developed in the 1920s with Weimar Expressionism in mind, then Lang's modernism—the formalism of his mise-en-scène—might be regarded as itself allegorical, with respect to German Romanticism. The "exaggeration" of the arts of this period was, for Benjamin, an "expression of desire for a new pathos."[36]

The duality of mythic classicism and allegory in *Le Mépris* is a formal distinction implicit in the narrative structure. It is perhaps more evident in the source novel's distinction between two interpretations of *The Odyssey*. The two theories, in Godard's adaptation, correspond visually to the two parts of the film: the Roman interiors and the Mediterranean exteriors.[37] The former corresponds to the "boudoir drama," which is one interpretation of *The Odyssey* put forward in Moravia's *Il Disprezzo*. This is countered by the classical interpretation, that the events in the Homeric epic are to be taken at face value. The "modern" theory that Ulysses left Penelope alone for so long in order to test her faithfulness with potential suitors offers a plausible parallel between Ulysses and Paul, whose delayed arrival at Prokosch's villa allows Camille to spend time alone with Prokosch. Paul's story that his taxi had an accident is unconfirmed, thus introducing the possibility of deception and also a revisionist psychological interpretation of *The Odyssey,* one in which "secret second meanings" are ferreted out from the "uniform illumination" and "fully externalized description" of the Homeric poems, in which "nothing is hidden."[38]

These two interpretations of *The Odyssey* are in fact related to Benjamin's distinction between the novel and the storyteller's tale. Insofar as it is grounded in the experience of the storyteller and has an indexical relation to history, the auratic element of the story involves the adequacy of language to account for reality, and therefore corresponds to the Homeric discourse in *Le Mépris*. The novel, on the other hand, *separates* meaning from life and becomes a "struggle against time."[39] Benjamin is indebted to Lukács's *Theory of the Novel* for this distinction, which, for Lukács also, is originally located in the Greek epic as it is transformed into tragedy. "This indestructible bond with reality *as it is,* the crucial difference between the epic and the drama, is a necessary consequence of the object of the epic being life itself."[40] "The 'meaning of life,' the center about which the novel [derived from the drama of tragedy] moves," not only insists on a radical separation of inward subjectivity and historical experience, but situates their desired unity as the telos of narrative.

Narrative mortality in *Le Mépris* invokes both narrative modes, which are distinguished stylistically as well as structurally. Fritz Lang is both the "director of destiny and fate" and the classical auteur. Bellour says that Godard's treatment of Lang in *Le Mépris* is "two-faced," pointing to the idealism that Lang espouses but cannot realize.[41] Lang's film, or all we see of Lang's film in *Le Mépris,* consists of low-angle shots of classical sculptures with painted eyes and scenes enacted by overly madeup actors in quasi-Greek dress. They perform speechlessly in front of blank walls and expansive Mediterranean landscapes. The epic that Lang wants to make is not the mythic spectacular that Prokosch envisions, but an allegorical production that is highly reminiscent of *Trauerspiel.* One sequence screened in Prokosch's studio suggests that Ulysses kills one of Penelope's suitors. There is a ritualistic aspect to Lang's faithfulness to Homer's original, a "cult value" that is reinforced by the insertion of the shots of gods into the narrative of Paul and Camille, marking critical moments in their relationship (e.g., the ill-fated ellipsis between the studio and the Roman villa in which Paul says he had a taxi accident).

Of the baroque dramatists, Benjamin remarks that without allegorical interpretation "in an unsuitable, indeed, hostile environment ... the world of the ancient gods would have had to die out, and it is precisely allegory that preserved it."[42] The redemption of *The Odyssey* and its Greek deities occurs with great difficulty in *Le Mépris,* despite the allegorical structure of the two interpretations. As the agent of the rescue, Lang is severely limited by the hostile environment of Prokosch's crude commercialism. More than the conventional auteurist mythos of Hollywood tension between auteur and industry is at stake here, however, given Lang's particular preoccupation with the theme of destiny, which is referred to repeatedly in the film—by Lang himself and by quotations from *Cahiers* critics on Lang's oeuvre.[43]

The redemptive strategy at work in *Le Mépris* involves a transposition of the idea of "the gods," the power over reality, the myth of destiny, to that of the filmmaking auteur. It is a strategy doomed to fail, because the difference between divine omniscience and filmmaking is precisely the difference of representation. Over a shot of a huge camera with eyelike lights protruding from it, an offscreen voice announces "the Cyclops scene." Godard makes the parallel explicit: "I filmed a spiritual odyssey: the eye of the camera watching these characters in search of Homer replaces that of the gods watching over Ulysses and his companions."[44]

Lang provides the fulcrum for the parallel between omniscience and authorship. Godard's casting of Lang is a principal means by which he alludes to the lost ideal of the classical cinema. In 1962 he wrote: "I would like to compose shots that are magnificent in themselves like Fritz Lang, but I can't."[45] Some of Godard's shots of architecture in *Le Mépris* (the Javals' apartment building, Prokosch's Roman and Mediterranean villas) echo the monumentality of Lang's *Die Niebelungen*,[46] and yet the style is also visually parodied in the kitsch shots of Lang's gods, which are always accompanied by the melancholic sound track. Early in the film, Prokosch asks Paul what interests him about *The Odyssey*. Although Paul answers, "to go back to the traditions of Griffith and Chaplin. Back to the time of the old United Artists," equating myths of authorship, origins, and classicism, neither he nor Lang is able to realize this desire.

The camera, in *Le Mépris,* retains the omniscience and determinism of divine destiny, but struggles to acquire the mythic potential of such a schema. Godard is not Lang, lacking his faith in the image, but neither is he Benjamin, whose philosophy of history is profoundly messianic. The future that is to be found in the past is one informed by faith, which is, above all, a faith in language. If the characters in *Le Mépris* are "survivors of the shipwreck of modernity,"[47] they survive only as representation.

The camera is responsible, according to Benjamin, for the pervasiveness of the *mémoire volontaire* in modernity. The camera, a "deadly" device that fails to return the gaze, "gave the moment a posthumous shock."[48] The melancholy tone of *Le Mépris* is perhaps directed ultimately toward this "already written" or mediated interface implicit in photographic reproduction. In the final car accident, the discourses of Bardot and Lang are crystallized in the emblem of death. Narrative desire and fatalism are jointly mortified in an image that finally abandons "realism" altogether for an allegorical rendering of tragic fate.

The accident scene begins when Paul wakes up, leaning against a rock. In a cut from long shot to medium shot, an ellipsis in which he has slept (and during which Camille has been apparently more active than we have seen her in the entire film) has passed. As he awakes, finds the note she has left for him, and reads it, Camille says in voice-over, "Dear Paul, I took the bullets out of your revolver. Since you don't want to leave, I'm going myself. Jeremy Prokosch is driving to Rome, so I'm leaving with him. I'm going to live in a hotel alone. Je t'embrasse ... adieu ... Camille." A brief scene with Camille and Prokosch in a gas station follows, and a close-up of the handwritten words "Je t'embrasse" is inserted before they pull out onto the highway. Another close-up of Camille's "adieu" accompanies the sounds of honking and metallic crashing. The lateral pan over the handwriting continues with a cut to a stainless-steel tanker truck until the crumpled red Alfa Romeo is center-screen. The shot then closes in on Camille's body draped over one side of the car, with Prokosch's to screen left.

Georges Delerue's background score comes into its own in this scene. Throughout the pan over the smashed vehicles and the fixed thirteen-second shot of the bodies dotted with blood, it rises and groans. In the mise-en-scène, the redness of the Alfa Romeo, a redness that has also been prominent in the Javal apartment's furniture and towels, is extended to the blood splashed over the windshield, Prokosch's sweater, a blinking light, and a trickle down Camille's exposed white neck. Instead of the violent action of the crash, Godard offers a tableau of its aftermath.

Far from an aestheticization of death, the stylization of the car accident points to the absence of death. The profilmic is still limited to Brigitte Bardot, actress: we have seen that white neck before. Compared to the speed and light of Lang's car accident in *Beyond a Reasonable Doubt* in which there is no body, compared to the accident that Belmondo/Michel carelessly witnesses in *A bout de souffle,* the representation of this accident involves what Benjamin says was, in the seventeenth century, "a contemplation of bones." Godard describes the characters in *Le Mépris* as "cut off," "shipwrecked," but in fact this sense of alienation extends beyond the characters to the undermining of the mimetic capacity of the film itself to penetrate existence to essence. The car may be ruined, but Bardot is only acting. Bardot and Palance were not required to act but simply to "be in" the narrative of *Le Mépris.*[49] As corpses, their status as mere signs of characters is made explicit.

The car accident also subverts what we might call the novelistic version of *Le Mépris*—the mythic narrative in which Paul would kill Prokosch, and thereby mimic *The Odyssey* and the scene we have already seen of Ulysses killing Penelope's suitor. The earlier apartment scene ends with Paul taking a revolver out of its hiding place. Camille's and Prokosch's *accidental* deaths thus explicitly *replace* Paul's hypothetical action. The narrative would have then been, indeed, one of the individual struggling against his circumstances. Paul's character, whether it is marked by modern neurosis or classical hubris, would have taken on a truly tragic aspect. Epic remembrance would have closed the representational gap between Paul and the mythic Ulysses.

Instead, the narrative of *Le Mépris* exerts an unrelenting control over the trajectories of these characters, culminating in the arbitrariness of the final accident. The thematic of contingency is, however, undermined by the intentionality of the cinematic process. In narrative cinema, the profilmic can never be contingent (of the status of Benjamin's "reminiscence") because of the photographic basis of the medium. Godard cannot "in good faith" represent a car accident in a present tense: if it is in a film, it has always already happened. The representation of accidental violence becomes, in a sense, an ontological obscenity. The accident scene equates written and cinematic language and situates the film, finally, in the camp of the allegorist, for whom myth is inevitably second nature, accessible only at one remove, a story for the teller of tales. The dissolution of the filmmaker's vision as an autonomous and viable category is at once a loss of truth and a loss of the possibility of mythic narrative in the cinema, and so the dissolution of matrimonial bliss is accompanied, in *Le*

Mépris, by a dissolution of the mimetic capacity of film language. The mortification process is completed with the final gesture of the film, the pan out to sea.

In the emptiness of the last shot the mythic qualities of aura and experience are nevertheless realized outside the second nature of the spectacle. With Ulysses' presence in the frame, a performance of heroism, history is a "petrified landscape" holding no possibility of renewal. Ulysses returns home as he has returned home since the dawn of Western culture, but the camera pans past him to the Mediterranean horizon. Precisely in its placement at the end of the narrative, after the scenes of death and return, the shot articulates the hope for transcendence and discovery of eternity in the image. It is an empty frame, though, suggesting the limitations of nature and history beyond their subjection to death. Narrative, too, decays, and in the process its images, like the ruins of the profilmic, are robbed of their "accordance with our desires." The shininess of the glittering ocean at the end of *Le Mépris,* like the shine of the commodity, may return our gaze — unlike the actors — but its "freedom from equipment" is only a gesture, and it too is a mechanically reproduced image: an image of endless space and time and the "eternally the same." The film thus ends on the threshold that Benjamin envisioned, bringing together in one dialectical image the new and the dead: "It is the appearance of the new [that] is reflected like one mirror in another in the appearance of the 'always-the-same.' "[50] If the shocklike segments of empty time in Baudelaire's poetry constitute a challenge to the historiography of progress, a similar sense of being stranded in an infinitely open history completes *Le Mépris.*

It is crucial that Godard's allegory of classicism does not succumb to nostalgia, but evokes a passion for the unknown and the new. "For people as they are today [1939]," says Benjamin, "there is only one radical novelty — and that is always the same: Death ... To one filled with spleen, it is the entombed person who is the transcendental subject of history."[51] A historical threshold is finally realized in the fully ambiguous closing shots of *Le Mépris.* Through the allegorical structure of narrative mortality, the auratic ideals informing both the telos of destiny and the mythos of femininity are split from the discourses informed by them and rendered dead. Beyond the melancholy of this film is the craziness of *Pierrot le fou,* which takes the modernist ressentiment or binarist conception of history (the romantic past versus the "new" present) into the more apocalyptic, crisis-oriented aesthetic of the postmodern.

Pierrot le fou: Carnival of Closure

Pierrot le fou can be plotted on two crucial grids of Andreas Huyssen's map of the postmodern. On one hand, it demonstrates the temporal imagination of the "historical" avant-garde that resurfaced with the 1960s exhaustion of modernism. And it also indulges in that sense of loss which characterizes the poststructuralist recognition of "modernism's limitations and failed political ambitions."[52] It is a film, viewed from a twenty-five-year distance, in which discursive heterogeneity becomes a historical and cultural threshold of postmodernity.

This threshold, as it is manifest in *Pierrot le fou,* allows us to trace the movement beyond modernism in film history. Narrative mortality provides a means of analyzing this transition in terms of a transformation from an existential anxiety (in which death figures as a subjective quest for meaning and identity) to a cultural anxiety (in which death figures as the voiding of universal humanism). This is a film that emerged, in 1965, out of Bazin's anxieties of realism and the *Cahiers*'s Hollywood cinephilia, and began to transform that theory and criticism into a radical cultural politics.

Ferdinand's (Jean-Paul Belmondo) final gesture in the film's last scene is to paint his face blue, wrap his head with yellow and red dynamite, and blow himself up. In his adventures with Marianne (Anna Karina), bloody corpses are discovered littering apartments and landscape, and as the pathos conventionally associated with images of death is consistently subverted, so also is its narrative function of binding and totalizing. The adventures of Marianne and Ferdinand are built upon an archaeology of modern art and literature, with visual and verbal quotations from a gamut of sources, including Joyce, Baudelaire, Celine, Picasso, Faulkner, and especially Rimbaud. At the same time, there are multiple allusions to Hollywood gangster and noir films, as well as the ostensible source novel, Lionel White's *Obsession.*[53]

The interpenetration of intertexts from both "high" and "low" sources points to the intrinsically carnivalized nature of the film. For Bakhtin, "carnival" refers not simply to the authorized transgression that such festivals are devoted to, the "turning upside down" of social norms of decency and respectability, an incursion of the margins and underclasses into the cultural center, but above all, "a sense of the world." As such, it can be identified outside the designated performances of community from which carnival originates; Bakhtin discovers it, for example, in Dostoyevski.

An important aspect of carnival is a conception of death as renewal, which involves, for Bakhtin, both reversal (ambivalence, negation, etc.) and corporeality (scatology and the "bodily lower stratum"). The body in carnival becomes a source of laughter. "Ritual laughter was a reaction to *crises* in the life of the sun (solstices), crises in the life of a deity, in the life of the world and of man (funeral laughter). In it, ridicule was fused with rejoicing."[54] The specific form of "laughing at death" that Bakhtin finds in Rabelais derives from Menippean satire, a genre dating back to ancient Greece and canonized in the carnivalized dialogues with the dead of Lucian (ca. A.D. 120–80).[55] Bakhtin lists fourteen characteristics of Menippean satire,[56] which are all strikingly apparent in *Pierrot le fou.*

These include comedy, a "freedom from plot," a "slum naturalism," a depiction of an underworld (a mixture in this case of Rimbaud's "Une Saison en Enfer" and the gangster genre), an experimental fantasticality ("musical" digressions), insanity, madness and doubleness (i.e., Ferdinand/Pierrot's double name), violations of etiquette (directed here at bourgeois society), juxtapositions of disunited things, references to utopia, and generic multiplicity. The Bakhtinian Menippean narrative is about "the adventure of an idea or truth in the world"; it is a genre of "ultimate questions" that articulates a new relationship to the contemporary world and the material of representation. This is precisely the project of *Pierrot le fou,* although the film also has a sense of impending crisis that is lacking in Bakhtin's description.

The Menippean character of *Pierrot le fou* is an extensive play with cultural and textual conventions that has the effect of situating Ferdinand's anxiety of identity (a typically modernist subjectivity) as a symptom of, rather than a response to, cultural pluralism. The Menippean crisis of representation is specifically linked, as Bakhtin suggests, to a destabilized notion of heroism and selfhood. The Menippean apoc-alypticism that is finally delineated in *Pierrot le fou's* carnival of closure is achieved through a radical treatment not only of modernism, but also of the ongoing war in Vietnam, of gender, and of the romance genre.

On one level, these references to Vietnam inscribe a "refusal to for-get" political reality into the film, a refusal to divorce fiction from lived experience, particularly lived oppression. But within the Menippean context of *Pierrot le fou,* the inscription of Vietnam is parodic. In the case of Karina's performance of a chattering Asian peasant, it is ex-ploitative, perhaps even surrealistically transgressive. The references to the Vietnam War stress its distance and its exoticism, but the at-tempts at representation can only fail to actually locate it. The marines in the movie theater disappear into a tropical jungle; Marianne com-ments on the daily body count on the radio: "We know nothing. They just say 115 dead. It's like photographs. They've always fasci-nated me."

The representation of death and the references to the war are in-strumental to the film's quest for "poetry," a "metaphysical material-ism" that conjoins representation and desire.[57] The poetry of *Pierrot le fou* is to be found beyond pathos and the myths of harmonious mimeticism and romance, and must be dialectically wrenched from the continuum of images and history. Marie-Claire Ropars Wuilleu-mier has written eloquently about the tension in *Pierrot le fou* be-tween the movement of narrative progression and the search for a poetic means of expressing "totality" and "essence" in an instant.[58] Given the intimate relationship between narrative and historical tem-porality, the poetic ideal "represents the impossible image of [a] stop-page of time, of [a] projection into a world that escapes, once and for all, from history."[59] Moreover, the film ends, after Ferdinand's sui-cide, with Marianne's and Ferdinand's voices whispering Rimbaud's poem "L'Éternité" over the closing shot of sea and sky:

> Elle est retrouvée!
>
> Quoi?—L'Éternité.
>
> C'est la mer allée
>
> Avec le soleil.

Georges Bataille has best explained the resonance of this particular poem, which he also quotes in *L'Érotisme*:

> Poetry leads to the same place as all forms of eroticism — to
> the blending and fusion of separate objects. It leads us to
> eternity, it leads us to death, and through death to continuity.
> Poetry is eternity; the sun matched with the sea.[60]

The violence of the poem consists in its dissolution of difference, a
violation taken up in the very perversity of Marianne and Ferdinand's
meeting in the afterlife. The juxtaposition of Ferdinand's spectacularly meaningless suicide with the romantic quotation of the Rimbaud
poem is perhaps the most succinct example of the dialectical edge of
narrative mortality.

The apocalyptic dimension of Ferdinand's death (which echoes the
fireworks over Paris that occur after he has turned a cocktail party
topsy-turvy) recalls Benjamin's advocacy of a "blasting out of the historical continuum." This is the secret promise of dialectical images
and the passage through time of the *mémoire involontaire*. If historical hope is grounded in the image of the past, rather than the teleology of progress, "the utilization of dream elements upon waking is
the canon of dialectics."[61] The narrative of *Pierrot le fou* proceeds by
way of montage, interruption, and episodes, and so the final death
cannot be read back into any logic of causality; myths of fate and
destiny abound in *Pierrot le fou* as stories told mainly by Marianne,
from which Ferdinand stands aloof. For Benjamin, "modernism must
be under the sign of suicide." The modernist suicide is "not a resignation but a heroic passion. It is *the* achievement of modernism in
the realm of the passions."[62] The carnival that Ferdinand, the flaneur,
makes of his death at the end of *Pierrot le fou* is precisely the image
of such a passion, but its excess is also the terms of its irony, and
Ferdinand's heroism is likewise displaced by Marianne's dream of
closure: the whispered Rimbaud poem.

The void opened up at the end of the film follows the total destruction of Ferdinand's body, a sight withheld from the viewer but
nevertheless shocking to the imagination. If, for Benjamin, "the only
good body is a dead body," for Bakhtin "carnival involves above
all a pluralizing and cathecting of the body ... a vulgar, shameless

materialism of the body."[63] For both writers, the body enters into language, becomes a discursive element of cultural signifying practices, when it is most radically divorced from categories of subjectivity: the corpse for Benjamin, the "bodily lower stratum" for Bakhtin. Only in the work of the surrealists, according to Benjamin, do "body and image so interpenetrate that all the bodily innervations of the collective become revolutionary discharge."[64]

Surrealism, "the death of the last century through comedy,"[65] like carnival, desacralizes the body and brings it down to earth. Likewise, in *Pierrot le fou,* the numerous bodies dripping with red paint, including Marianne's own, prevent the "sphere of images" that the film is in search of from spiraling off into idealism. If "for Benjamin and Bakhtin, images are material, and matter—the body above all—imagistically constructed,"[66] for Godard the materiality of images consists in their documentary and "nonillusionist" qualities. The absurd representation of violent death is instrumental, in this respect, in maintaining a duality of performance; it is always the body of an actor, not a character, that is found slathered in blood.

Narrative mortality involves more than imagery, style, and philosophy; it also pertains to the narrative deployment of death. Narrative in *Pierrot le fou* evolves as a dialectic between the stasis of poetic imagery and the movement of adventure and desire, a dialectic that is coded in terms of gender. Ferdinand says toward the end of the film that all he wants to do is to "stop time." Marianne, on the other hand, calculates the number of seconds in an individual life. She is a classic "femme fatale" insofar as she plays upon Ferdinand's attraction to her in order to lead him more and more deeply into a criminal world, leading him inexorably away from "poetry." As they reenter the gunrunning adventure in the Midi, Marianne tells Ferdinand a story about a man who tries to escape his death in Paris, travels to the Midi, and dies in a car accident, a foreshadowing of Ferdinand's and Marianne's own deaths. But the notion of "fatality" extends to the narrative momentum that Marianne generates with an extremely high energy level.

In, or against, the frenetic movement of the film from one place to another, from one vehicle to another, even from one discontinuous shot to the next, Ferdinand is repeatedly found sitting, stationary, either writing, reading, watching movies, eating, or simply waiting. As a flaneur, Ferdinand allows the world to move by him; the "crowd" of discursive voices flows around his watchful, meditative posture. In his musings, death has an immanent meaningfulness that is lacking in Godard's disrespectful representations of corpses. For example, on discovering a midget executed bloodily in an apartment, Ferdinand says: "such a beautiful, magnificent death for such a little man." The disparity between the magnificent death and the little man encapsulates this attribution of significance and anticipates Ferdinand's own spectacularly explosive death, which compensates visually for its existential meaninglessness. His spoken and written introspective commentary on mortality is an obsessive musing that is out of keeping with the garish and casual world of Marianne.

The movement of the film toward a "mingling" of these two characters' voices suggests that they represent a discursive difference that the film dialogizes. Marianne may be closer to the popular culture intertexts (she is introduced reading the comics) and Ferdinand may have more affinities with his high-modernist heroes, such as Joyce and Picasso, but there is an important difference between their respective affinities. While Ferdinand desires to write better than Joyce, while he wants to see Marianne as "Renoir's" Marianne, and while he imagines himself as a Céline or Verne protagonist, Marianne lacks this distance from her intertextual sources. The immediacy and spontaneity of detective novels that Marianne embodies turn out to be exactly what Ferdinand is looking for in a literature that is "better than Joyce" because it is "not about people's lives but about life itself."

Godard describes *Pierrot le fou* as a film that is "about the adventure rather than the adventurers," and invokes Sartre to explain this: "It is difficult to separate one from the other. We know from Sartre that the free choice which the individual himself makes is mingled with what is usually called his destiny."[67] This "mingling" is represented in *Pierrot le fou* through the convention of popular romance, in which Marianne, the femme fatale with the "line of luck," seduces the anxious modernist protagonist. But although the film may well fall into the modernist trap of feminizing popular culture,[68] the textual seduction that takes place produces an exemplary marriage of existential "knowledge" with the utopian truth-values of romance. If the courtship ritual that informs the American film musical is constitutive of a redemptive impetus in American popular culture, "a sort of secular religious feel, a sense of restoring Eden in a fallen society,"[69] it might be argued that Godard recognizes and attempts to extract precisely this "auratic" experience from the romance genre.

One of the central characteristics of narrative mortality is irony, a specific form of allegorical representation that has been noted in discussions of Lang and Wenders, and even in *Le Mépris*. The more overt recourse to comedy in *Pierrot le fou* allows for a more extensive theorization of irony in relation to narrative mortality. As carnival is sanctioned disruption and authorized dehierarchization, and as auratic experience is only available as allegory, so also is the "triumph of desire" in *Pierrot le fou* profoundly ironic. Belmondo/Ferdinand survives only as voice. In this way the ironic consciousness that has been developed over the course of the film is maintained by the gesture of detachment from mythic existence.

Reworking the categories of existentialism in terms of representation, Paul de Man argues that

> the prevalence of allegory always corresponds to the unveiling
> of an authentically temporal destiny. This unveiling takes
> place in a subject that has sought refuge against the impact of
> time in a natural world to which, in truth, it bears no
> resemblance.[70]

In his discussion of Romantic poetry, de Man makes a distinction between allegory and irony, defining irony as a language in which the self-consciousness of the "doubleness" of humanity, its lack of unity with nature, becomes a tenet of self-definition: "The ironic language splits the subject into an empirical self that exists in a state of inauthenticity and a self that exists only in the form of a language that asserts the knowledge of this inauthenticity" (p. 213). De Man's point is that consciousness is neither mythic nor eternal, but is language/representation that unfolds in time. Ironic narrative thus strives to move "beyond and outside itself," but is always aware of the impossibility of doing so.

De Man's distinction between allegory and irony is drawn in part from Baudelaire, whose comments on a pantomime performance (that includes a Pierrot) indicate the temporal form of modernist irony:

[The characters] make their extraordinary gestures, which demonstrate clearly that they feel themselves forced into a new existence. . . . And they leap through this fantastic work, which properly speaking, only starts at that point—which is to say, on the frontiers of the marvellous.[71]

For de Man, irony is unlike allegory in its "madness" or recognition of the nonconscious status of language and representation; the passage suggests to him that "irony is unrelieved *vertige,* dizziness to the point of madness" (p. 214). Both allegory and irony "pertain ultimately to a subjective experience of time." Irony is "essentially the mode of the present, it knows neither memory nor prefigurative duration, whereas allegory exists entirely within an ideal time that is never here and now but always a past or an endless future" (p. 220).

Benjamin's theory of allegory embodies both of de Man's structures of allegory and irony in a dialectical relationship. Both Benjamin and de Man define allegory in opposition to symbolic representation, as a recognition of the nonunity of image and referent, which in the nineteenth century extended to the relationship between man and nature. It is precisely the romantic disavowal of mortality that is unveiled in Benjamin's allegory, the temporal structure of which is most eloquently described in terms of decay: "Allegories are, in the realm of thoughts, what ruins are in the realm of things."[72] Benjamin's Baudelaire is far from mad, and sees in the pantomime figures (dead objects, which, like puppets, imply dead conventions) the past and the present combined dialectically to produce a historically different future. It is above all in the commodity that Benjamin's Baudelaire confronts the new "just as the seventeenth-century allegorists confronted antiquity." For Benjamin, "The devaluation of the world of objects within allegory is outdone within the world of objects itself by the commodity."[73]

In *Pierrot le fou,* the gender duality represented by Marianne and Ferdinand also corresponds to two experiences of temporal rhetoric, which are carnivalized, or mingled, in a quite different narrative time than the novel (where de Man finds them linked). Whereas Ferdinand may indeed be a Baudelairean flaneur, for whom alienation becomes an authentic experience of inauthenticity, the figure of Marianne and the role of allegory function in a more Benjaminian, that is, historical, way. Sam Fuller's cameo appearance in the film as the director of *Fleurs du mal* indicates that it is not "nature" but Hollywood that is allegorized, mortified, or lost in *Pierrot le fou*. Marianne is like the pantomime figures that Baudelaire describes, moving freely within and beyond the genre conventions of Hollywood musicals, gangster films, and melodramas. For Godard, intertextuality is a historical structure with which he excavates auratic experience among the ruins of modernist and popular culture. While he derives his archaeological method of irony from the "high art" sources, the qualities of Hollywood at stake here are those of mimeticism and closure — precisely the symbolic orders of Romanticism that both Benjamin and de Man find relinquished in allegory.

The final shot of *Pierrot le fou,* the "empty" image of sea and sky with the whispered Rimbaud poem about eternity, is an allegory of transcendence, a recognition of its own inauthenticity. The freedom of the film is not, therefore, a freedom from history. It is unlike the silent spectacle of sea and sky at the end of *Le Mépris,* in which language is drained by narcissism and melancholia, and it is not a "dream of disappearance" or terminality. If it is the shot that is not shown but described at the end of *Bande à part* as a "horizon without limits or contradictions," the excess of "harmony" and transcendence echoed in the voices from the afterlife is what constitutes its irony.

What is "mingled," finally, in the carnival of closure is the existential consciousness of Ferdinand — free but anxious, wise to his inauthenticity but restricted to his own, mortal experience of time — and Marianne as an intertextual access to romantic disavowal, desire, and imagination. Together they create an image of utopia, its naïveté bracketed through irony, but its historical promise grounded in allegory. If the last half hour of the film conveys that randomness that Godard insists informs it ("Two shots which follow each other do not necessarily follow each other. The same goes for two shots which do not follow each other. In this sense, one can say that *Pierrot* is not really a film"),[74] then an astonishing teleology is restored with the final double deaths.

The cathartic surprise of this "goal" of the film's end is partially due to the extraction of Eros from the myth of romance; but equally important is the role of Thanatos, violence, and death, the privileged signifiers of narrative mortality. In this respect, Sam Fuller is not just any Hollywood filmmaker but one whom the *Cahiers du Cinéma* critics appreciated especially for the excessive violence of his films.[75] Fuller describes cinema as a "battleground," and it is indeed through the representation of death that the film engages questions of phenomenology and spectacular representation in a way specific to the mid-1960s intellectual climate. The existential "freedom" of *Pierrot le fou* is achieved through violence, a violence of historical discontinuity (Benjamin's "shock" effect), as much as it is through the imaginary of eternity.

Blasting himself out of the momentum of narrative, the continuum of history, and the finitude of existence, Ferdinand also blows himself out of representation. There is no corpse, no body at all to organically "reenter the world" because, of course, it would not be a dead body at all, but Belmondo acting dead. The "renewal" of this carnivalized death is not organic but spectacular. Throughout the film, death is at once ironic, spectacularly "fake," and yet instrumental to the film's momentum, driving the couple on to further adventures, reversing expectations, generating action: a crucial decoration of the underworld that Ferdinand traverses. Finally, a sense of rebirth pervades the couple's own deaths. Ferdinand shoots Marianne, perhaps by mistake, as they are running through some complex geography, or perhaps because she double-crossed him (figure 9). He carries her limp and bloodstained body into a villa and she repeats a line she has said at least once before — "It was the first, it was the only dream" — before dying on the bed. The film's apocalypse is the awakening from this dream.[76]

That this is also an "awakening" from a certain kind of modernist anxiety can be illustrated by comparing the end of the film to Rimbaud's poem "Une Saison en Enfer." Ferdinand's response to Marianne's enigmatic words is to paint his face blue, phone home, cite Balzac, and wrap his head in yellow and red dynamite. His attempt to frantically put out the fuse before the final cut to a long shot of the explosion is taken in part from Rimbaud:

No! No! at present I rebel against death! Work seems too easy for my pride; my betrayal to the world would be too brief a penalty. At the last moment I should strike out right and left . . .

Fig. 9. *Pierrot le fou*: Ferdinand (Jean-Paul Belmondo) shoots Marianne (Anna Karina) at the end of their adventure. Publicity still courtesy of Cinémathèque Québécoise.

Then—Oh!—dear, poor soul, would eternity not be lost to us!

And, from the last "chapter" (like *Pierrot le fou,* Rimbaud's prose poem is divided into short subtitled sections), called "Adieu":

It is necessary to be absolutely modern.
No canticles: hold to the step you have gained. Sore night!
The dried blood smokes on my face, and I have nothing at my back but this horrible bush!... One advantage is that I can laugh at the old, false passions, and put to shame those lying couples, — I have seen the hell of women down there; — and it will be legitimate for me to *possess the truth in a soul and body.*[77]

Besides the many other imagistic allusions to "Une Saison en Enfer" in *Pierrot le fou,*[78] Rimbaud's prose poem provides Godard with the attitude of laughter directed toward those structures of language, behavior, and narrative from which the film is in flight. As in "Une

Saison en Enfer," the necessity to be modern is accompanied by a desire to be whole, a unified entity of consciousness and world, an existentialist quest for an "authentic" union of action and choice. In keeping with Rimbaud's misogyny, Ferdinand's bourgeois marriage and adventures with Marianne are both "hells" characterized by a loss of mastery over willful women. His escape from his particular hell involves the death of the woman, Marianne, but also the inter- mingling of his voice with hers after death. And this is perhaps where Godard moves beyond Rimbaud's modernism, in a movement be- yond subjectivity as an autonomous category, toward the romance of intersubjectivity.

The absurdity of Ferdinand's suicide, followed by the resurrection of the self "outside of this world" is at once a renunciation of the empirical self and a concession to the linguistic construction of sub- jectivity. It is precisely the stylized, excessive violence that enables the film to transcend Rimbaud's modernist conception of mortality. Rimbaud may "write himself" against the void of death,[79] but for Go- dard it is a void of representation, figured in death, against which sub- jectivity is "written."

Moreover, subjectivity in *Pierrot le fou* takes on a temporal struc- ture. "Authentic subjectivity" is relegated to the flaneur and his pos- ture of aloof nonparticipation in the teleology of modernity. This pos- ture may be rendered inadequate, but it nevertheless resonates in the film's "poetry." Consciousness is finally radically separated from mortality in the cut from the close-up of Ferdinand's hands groping for the fuse wire on the ground to a long shot of the explosion on the hillside. The death is structured metonymically, displacing the ex- perience of death from the spectacle of death, making it "an objec- tive fact for another consciousness."[80] Rather than metaphorical mean- ing, we get a performance. Again, one of the key effects of narrative mortality is the inscription of temporal/historical difference between the profilmic and the eternal present tense of the narrative.

Before wrapping his head with the dynamite, Ferdinand says to the camera, "I just wanted to say ... I am stupid ...", a final instance of the Brechtian theatricality of *Pierrot le fou*. The frequent instances of visual and voice-over direct address maintain a constant, if sporadic and somewhat one-sided, dialogue with the spectator. Comedy and heteroglossia likewise inscribe a plurality of voices into the text in a cacophony of consciousnesses rendered as languages. The carnival of closure in *Pierrot le fou* does not produce an idealized image of utopia, an alternative representation to the sterile world of bourgeois cocktail parties, nor an anarchist rejection of reason, but a fragmented image of existence and essence, body and consciousness, things and words, material reality and utopian imagination. None of the film's various binaries are irrevocably divided in death, but, like Ferdinand and Marianne, they are ironically and comically dialogized, so that they might be recombined differently, in a future that lies beyond the film—in the viewer's mind, in eternity.

Godard's "allegory of the body" is precisely a matter of subjectivity construed as perception. The sustained duality of Belmondo/Ferdinand and Karina/Marianne, achieved through voice-over, narrative, direct address, and performance, is carried through to the characters' deaths, which are shocking precisely because we have been drawn inside the characters in spite of all the strategies employed to keep us outside. Like the baroque dramatists, Godard's obsession with death "would be quite unthinkable if it were merely a question of reflection about the end of their lives." The corpse, arrayed in tableaux of the ruins of late capitalism, is, for Godard, "the pre-eminent emblematic property,"[81] because in it is registered the limitations of cinematic language to realize the image of authentic experience, the inability to reach the soul through the image, and the inability to "capture life."

Within the particular intellectual climate within which *Pierrot le fou* was produced, Godard's carnival explodes the categories of existence and essence to take from death the knowledge of their dialectical possibilities of history and desire. As the threshold of discovery and repetition (the always-the-same), the ruin of the body is, in a flash, a renewal. The mourning of immortality and mimeticism that takes place in *Le Mépris* is transformed in *Pierrot le fou* to an allegory of desire. The closing shots of the Mediterranean horizon are the same in the two films, but the mortals in *Le Mépris* are embroiled in language; the discourses of myth and cinema have them thoroughly enmeshed. In *Pierrot le fou*, "the forces of the mythical world"—and the limits of representation—are indeed met "with cunning and with high spirits."[82]

At the limits of modernism, transcendence can only be perceived in the form of loss from the perspective of history as itself a form of mortality. The dialectic between the immortal and the mortal is situated by Benjamin on the plane of representation, between symbolic correspondence (mimeticism) and the signifying processes of language. The Mediterranean is a privileged site of the ruins of history, demonstrating the submission of history to nature, which for Benjamin is "always allegorical":

> In the ruin history has physically merged into the setting. And in this guise history does not assume the form of the process of an eternal life so much as that of irresistible decay. Allegory thereby declares itself to be beyond beauty. Allegories are, in the realm of thoughts, what ruins are in the realm of things.[83]

If the "death's head" is the baroque emblem of nature's claim on history, for Godard the car accident performs a similar role in the twentieth century. The wrecks of cars will never entirely return to nature, but will mar eternity with their rust. One technique of baroque allegory as a ruin of history is "to pile up fragments ceaselessly, without any strict idea of a goal,"[84] and indeed, highway death is likewise contingent; the subjection of *travel* to death transforms the temporality of progress, in an instant, to that of decay. Equally important, however, is the status of the automobile as a commodity. If the allegorization of Bardot involves the distantiation of her sexuality, the melancholy gaze is equally directed at the fetish of the shiny red Alfa Romeo. The disjunction implicit in allegory between signifier and signified is a historical one, inscribing a difference in historical moments; but the commodity, too, is allegorical. "Just as in the 17th century allegory becomes the canon of dialectical imagery, so in the 19th century does novelty."[85] Under the melancholy gaze, the commodity, separated from its use-value, becomes, like the baroque death's head, a signifier of a transient signified—in this case, the cult of the new.

The detritus of capitalism, its ruins and discarded commodities—represented, for example, in the wrecks of smashed cars that litter Godard's films of the late 1960s (e.g., *Weekend* [1967])—are thus allegorical; in them is fixed the erotic charge of novelty—the illusory totality of the fetish—now separated from its rusting material basis. Thus the "death's head" and the commodity become one in the final car accident in *Le Mépris,* and, moreover, the melancholy gaze belongs to the camera. The transience registered in this allegory is less the face of nature than that of the profilmic because, in the twentieth century, the spectacle as emblem has itself been commodified.

Just as Benjamin's and Bakhtin's theories of cultural utopias were conceived within the totalitarian nightmares of Europe between the wars, in the fading light of the avant-gardes of the 1920s, the threshold delineated here also has its dangers, many of which (as we will see in the final chapters) have been realized in postmodern cinema. From *Le Mépris* to *Pierrot le fou,* the sense of loss begins to be lost, a process that is instrumental to the radical potential of narrative mortality. And yet it has to be recognized that postmodern apocalypticism and intertextuality carry with them the threat of historical amnesia. Memory is crucial to the potential of narrative mortality to "ruin" crisis and transform it into the desire for a different future. Redemption is simply the structure of radical memory that may be identified within the dialectical relations between these two films, even if it is not fully developed in either one of them.

It may well be that the carnival of *Pierrot le fou* was Godard's last laugh; certainly his subsequent films adopted a more resigned tone. The apocalyptic *Made in USA* is a full-color allegory of Hollywood, but without the ironic existentialism of the Ferdinand character; it is a film only about a loss of vision, which may make it more "postmodern," but it lacks the exhilarating speed of a film going nowhere. In *Pierrot le fou,* one finds the traces of modernism still potent, instilling a memory of materialism, the hint of a historical referent informing its apocalypse. But what is perhaps most intriguing about the threshold that is delineated in *Pierrot le fou* is that it also anticipates the crisis of historical vision of the postmodern apocalyptic and allows us to situate that crisis within the philosophical, political, and aesthetic framework of the Nouvelle Vague and the *Cahiers du Cinéma* critics' "necessity to be modern."[86] The spectacle of death and the poetry of eternity are finally separated from each other with the cut away from the protagonist's explosive body, and it is perhaps in that cut, in that which is not representable, that the future of the society of the spectacle might be hidden.

FIVE

AMERICAN APOCALYPTICISM
The Sight of the Crisis

● ───────────────────────────────

> The disaster is separate; that which is most separate. When the disaster
> is upon us, it does not come. The disaster is its imminence, but since the
> future, as we conceive of it in the order of lived time, belongs to the
> disaster, the disaster has always already withdrawn or dissuaded it;
> there is no future for the disaster, just as there is no time or space for its
> accomplishment. — MAURICE BLANCHOT[1]

Violence to the body, represented in ever more vivid anatomical detail, through the use of ever more special effects, has come to signify death in contemporary American narrative film. As the substantial lived body is wrenched apart, it is anatomized through wounding and ejaculating blood, and becomes the producer of its own excess. This strategy involves a shift of emphasis from the more abstract sense of the individual to a biological, organic sense of the finite self. Moreover, it represents a very different fear of death, replacing the existential anxiety of the European "art" film with a fear of "unnatural" and abrupt curtailment of life.

We have already encountered this distinction in our discussion of

173

The State of Things, in which the pressure of mortality suggested by ticking electronic instruments in Europe is banished with the transition to an American road movie. The fear of violent death, which hangs over the last scenes and which is eventually realized, is not a "metaphysical" fear but a fear of discontinuity. It is not a sense of time that contradicts consciousness, but a fear, simply, that there will no longer be a body, a subject, or a film.

It is within the breakdown of genre within the American cinema that apocalyptic violence terminates films that can no longer end in the safety of "home." This process of disintegration might have begun after the Second World War, and maybe even in the 1930s gangster genre, but it becomes ironically perfected in the late 1960s and early 1970s. Apocalyptic closure might be defined as a terminal form of closure in which the narrative has traveled somewhere, but not to where it began. In the alterity of space and time of the road movie, which has been described as Hollywood's most "desperate genre,"[2] "identity" cannot be secured, despite the isomorphism of death and closure. Spectacular violence often becomes an attempt to restore a sense of ending to narratives that travel beyond the securities of genre.

In the preceding pages, death has been discussed as something quite separate from violence. And indeed, in film as in life, death is not always violent—although it certainly is so more often in film than in life. The moral objection to violence in the mass media, raised since the earliest days of the cinema, does not often speak of death per se.[3] Although numbers of murders per televisual hour have been dutifully tabulated by sociologists since the 1950s, death in the sociological discourse is a heightened form of violence, and not a phenomenon in itself.[4] A possible explanation for this tendency is that violent action and death have a similar *narrative* function in advancing plot, a function that should distinguish them from lived violence and actual death. In content analyses, however, they advance yet another plot: the deleterious effects of the mass media on "society."

More pertinent perhaps than quantification is the question of why so much narrative discourse revolves around violent action and death. The development of narrative codes in early American film takes place in stories that involve both the speed and the drama of opposed forces, symptomatic of violent action. Porter's *The Great Train Robbery,* Griffith's *Birth of a Nation,* and the plenitude of early films based on chases and rescues often depend on violent action and the threat of death for the deployment of those innovative formal strategies for which they are generally known.[5] This is something that Eisenstein appreciates in Griffith, and indeed Eisenstein's early theorization of montage was derived from the representation of violent death on the steps of Odessa.[6]

The prevalence of violent death in the mass media is thus immediately attributable to the demands of the medium: speed and spectacle, but also to the melodramatic desire to "see the unseeable." It has been pointed out that violence gives death "a perceptible form," endowing the mysterious transition from being to nonbeing with the dynamics of movement, color, and sound.[7] Paul Virilio has rewritten the history of cinema as a history of military technology designed to transform the enemy into a system of representation. In the "logistics of perception," visibility effectively becomes a form of violence.[8] In the late 1960s and early 1970s in the United States, when narrative closure becomes synonymous with spectacular death in the cinema, a discourse of apocalypse appropriates the violence of visibility as the end of history.

The reliance on the star system and on realist performance styles in this cinema insists on metaphors of psychology and desire, giving back "the sense of an ending" to historical allegories. The bodies of American movie stars cannot be sacrificed as documentary or ethnographic subjects. In the genre revision of the late 1960s and early 1970s — the cinema of Coppola, Scorsese, Penn, and Altman — narrative mortality emerges as an allegory of the debased myths of American culture. The argument of this chapter is that the excessive representation of violence reinstates the mythology of death as closure within the allegory of narrative mortality; that is, the potential mortification of genre is curtailed by the resurrection of the spectacle in the excessive closure of this American apocalyptic cinema.

From *Kiss Me Deadly* (1955) to *Apocalypse Now* (1979), a rash of films from a revived Hollywood of auteurs repeatedly end with spectacularly violent multiple deaths. The films under discussion in this chapter — *Bonnie and Clyde* (Penn, 1967), *The Wild Bunch* (Peckinpah, 1969), and *Nashville* (Altman, 1975)—are in this respect exemplary of a group of films that also includes *The Godfather, Night Moves, Taxi Driver, Dirty Harry,* and others. The analyses of these films should demonstrate the parameters of narrative mortality as a discourse of apocalypse in the Vietnam and Watergate periods of American history.

The New Testament Apocalypse of Saint John, renamed the Book of Revelation, is about catastrophe and revelation couched in the terms of vision. Visions of the end of the world are generally produced during periods of social upheaval and accelerated change, and the history of false predictions is a history of social anxiety.[9] The "modern apocalypse" differs from previous anticipations because it is informed by the dread of uncompassionate science and technology, but, like other mythologies of ending, it is both "transforming and concordant";[10] that is, it is a means of understanding the experience of history, an anticipation of the future within the limited terms of present experience.

To the extent that the mythology of apocalypse implies a theory of history, of social change (to a future of either heaven or hell, paradise or suffering),[11] in the society of the spectacle "neither death nor procreation is grasped as a law of time. Time remains immobile, like an enclosed space."[12] That which might be described as the postmodern apocalyptic vision effectively turns in on itself, curtailing both the promise and the threat of apocalyptic historiography. Rather than lamenting the dystopic scene of terminality à la Baudrillard,[13] the impotent apocalyptic vision of this cinema can be analyzed in terms of cinematic realism, excess, and history. Key differences between the three films *Bonnie and Clyde, The Wild Bunch,* and *Nashville* demonstrate the range of relations between apocalyptic violence and history in this period. While the "fracturing of the male subject" implied in the term "impotent" is a key feature of the disintegration of genre cinema,[14] we shall see that it is also the failure of the white American subject that is allegorized in these films.

In American apocalypticism, narrative mortality is the allegory of a crisis of historical vision. In the secular world of late capitalism, apocalyptic discourse points, in most cases, to a loss of social consensus, but the "loss of myth" that informs Godard's work is figured quite differently in American genre revisionism, which generally fails to question the status of the image in its deconstruction of myth. Death and closure converge more teleologically in the American apocalypse, as crisis is institutionalized as commodified spectacle. Although the excesses of the representation of death and violence point to an anxiety provoked by the "loss of myth" involved in genre revision, this loss tends to be mystified once more as "meaningful loss." This apocalyptic cinema spearheaded by auteurs is itself the redemption of an American "art" cinema, its national character ironically guaranteed by the generic discourses of the Western, the musical, and the gangster film. Narrative mortality assumes an anxiety or hysteria that will be defined in terms of sacrificial crisis.

Dances of Death

Bonnie and Clyde (1967) and *The Wild Bunch* (1969) were particularly "shocking" to contemporary audiences. It is instructive to analyze the representations of death in these films because they are symptomatic of the tendency of the American mythos of "regeneration through violence" to disintegrate into an aesthetic discourse of "excess." Stylization takes up where coherent belief systems dissipate, and death, likewise cut off from those metaphysical, religious, and melodramatic discourses in which it had been "tamed," explodes in a violent destruction of the body. However, the two films also differ in important ways. Narrative mortality in *Bonnie and Clyde* succumbs to a circular, self-referential myth of American history, whereas in *The Wild Bunch* it becomes more allegorical in the Benjaminian sense, opening onto a discourse of historical transformation. A "gangster" film and a "Western," both films are also exemplary road movies, traveling physically and geographically to their narrative goals of death and destruction.

Bonnie and Clyde includes scenes that were described at the time as "the most brutally violent ever filmed,"[15] mainly because of the amount of blood involved.[16] Most spectacular of all is the last scene, in which Bonnie and Clyde are machine-gunned to death in a complex montage of very short shots. Crosscutting between Clyde (Warren Beatty) falling and rolling on the ground in front of the car and Bonnie (Faye Dunaway) hammered into the front seat with bullets and finally dropping headfirst onto the running board, to the accompaniment of a loud machine-gun rattle, the scene consists of thirty shots in one minute. The film ends immediately after the police emerge from the bushes and drop their guns to their sides.

This is an entirely different order of violence from *Pierrot le fou*. Godard uses great amounts of red on static, motionless bodies to signify death, as well as the impossibility of signifying death. Penn uses codes of motion and movement that represent life in its last vestige of being, a violent movement through which the body is transformed from subject (facial expression) to inert and lifeless object. The sequence moves from four extreme close-ups alternating between Bonnie's and Clyde's faces, suddenly realizing the gravity of the situation, to Bonnie's limp hand finally signifying death. (The emphasis on the weight of the bodies is a familiar Hitchcock technique.) As Penn explained to an interviewer:

> I wanted to get the spasm of death, and so I used four
> cameras, each one at a different speed, 24, 48, 72 and 96, I
> think, and different lenses, so that I could cut to get the shock
> and at the same time the ballet of death.... I wanted two
> kinds of death: Clyde's to be rather like a ballet, and Bonnie's
> to have the physical shock.... We put on the bullet holes—
> and there's even a piece of Warren's head that comes off, like
> that famous photograph of Kennedy.... [I asked the actress]
> simply to enact the death, to fall and follow the laws of
> gravity. Faye was trapped behind the wheel. We tied one leg
> to the gear shift so that she would feel free to fall.[17] (Figure 10).

The fact that the film ends immediately after the stoppage of bodily movement delimits representation to subjectivity. It is a classic instance of death as closure. In Bonnie and Clyde's deaths, the emphasis on movement and the last energetic spasms of life as it is reduced to automatic reflexes may be an example of an attempt to represent death from within: the special effects of slow motion and the use of close-ups distend the mimesis of subjective experience. Despite the use of these effects, however, in conjunction with the crosscutting and blood, the scene is very much a stylized spectacle for a viewer: another instance of death from without. Bonnie's silent scream "answers" the first death in the film, a man whose bloody face is fixed in a silent scream (Potemkin-style), framed by a car window. The simul-

Fig. 10. *Bonnie and Clyde*: Bonnie (Faye Dunaway) and Clyde (Warren Beatty) and their dead car at the end of their adventure. Publicity still courtesy of Photofest.

taneity of the two modes, death from within and death from without, is crucial to the naturalization of the spectacle, legitimating the pleasure in violence and codifying its excess as "expression."

Penn may have drained the myth of its romantic impetus in the physical depiction of the bodies, but the spectacle of blood is excessive rather than allegorical and the legend remains intact. Whereas allegory points to the doubleness of representation, excess, in Roland Barthes's words, "sterilizes" not only meaning, but metalanguage and criticism as well.[18] What he calls "the third meaning," beyond denotation and connotation, is "obtuse" because it opens the field of meaning "totally, that is infinitely." Where allegory "mortifies," excess "liberates." The antiauthoritarian stance of *Bonnie and Clyde* is ultimately diffused in its violence, displaced from history onto the "liberation" of the image itself. The narrative collapses under the weight of a violence that strains the codes of realism that the film has so faithfully upheld. Significantly, unlike the Eisenstein film that Barthes discusses (*Ivan the Terrible*), this rupture occurs only at *the end* of *Bonnie and Clyde*.

Moreover, both subjectivity and the film are abruptly curtailed in a dead car. Bonnie and Clyde drive even more cars across this film than Ferdinand and Marianne do in *Pierrot le fou*. The terminal nature of the final stoppage of the car is accentuated by the union of Bonnie's body with the driving apparatus. At the end of the film's journey, there is really nothing but the characters' deaths. The lack of destination, which has haunted the narrative throughout, is finally eradicated in the spectacular eruption of blood, as if this were the end of the road of desire and not just the end of the road. At first the beautiful bodies of Warren Beatty and Faye Dunaway survive the ugly deaths of the Gene Hackman and Estelle Parsons characters. The horror of *Bonnie and Clyde* is finally the destruction of their lovely faces. The body of the film, its smooth surface, its very coherence and consistency, are synonymous with the smooth skin of Faye Dunaway's cheeks. Like the shiny surfaces of the period cars that are riddled with bullet holes throughout *Bonnie and Clyde,* but are continually replaced with new cars, the film itself is a body that suffers and finally dies.

Once Dunaway and Beatty are irreparably punctured, torn, and bloodied, the film too is finished. This is why the excessive rupture of violent death can happen only at the end of the film. If the fragmentation of the film's spatial and temporal unities through the multiplicity of speeds and focal lengths is a literal disintegration of the image, the failure of subjectivity and desire is also the failure of representation. When it can no longer signify *anything,* the film signifies itself within the very code of excess (as Barthes has said of Japanese melodrama),[19] but it does so only at the end. Violence here does not become a form of "writing" because it says nothing, except that this is the end. The desire repressed in the narrative (Clyde's impotence) is finally realized in the desire for closure, for these deaths that were anticipated all along. The telos of the myth of fate is celebrated in the excesses of representation, which give to the spectator precisely what was missing when Bonnie and Clyde went offscreen, out of frame, to make love.

Pauline Kael ended her long and enthusiastic review of *Bonnie and Clyde* with the observation, "Maybe it's because Bonnie and

Clyde, by making us care about the robber lovers, have put the sting back into death."[20] It is precisely this "care" that distinguishes Penn's ending from that of Lang's *You Only Live Once* (1936) (to which Kael quite rightly compares it), in which Sylvia Sidney dies in Henry Fonda's arms while a burst of light and heavenly music accompany the couple to "freedom" and they are ushered into the netherworld by the voice of a dead priest. Partly because Lang's characters are cartoon characters from the outset, their deaths are inherently allegorical. His film does not ask us to believe in the characters or the image, but in something else, beyond representation. Against Lang's allegory of transcendence, in 1967 Bonnie and Clyde preserve in their deaths a belief in the image on the screen; the "sting," as Kael puts it, is born of an intense identification with the image and/as the characters on the most libidinal level, which is suddenly broken. With the puncturing of its skin/illusion, the film becomes an object, subject to the laws of gravity and narrative.

It may well be argued that the heightened realism of *Bonnie and Clyde* gives a strong utopian thrust to the gangster genre's conventions of antiheroism. The rupture of identification in the melodramatic ending can, and often does, make the viewer cry, which may be understood psychoanalytically as the restaging of an originary experience with the mother. According to Steve Neale, the pleasure of tears provoked by melodrama is bound up with the belief that "there might be an Other capable of responding to them." Following Peter Brooks, Neale observes:

> The cry and the gesture indicate 'a kind of fault or gap in the code, the space that marks its inadequacies to convey a full freight of emotional meaning.' Tears very often come in this gap.... One of the reasons instances of this gap can be so moving is that they mark a form of failure of the fantasy of union.[21]

Neale notes that this "gap" is often produced by the noncoincidence of points of view and knowledge—for example, the viewer's prior knowledge of Bonnie and Clyde's imminent deaths. In melodrama it is "always too late" because the film is always finished before it is screened; and it is this situation of powerlessness on the part of the viewer to control or alter the destinies of those on-screen that is so often restaged in melodrama. Tears, however, preserve the fantasy of possibility and the reality of desire.

The "unhappy" ending, especially, says Neale, "may function as a means of satisfying a wish to have the wish unfulfilled—in order that it can be preserved and re-stated rather than abandoned altogether" (p. 21). If Bonnie and Clyde were to live happily ever after, there would be no more legend to replay, no fantasy to indulge in. The "mythical, legendary, balletic ending" (Penn's words) preserves the failure of desire that the narrative has enacted, and thus the possibility that "the loss can be eradicated"—the loss of "the Other," but also the loss of history. It is precisely this resurrection of history that distinguishes *Bonnie and Clyde* from both *The Wild Bunch* and *Nashville*. Corrigan aptly historicizes the circularity of this film:

> If *Bonnie and Clyde* is based on a historical account, it is more accurately a historical account of modern perception, perception that in the sixties is already beginning to reduce history to the material of images, material in which a culture must obsessively act itself out in order to displace the return of more threatening histories.[22]

Several parallels exist between *Bonnie and Clyde* and *Cruel Story of Youth*. In both narratives, the young couples are criminals outside the law of the state and the law of the family, betrayed by fathers and father figures. In both cases, their love for each other cannot be contained by a corrupt society, and they die bloodily and separately, subverting the possibility of a transcendent, utopian realization of desire. The key difference between the two films is their settings. Oshima's redirection of the politics of death from social submission to social opposition is accomplished through a demystification of history. Where Oshima's narrative is set in a highly stylized yet historically specific contemporary Japan, Penn's is set in a never-never land of the 1930s.

Depression America is represented as a timeless zone of poverty and social ills in which Bonnie and Clyde will die over and over again. That mythic time when gangsters were the heroes of the underclass, a New Deal America in which "the people" were a viable unified collective (however impoverished), is preserved as a fantasy outside the irreversibility and cruelty of history. In the displacement of the melodramatic excess of unfulfilled desire onto the bodies of the actors, and the body of the film, desire is turned back on itself. It becomes a desire for the fantasy of coincidence, timelessness, and return. Despite the emphasis on vision and catastrophe, this apocalyptic ending curtails the very possibility of historical anticipation, displacing teleology onto visual pleasure. In Penn's imaginary return to history, the historical alterity of future and past are transformed into the phenomenological and terminal space of the screen. There are so many markers of the couple's fate that the narrative is, in Penn's words, a matter of "waiting out history."[23] If this is historiography, Penn's narrative mortality allegorizes the wait for the spectacular end of history.

If *Bonnie and Clyde* was the "first" film to represent death in anatomical detail, opening the "bloodgates" of American film, *The Wild Bunch* is the mythic initiator of a "celebration" of violence.[24] Although such a historiography of cinematic "firsts" is undoubtedly suspect, it is worth comparing the two representations of violent death. In comparing the two films, Robert Kolker is typically moralistic. Peckinpah's sensibility is "vicious," and *The Wild Bunch* is "a film to admire and despise simultaneously." His condemnation of Peckinpah's misogyny is certainly apt, as is his observation that his "narratives require more and more exploding flesh to prove that [his] male bond[ing] cannot succeed past its repressions."[25] However, the narrative and historiographic form that these cruelties and contradictions take is illuminating. Even for Kolker, Peckinpah's violence "permits one to be excited by dynamic movement and offers ... a vicarious thrill.... More than the violence itself, the *image* is important, the fact that one is permitted to see the unseeable" (p. 56). In fact, this is also true of *Bonnie and Clyde,* but Peckinpah prolongs the spectacle, adding temporal duration to the excesses of representation.

The apocalyptic violence in this instance really does overwhelm its narrative function. Stylistic excess takes on a particularly ambiguous function in *The Wild Bunch,* an ambiguity that is crucially related to the representation of history. In this film, as well as in *Nashville,* ethnic difference enters into the mythology of Americana, and narrative mortality allegorizes an inability to "return home" to homogeneous cultural nationalism. The end of the road of this Western, like that of *Butch Cassidy and the Sundance Kid,* lies outside America, in Mexico, only here it is less a "foreign" country than an extension of postcolonial American economic imperialism.

The Wild Bunch is about a group of outlaws who have run out of opportunities to exercise their heroism in the late nineteenth century American West. The frontier has closed, and there is little geographic or ideological space for their particular brand of individualism. They meet their deaths with an attitude of nihilism that is nevertheless marked with the pride of adhering to a code of fraternity and outlaw ethics. In the complexity of the film's historical setting, however, the romance of heroism encompasses a utopian vision of social transformation and the apocalyptic finale, with all its visual excess, does not completely overwhelm historical possibility.

The group's decision to take on a Mexican village and the army that occupies it is initiated by Pike (William Holden), who simply says "Let's go." The response, "Why not?" is the only verbalization of the unspoken agreement among the four men to avenge the cruelty that the Mexicans have committed against their buddy Angel. Angel's "crime" was to have skimmed a box of rifles from the military loot that the bunch has just sold to Mapache, the Mexican general who runs the village. The weapons were for Angel's "people" — Mexicans oppressed by Mapache. The bunch is complicitous with Angel's guerrilla action, if not enthusiastic about it, appreciating the nobility of the act more than the cause for which it is perpetrated. Mapache slits Angel's throat, upon which the Americans shoot the general in front of his entire entourage. The ensuing shootout between the four members of the bunch and the hundreds of armed Mexicans "answers" the shoot-out between the bunch and a small American town, whose railroad office they rob in the opening scene of the film. As in *Beyond a Reasonable Doubt,* an initial death is rhymed by a final death, although in this case both are virtual massacres, and where death was invisible and offscreen in the 1956 film, visibility supersedes narrative in 1969.

Both battles in *The Wild Bunch* include individual confrontations of point-blank shooting, isolated in the mise-en-scène by the camera's adoption of rifle sights. In the final shoot-out, the heroes are each shot several times, falling back from the force of the bullets again and again, while the Mexicans fall mainly in slow motion waves of men (figure 11). The scene lasts five minutes, beginning with the slitting of Angel's throat and ending with a close-up of Dutch's (Ernest Borgnine) bloody face calling the name of his buddy Pike, who dangles by his finger from the machine-gun with which he has slaughtered dozens of Mexicans. As in *Bonnie and Clyde,* the *Wild Bunch* shoot-out is filmed from multiple perspectives with a variety of lenses, speeds, and distances. One cutaway to Thornton (Robert Ryan) in the hills with binoculars suggests a diegetic witness to the carnage, but his long shot of scurrying men and puffs of smoke bears no relation to the medium close-ups of slow-moving bodies that dominate the sequence. This is less a celebration of death than of the male body, displayed acrobatically. Again, it is "ballet" that is often evoked by critics to describe the sequence.

Lawrence Alloway has suggested that in the Westerns of the 1950s,

Fig. 11. *The Wild Bunch*: Butch (Ernest Borgnine) and Pike (William Holden) take a breather in the middle of the massacre. Publicity still courtesy of Cinémathèque Québécoise.

"the witty athleticism of stunt men defends the audience from dismay; the shock of life's extinction is overwhelmed by admiration of the gymnastics."[26] Alloway goes on to observe, "However, as the motives of Westerners have become more naturalistic, death has become more a physical fact and less a form of play." He cites "the impact of bullets and their exit on the other side of the body" as evidence of this naturalism, but this is precisely what Robert Kolker points to as a lack of realism.[27] Since notions of realism are inevitably historically determined and each writer here assumes a different definition, we might do better to look at specific instances of the relation between death and violence. Since the mid-1960s, the body has become the site of a violence that, in the 1950s, was more often directed against locations and objects: the cracked mirrors of *The Lady from Shanghai*, the scores of ransacked apartments, the car crash in *Beyond a Reasonable Doubt*.

Once death is represented as a violence to the body, a destruction of the skin that holds body and soul together, the look of death becomes potentially repulsive. One of the conventions by which the gruesomeness of this form of death is "contained" in narrative is slow motion, also a key means by which violence can be construed as ballet.[28] As an analytical dissection of the moving image into constituent parts that approximate the condition of individual frames (even if they do not achieve that condition), slow motion fails to jeopardize the illusion of reality when it is used to represent death, precisely because of the affinity of these "still" elements with the state they portend to represent. In other words, although slow motion is "less real" than twenty-four frames per second, when used to depict death, it achieves a degree of realism. Furthermore, the distinction between death from within and death from without also breaks down as the spectacle assumes the codes of subjectivity, as in *Bonnie and Clyde*.

Rarely, if ever, does one find a slow-motion death scene that ends with a freeze-frame of the corpse. The photo finish is reserved for the body caught in a posture that is virtually caused by the force of the bullet. And yet the principle involved in slow motion and the freeze-frame is similar. Garrett Stewart writes of the "arrested bodies" of *Butch Cassidy and the Sundance Kid* (1969), *The Parallax View* (1974), and *Gallipoli* (1981):

Stop-action does just what its name suggests; within the
textual system, it stops the narrative action itself, not just the
representation of movement. Hence the totalizing force of the
freeze-frame in such closing death "scenes," its power to
subsume narrative entirely to graphic figuration.[29]

In the particular films with which Stewart is concerned, the freeze-
frame *replaces* the corpse, preserving the living body in the ontology
of the photographic image. The mythic subject is thereby saved from
history, allegory, and decay.

Likewise, the slowing down of the film corresponds to a slowing
down of life. As in the freeze-frame, the representational illusion is
preserved through the identification of the body of the film with the
body of the actor. The protraction of the dying process that occurs
with slow motion does not represent pain but, in the freedom from
gravity, its opposite: movement without friction. Neither film nor life
is actually retarded, but in the equation of the two, and in the "grace"
achieved by the falling body, death and stasis are virtually effaced
and disavowed. Death in slow motion, especially when it occurs at
the end of a film, participates in a "code of excess." The shift into metaphor preserves the image at the moment it is threatened with disintegration.[30] In the case of *Bonnie and Clyde,* in the codification of
excess, the apocalypse is effectively postponed.

While this codification of excess through metaphors of mortality
certainly occurs in *The Wild Bunch,* the limits of cinematic realism
are pushed much farther than in either *Bonnie and Clyde* or *Butch
Cassidy.* Slow motion in the climactic scene of *The Wild Bunch* takes
variable speeds and alternates with "normal" speed. It is this choreography of dying that has been charged against Peckinpah. The
exploding blood bags and swooning bodies that represent death in
The Wild Bunch constitute an iconography of death that can even be
described as baroque in its excess. Slow motion interrupts the narrative momentum for a veritable *danse macabre,* and indeed two features of the sixteenth-century iconographic mortuary frescoes seem
pertinent here. Philippe Ariès notes that the dance of death involves
a mixing of the living with the dead: "The dead lead the dance; indeed, they are the only ones dancing.... The art lies in the contrast
between the rhythm of the dead and the rigidity of the living."[31] In
what was fundamentally a depiction of destiny as rebirth, an energized

representation of mortality, the *danse macabre* evolved into violent and erotic celebrations of sensuality in the eighteenth and nineteenth centuries. Ariès describes it as an intermingling of "pleasure and pain that will later be called sadism" (p. 370).

Likewise, in *The Wild Bunch,* the dying leap and bleed while the living cower, and Thornton, the survivor, learns about death and desire from the dance that he witnesses from afar. Pike and Dutch come closer in their final moments to articulating their libidinal relationship than they have over the entire course of the film. Once again, violent death involves a melodramatic displacement of the desire that cannot be fulfilled or sustained in the narrative. In this case it is the impossible homoerotic desire of the "buddy system."[32] Kolker's claim that Peckinpah reveals the "unseeable" indicates the melodramatic impetus of the violence, its excessive attempt to exceed the limit of the visible. Sexual desire is displaced onto excessive violence in this Western, but so is the unrealized historical desire of the collective antihero that is the "wild bunch." The excessive gesture of the ballet of violent death restores to the dead heroes the dynamics of these desires as valid wishes, despite the impossibility of their realization.

Unlike *Bonnie and Clyde,* the apocalyptic discourse of this film does possess a form of historical vision. The crisis might become a threshold onto historical change insofar as the spectacular death scene not only constitutes an intrusion into the diegesis, but it lasts five minutes, over which time the "code" of excess cannot quite be sustained. In the severe retardation of the film's movement, and in the splashes of red liquid across the screen of the protracted bloodletting, pleasure is compromised by duration. The number of bodies alone challenges any plausibility theory of narrative realism and points to a *discursive* excess and ideological counterpoint to the "regenerative" epilogue, thus rendering it discontinuous, if not ironic, with respect to the rest of the narrative.

The point at which stasis is finally reached is a stoppage of Dutch's body (and an end to the sound of guns), not a stoppage of the succession of frames. Before the final close-up of Dutch's face, an out-of-focus point-of-view shot is inserted, but it has the opposite effect of representing the subjective vision of a dying man (death from within). As the only such shot in the entire sequence, it restores narrative discourse (a metadiegetic "voice") to the temporarily threatened movement of the film. The scene then continues with the slow, silent resumption of movement as the scattered survivors emerge from the carnage.

On one level it might be said that *The Wild Bunch* participates fully in the myth of "regeneration through violence," which has been described as constitutive of American Western narratives. When manifest destiny is transposed into the psychological terms of heroism, the savagery of the wilderness becomes part of the identity of the conqueror. Self-annihilation through aggression is a transcendence of the ineffectual "Eastern" (cultured) self, but also remains in the service of the civilizing teleology.[33] The wilderness is thus conquered by the internalization, through violence, of its "uncivilized" values, a theme played out most explicitly in John Ford's *The Searchers*. Violence assumes the character of "moral necessity" in its perpetuation of manifest destiny, and as such has become an archetype of American culture.[34]

A transcendent, regenerative function of the violence is certainly suggested in *The Wild Bunch* through the conversion of Thornton from vigilante back to outlaw after the massacre. Moreover, after their deaths, a series of superimposed flashbacks of each of the five dead members of the gang is superimposed over Thornton's ride back into the wilderness. Insofar as their suicidal action results in the perpetuation of their values through the staging of violence, the death of the wild bunch is sacrificial. Their values of fraternity and outlaw ethics survive in Thornton and his ragged bunch of outlaws *despite* the fact that the film has demonstrated the historical anachronism that those values embody.

And yet an important shift has taken place, and "the work" that the group of survivors at the end of *The Wild Bunch* have to do is not simply to terrorize the landscape. Sykes, the old man who Thornton finally joins up with (an ex-cohort of the bunch), says, "It ain't like it used to be, but it's better than nothin'." The men with him are from Angel's village, Mexicans whose outlaw status is that of revolutionary guerrillas, so it is Che Guevara on whom the heroism of the film is to some extent modeled.[35] The bunch do die out of loyalty to Angel, although not necessarily to his cause, and as Sykes's words suggest, the recourse to revolutionary action is a reluctant one. In this sense, the "necessity of violence" implicit in the heroes' moral code is ironically pushed to a limit at which it might accommodate revolutionary violence. Capitalism is represented in *The Wild Bunch* as sheer greed, which has totally corrupted the once-open frontier, and in order to preserve the frontier ideology of individualism, the narrative is literally forced into the defense of the oppressed and an embrace of history. The memory of Angel's village, a pastoral "folk" utopia, preserves the possibility of social change, and while it may be an ideal, it is nevertheless quite different than the culture that gave rise to these heroes.

This ending is in fact neatly balanced on the verge of allegory. The historical past is much more fully lost here than in *Bonnie and Clyde,* and the bodies that die over and over again in the "ballet" testify to the different historical time of representation. In the sheer length of the interruption that the massacre occupies, time is felt to be passing; narrative time and viewing time are radically collapsed into a present tense from which the mythic time of the American wilderness is absolutely excluded. The corpses of the aged heroes in their final dance are the very ruins of history. At the same time, there is the coda of regeneration, return, and transcendence awkwardly tacked onto the bloodbath. In the spectacle of the dance itself, the pleasure in fantasy that was noted in *Bonnie and Clyde* survives as the historical desire of the genre. In the autonomy that the death scene achieves through its excesses lies a resistance to the law of narrative and the law of history that demands the heroes' deaths. Their outlaw status takes on the proportions, however briefly, of a challenge to the norms of visual pleasure. And yet any radical potential of this discourse is, like the suggestion of revolutionary activity, ultimately enfolded within the structure of myth: the regeneration of the buddy system and American patriarchal individualism. It is most definitely "Che," the (beautiful) male revolutionary hero, and not Marx who lurks outside this Western.

Peckinpah leaves the viewer on the very threshold of history as it escapes from myth. As many critics have noted, the body counts and disabled men returning to the United States from Vietnam during this period rendered the myth of manifest destiny inadequate and dangerous. The depiction of death as a violation of the body was undoubtedly a response to the war experiences and media imagery of Vietnam, and yet it is a mistake to label a film like *The Wild Bunch* "an allegory of the My Lai Massacre."[36] The lingering faith in the image and its myths of pleasure, desire, and closure have nothing to do with the horrifying televisual imagery. In the very excess that verges on allegory, the possibility of regenerative violence remains in the desire to see, a desire encouraged by the careful choreography of cameras, bodies, and blood. Moreover, this vision is linked to an apocalyptic historiography in which social change resides, however awkwardly, with repetition. The cataclysm of the massacre is offset by the pressure of memory, visually represented in the final series of superimposed flashbacks.

It may be fair to say that narrative mortality subsists in *The Wild Bunch* as an allegory that remains closely knit with the mythology of death as closure. The dialectical thresholding that was identified in the films of Oshima and Godard cannot be realized here because of the realist codes that effectively close off the narrative from historical desires. The reading of narrative mortality in *The Wild Bunch* is only possible through criticism that is prepared to perform the mortification—to move beyond the pleasure principle of narrative realism. If this violence can be construed as allegorical ruins, it is not due to the slow motion itself, or to any other isolated technique employed by Peckinpah, but principally to the scale and duration of the violence. A causally organized narrative suddenly gives way to a non-linear sequence of shots in which time, space, and bodies are fragmented. It is to the extent that the violence against the characters extends to a violence to and of the image that the scene may be described as autonomous and allegorical.

On the other hand, *The Wild Bunch* demonstrates the reluctance of American culture to let go of the myths of regeneration that have informed the nation's narratives since the first encounter with native peoples. After John Wayne has saved Natalie Wood and scalped her Indian captor in *The Searchers,* he returns to the clean white screen of the desert. Natalie retreats into the darkness of history. In films such as *Bonnie and Clyde* and *The Wild Bunch,* the structure of apocalypse indicates a certain exhaustion of mythic, regenerative violence as valid social discourse, and yet the spectacular nature of these apocalypses tends to close off historical possibility.

The fetish made of the image and of vision itself, articulated as excess, contains (and organizes, in the form of slow motion) the violence to the body. The fragmentation of both image and body is disavowed in the pleasure of the spectacle. At the same time, the spectacular codification of excess prevents the recognition of ethnic difference (e.g., the Mexicans in *The Wild Bunch*) from fracturing the integrity of American mythology. Despite the enactments of catastrophe, the films end without forsaking the promise of the return of the spectacle and the replaying of the myths in imaginary form.

Nashville: The Show Must Explode

Of all the apocalyptic films made during this turbulent period in American history, *Nashville* comes closest to articulating a discourse of narrative mortality because it is a text that is most aware of its own limitations as a realist Hollywood film. The disintegration of American cultural myths and institutions is narrativized through the corruption of the country music industry, but equally important is the narrative structure of fragmentation and apocalypse. Lacking a central protagonist, subjectivity is dispersed over twenty-four characters. In Hollywood terms, this constitutes a radical decentering of narrative. The center is eventually restored in the enactment of death as closure, but it is a very empty center that is signified by the final death.

The possibility of this being a road movie of any kind is abruptly curtailed in the massive traffic jam of the second scene. This narrative "jamming" also pertains to the structure of desire, which is not that of romance or travel but strictly a desire for spectacle. The spectator of *Nashville* is implicated in a form of terminal pleasure, the ultimate apocalypse of which pertains beyond subjectivity to the "family" of American popular culture.

Wandering through a mountainous junkyard of cars in *Nashville*, Opal (Geraldine Chaplin) eulogizes the dead metal ("Without coffins ... their vast and vacant skeletons sadly sighing to the sky ...") into her tape recorder. She concludes: "Oh cars, are you trying to tell me something?" Her demand for meaning from these ruins is a futile demand for a mythic symbolic counterpart to mortality, a demand that is never met by the film. When Kenny eventually shoots country-music star Barbara Jean from the audience of a political rally at the Nashville Parthenon, the cynicism of the junkyard sequence is absent. The final death is represented neither in close-up nor slow motion, but from the detached perspective of a surprised witness or spectator.

The onstage assassination of Barbara Jean, typical of the apocalyptic violence of so many of the films of this period, should be considered within the context of the history of the spectacle of violence. This history includes the ritual sacrifices of ancient cultures, Roman circuses, public executions, tortures, and witch hangings, as well as organized sport.[37] Both Georges Bataille and René Girard have identified ritual sacrifice as a constitutive feature of social representation. Bataille points out that the taboo of death is lifted for religious reasons and describes its sacramental element:

> Only a spectacular killing carried out as the solemn and
> collective nature of religion dictates has the power to reveal
> what normally escapes notice.... divine continuity is linked
> with the transgression of the law on which the order of
> discontinuous beings is built. Men as discontinuous beings try
> to maintain their separate existences, but death, or at least the
> contemplation of death, brings them back to continuity.[38]

Whereas Bataille emphasizes the erotic element of violent sacrifice, Girard emphasizes its role in the maintenance of the social order. The circular and mimetic tendency of violence as vengeance can only be curtailed with the murder of a surrogate victim, of which Oedipus is an exemplary figure. Violence, for Girard, is a fluid phenomenon that "moves from one object to another" and, unless it is checked, can destroy an entire society through mimetic acts of vengeance. Justice systems have supplanted sacrifice only by institutionalizing vengeance; therefore the "purity" of sacrificial violence has been completely lost and "impure" violence festers beyond the facade of justice.[39]

"Sacrificial crisis" is, for Girard, the failure of ritual to organize difference in society. The unleashed violence of reciprocal killing is an infectious crisis of mimesis, into which sacrificial violence constitutes an inoculation of "difference." When the ritual can no longer contain the spread of the infection and the reciprocity of judicial institutions has been unmasked, sacrificial crisis emerges as a crisis of distinctions. Girard points to classical tragedy as a paradigm of sacrificial crisis:

> The tragedians portray men and women caught up in a form
> of violence too impersonal in its workings, too brutal in its
> results, to allow any sort of value judgement, any sort of
> distinction, subtle or simplistic, to be drawn between "good"
> and "wicked" characters.... It is the act of reprisal, the
> repetition of imitative acts of violence, that characterizes tragic
> plotting.[40]

Certainly the Christian myth of the Crucifixion and its related ritual of Communion serve as examples of "good" violence that is all but lost in contemporary society. And although Girard can be accused of an unacknowledged Christian orientation, his notion of sacrificial crisis remains pertinent to the representation of death in contemporary American film.[41] From *Intolerance* to *Platoon,* the Christian mythology of sacrifice has informed Hollywood melodrama.

It is Girard's theory of sacrificial crisis, rather than Bataille's theory of sacrificial redemption, that has been invoked more often with respect to American film of the 1970s.[42] Girard's conception of "equilibrium" derives from an analysis of the identity and doubling of the antagonists in Greek tragedy, and from the superstitions regarding twins and fraternal resemblance in primitive cultures. But it is equally true that the American myth of "regeneration through violence" is based in a structure of mimetic, reciprocal violence. Indeed, in *Bonnie and Clyde* and *The Wild Bunch,* the final eruption of violence is not only a repetition of previous instantiations, but is motivated by revenge; the cop, Hamer, taking revenge against Bonnie and Clyde by assuming their violence for himself, and "the bunch" taking action against Mapache for his violence against Angel. In fact, most of the violence in contemporary American film is grounded in a cyclical, repetitive schema of vengeance, epitomized perhaps in the *Dirty Harry, Cobra, Death Wish,* and *Lethal Weapon* narratives in which the hero-killers aspire to the enemy's capacity for violence. The endless regeneration of sequels to these movies indicates their ritualistic impetus, and also the failure of the ritual to stem the tide of violence.

In *Nashville,* sacrificial crisis is directly linked with the failures of the American political process and democratic institutions. Watergate is explicitly invoked by the film's only nondiegetic song, "Trouble in the U.S.A.," which accompanies Walker's limo and his entourage's approach to the Parthenon. The Hal Phillip Walker "Replacement

Party" van babbles throughout the film about the crises of American society. If the reprisal of moralistic nationalism during the Watergate crisis was the transcendence of nationhood over its corporal debasement, if "in the end it was the soul of the nation that suffered most from the assaults of Watergate,"[43] then it must be within a civil-religious context that the sacrifice of a surrogate victim is performed.

Although the final shooting comes suddenly in *Nashville,* it is foreshadowed in several ways, including Lady Pearl's eulogies for "The Kennedy Boys."[44] The overt trajectory of the film is toward the appearance of Hal Phillip Walker, the "presence" behind the aggressive Replacement campaign. Barbara Jean's death is therefore a double displacement: it is the spectacle for which the audiences inside and outside the film have been surreptitiously prepared, and if—as the film's/Walker's opening words claim—no one can escape politics, it is also the political assassination.

Girard is careful to distinguish between the fiction of tragedy and the reality of history,[45] and we too must distinguish between the killing of the "kings" in the sixties—John F. Kennedy, Martin Luther King, and Robert Kennedy—and Altman's "poetic" gesture. In sacrificial crisis, "pure" and "impure" violence can no longer be distinguished, which, for Girard, means that ritual can no longer function independently of history. "The difference between blood spilt for criminal purposes and ritual purposes no longer holds" (p. 43). The theme of assassination might therefore be understood as an attempt to restore the ritual of sacrifice, an attempt to recover a "pure" violence. Symptomatic of its failure is the mimeticism inevitably attributed to it, exemplified in the Hinckley case in which Ronald Reagan's would-be assassin was reputedly inspired by Scorsese's *Taxi Driver.* Since Kennedy and Oswald in 1963, political assassination in America has been a reciprocal form of violence, emblematic of "contagious, reciprocal violence [that] spreads throughout the community" (p. 49). If Watergate can be understood as a failure of ritual and the myth of the presidency, it may be the real crisis alluded to by Girard. Altman, along with his contemporaries, supplies the tragic, if ineffectual, response.[46]

In popular ("hyperdermic") communications theory, violence on TV and in movies causes violence in the world. In this lack of distinction between the commodification of violence in the mass media and its intensification outside representation, all violence is either caused or causing, involving all individuals in a "total system" of universal violence. Most psychosocial studies of the "effects" of screen violence fail to distinguish between documented and fictional violence.[47] In the literature on the effects of violence, the debate is between imitation and catharsis,[48] which is simply a difference between externalized and internalized mimesis. The repetitive replaying of televised violence — such as political assassinations, the Vietnam footage, the exploding Challenger space shuttle in 1986, and the beating of Rodney King in 1991 — locates random and disordered violence within the ritual of the nightly news.[49] In endless repetitions, real violence enters into a discourse of mimesis through the doubling of multiple broadcast signals and media representations.

Girard claims that "if tragedy was to function as a sort of ritual, something similar to a sacrificial killing had to be concealed in the dramatic and literary use of *katharsis*."[50] Sacrificial crisis involves a disintegration of catharsis into mimeticism. The ritual displacement of violence in sacrifice gives rise to a reciprocity that cannot differentiate between the real and the representation, or the pure and the impure functions of violence. In *Nashville,* this reciprocity that represses the articulation of difference and distinction is present as a perverse or extreme form of catharsis: the film's representation of spectatorship ultimately embraces the film's own spectator.

The function of violence in ritual is, for Girard, the production of the mythology of individual as victim; for Bataille, it is a transgression of the mythology of individualism. What for Girard is the mimetic tendency of violence in its reciprocity (vengeance narratives) and cathartic forms is, for Bataille, an erotic transcendence of alienation. Narrative mortality in *Nashville* allegorizes both aspects of sacrifice: the eroticism of the spectacle and the failure of mythic violence to purify the cultural order. Through the lack of mythic values in the rituals of country music in *Nashville,* the film engages with the post-Watergate lack of American faith in America. The final staged assassination effectively replaces critical fragmentation with the simulacrum of unity, which is both binding and erotic. In Altman's ironic mode, the sight of death is a guilty, shared pleasure.

Violence in *Nashville* does not employ a pattern of vengeance, but instead aspires to the random violence of terrorism and assassination. The staging of the violence and the nature of the victim point directly to the practice of sacrifice as a social ritual enacted as a response to social disintegration. While it is horrifying, it is also spectacular, fully operative within the structure of scopophilic and narratological desire that the film has set up. The crisis of Barbara Jean's death is, moreover, couched in the terms of a discourse of the family, in which her assassin emerges as the troubled son of the post-Watergate, post-Vietnam, dysfunctional American family.

During Barbara Jean's last song, "My Idaho Home," at the Parthenon (Nashville is referred to as the "Athens of the South"), Kenny unlocks his violin case. A series of reverse shots between him in the crowd and Barbara Jean (Ronnee Blakeley) on stage punctuates the number. The shots of Barbara Jean move in to tighter close-ups, and before she finishes the song a screen-size shot of the American flag is inserted. When she finishes, she dedicates the song to "Momma and Daddy," and Haven Hamilton (Henry Gibson) joins her onstage. Over an extreme long shot of the stage, from an angle higher than the crowd, the sound of a whizzing bullet is heard, followed quickly by Barbara Jean sinking suddenly to the floor. Cut to a long shot of Kenny in the crowd, firing his pistol several times in the direction of the stage. After Private Kelly wrestles him to the ground, Barbara Jean is already being carried off, most of her body obscured by the men around her.

Kenny and Kelly, both bland young men in their twenties played by (then) relatively unknown actors (i.e., not-stars), are most perfectly equated as audience members (figure 12). Although these two characters do not meet until the shooting, both have come to Nashville, apparently, simply to watch. They are especially attracted to Barbara Jean and Connie White—or, at least, Altman's reverse shots suggest an erotic specular bond between these young men and the two icons of femininity: the virginal Barbara Jean and the red-dressed, primping White. In other scenes of *Nashville,* particularly in the two parallel edited scenes of Sueleen's striptease and Tom's love song to four women, the erotic potential of performance is subverted. Tom's various women, and Sueleen as well, are represented as the victims of their own self-deceit and of the male gaze.

Kenny and Kelly, however, are less developed as characters; situated among the masses of bland white faces at Opryland, at the Opry Belle, and at the Parthenon, they are the generic desiring subjects on

Fig. 12. *Nashville*: Kenny (David Hayward), Private Kelly (Scott Glenn), and Opal (Geraldine Chaplin) — far right — with a bored audience at the Opry Belle. Publicity still courtesy of Cinémathèque Québécoise.

whom the commodification of Barbara Jean depends. All we know of either character is their relations with their mothers. Barbara Jean is the love object standing in for Private Kelly's mother, who "saved" her. For Kenny, she stands in for a hated mother whom he argues with, the mother who, it is implied in his brief telephone conversation, will not release him from her care. Kenny roams Nashville looking for someone on whom to unleash the vengeance packed up in his violin case. To the extent that he is doubled with Private Kelly,[51] his oedipal crisis of a love-hate relationship to his mother is extended to the traces of the Vietnam War—the vengeance of its servicemen against American nationalism: a love-hate relationship to the mother country.

The rhetoric of family unity underscores many of the film's key songs, including "For the Sake of the Children," sung by Haven Hamilton (Henry Gibson) at Opryland, and "My Idaho Home," which Barbara Jean sings right before she is shot. The assumptions about familial security in these numbers are in blatant contradiction to the various disintegrated families in the film. Martha/"L.A. Joan" disowns her family from the moment she arrives in Nashville in favor of the larger, nebulous family of country music. Kenny and Mr. Green (Martha's uncle) arrive at the Parthenon rally directly from Mrs. Green's funeral, which Martha fails to attend. The token nuclear family in the film is a classic suburban time bomb of repression, adultery, and miscommunication, epitomized in the father, Delmer, who cannot understand his two deaf children's sign language.

The family of country music is represented as one in which ethnic and racial difference is disavowed. The film's opening credit sequence underlines the difference between American black music and American white music in the crosscutting between two studios, where Haven Hamilton records an epic, patriotic, bicentennial dirge in one and a choir-gowned black gospel group enthusiastically praises the Lord in the other. Linnea's lily-white, weak-voiced presence among the rollicking gospel group reminds Opal of a woman missionary she met in Kenya. Over the course of the film, Opal denounces the disabled (Linnea's deaf children) as well as servants (Norman, the driver), and constantly assumes class, cultural, and racial differences that no one in the film except Wade, the black chef, addresses or acknowledges.

Tommy Brown, the black country singer whom Wade denounces as "an Oreo cookie," epitomizes the dissolution of cultural difference. (Wade is headed for Detroit, where the integrity of black music is supposedly secure in the form of Motown.) In other words, what is at issue here is not racism and discrimination but the sterile homogenization of American culture. In keeping with Hal Phillip Walker's first words of the film, that "no one escapes politics," the various singers are assembled at the Parthenon through their ignorance of govern-mental politics. None of them endorses the candidate, but they agree to perform for reasons of self-promotion, within the polemics of show-business politics. In Nashville, there is no category of "the Other" except for the relation between spectator and spectacle. In Haven Hamilton's rhetoric, long hair, rock and roll, and death simply "don't belong in Nashville."

Sexual difference, however, remains in place as a dominant cul-tural code, institutionalized in the fetish of the spectacle. Kenny's ac-tion is psychologically motivated by the eroticization of the mother figure of Barbara Jean, the oedipal threat that the down-home lyrics of "My Idaho Home" finally fail to contain. When Barbara Jean is shot, her long white dress is stained with blood: the color scheme makes it that much more spectacular. If the virgin and the lamb are sacred precisely because they are defenseless and incapable of revenge, Bar-bara Jean's stain marks her as a sacred victim. And yet Girard claims that the taboo against menstrual blood in primitive societies is symp-tomatic of the fear of cyclical violence. In the sacrificial ritual, blood is contained and controlled (placed in a chalice) and prevented from running wild. The fear of sexual violence represented by menstrual blood suggests to Girard "some half-suppressed desire to place the blame for all forms of violence on women."[52] Haven's white cowboy outfit is also stained with Barbara Jean's blood, indicating the un-checked flow of her bloody wound. In other words, she *looks* like the sacrificial victim, dressed like a bride in a false couple beside Haven, but her death is the apogee of impure violence, marked by repetition and mimesis, and ensuring further violence.

Given the cruel exploitation of women that goes on in the film — Linnea's, Sueleen's, and Mary's especially — Barbara Jean's death points to the patriarchal structure of the music industry and "show busi-ness" in general. As Catherine Clément observes, "All the women of opera die a death prepared for them by a slow plot, woven by furtive fleeting heros, up to their glorious moment: a sung death."[53] Barbara Jean's death fulfills the promise of her collapse in the opening scene, and also, insofar as she is pushed into her performances by her ma-nipulative manager-husband Barnett, it is an "answer" to the men who con Sueleen into performing a striptease. Sueleen's misguided ambition to be a singer is in fact wholly motivated by her worship of

Barbara Jean. To many of the characters in *Nashville,* Barbara Jean is a sacred being, an icon of American wholesomeness, and (echoing the mythic Judy Garland) she inevitably crumbles under the pressure of fulfilling such expectations. Her appeal to the mother-frustrated Kenny and Kelly further entraps her in an oedipal mythos of purity, so that her collapse under the phallic thrust of a pistol is also a rape of the inviolable mother.

The woman as spectacle and sacrificial victim dies, like Carmen, for the spectator whose complicity with the murderer is bound up in the desire for her "otherness" to remain other, separate: on the stage and on the screen.[54] If the structure of the folk musical typically breaks down the distinction between spectator and performer in the interests of a "total" community, Altman gives this larger familial configuration an oedipal dimension. "Producer and consumer [of music] are not separated by a proscenium, they are part of the same family,"[55] but the individuating audience shots that mark every performance in *Nashville* culminate in the son's violence against his parents. The "crisis of distinctions" from which the violence erupts exists not only in the enforced homogeneity of the country-music "family," but from the unrelenting mimesis of the film's representational strategies, which continually conflate audiences in the film with the audience of the film.

It is this self-referential aspect of *Nashville* that enables it to be read as more than an example of sacrificial crisis, but also as an allegory of narrative mortality that articulates the limits and boundaries of narrative realism. Girard's notion of ritual enables us to address *Nashville* as a cultural ritual that understands itself quite consciously as such. Altman's irony lies in the knowledge of sacrificial crisis; the recognition that American ideology is a civil religion without a sacred character precisely because it cannot organize racial, ethnic, or sexual difference, or contain the violence with which it is preoccupied. The film is likewise wrapped up in its own realist aesthetic, presented as an attraction, a spectacle as empty as that within the film, equally incapable of breaking out of the apparatus of entertainment.

In keeping with the violent conclusions of *Bonnie and Clyde* and *The Wild Bunch, Nashville* also channels the revelatory potential and sacred power of apocalypse into the spectacle itself. As a film about show business, it seriously questions the politics of image production,

stardom, and industries of appearances, but fails to step outside the
society of the spectacle. Indeed, the film's real crisis pertains to this impossibility. The desire for spectacle survives and is perhaps regener-
ated, the crowd having got a little more than it bargained for at the
Parthenon that afternoon, and the audience of *Nashville* receiving a
sense of closure — or at least an explanation for Kenny's presence in
the film — and an explanation for the spectacle of the film itself. Displacing the categories of desire and the mythic archetypes represented
by the open frontier or the romantic couple, the show, in *Nashville,*
"goes on." The mythic Other that is supplied by this spectacle of violence is the phenomenological other of the stage and the screen.[56]

In its opening credit sequence, *Nashville* announces its participation in consumer capitalism by introducing its stars in the manner of
a cheap TV record commercial. It sells itself precisely by collapsing the
difference between the actors and the "stars" they portray. Within
the narrative, the differences between the political campaign and the
entertainment spectacular, between politician and star, are diminished.
The viewer is in a sense the victim of this process of matching; in
the end, there is no one to blame, nor any lesson to have learned,
merely the satisfaction of seeing Kenny do what it is he had to do.
One of the most critical aspects of the Nixon period from the perspective of civil religion was that "the public tended to look upon
the Watergate scene in terms of bemused spectators watching a game
in process."[57] As Thomas Elsaesser puts it, in *Nashville* "the spectacle
consumes the spectator in the end,"[58] and the revolutionary moment —
the potential of catastrophe — becomes the revolutions of repetition:
a restoration of myth.

A key implication of Girard's theory is that repetition and homogeneity are the price of pacifism. This is the bleakness of Altman's
Nashville, its reduction of social choices to violence and nondifferen-
tiation. The only valid distinction in *Nashville* is that between spectator and spectacle, a relation that is articulated as a structure of passivity, out of which Kenny's gesture erupts. Although its revisionist
practice involves the articulation of difference, disharmony, and contradiction within the context of "the musical," the representation of
the audience in *Nashville* is homogeneous and undifferentiated.

The final Parthenon scene begins with a TV broadcast, from which

Altman's camera slowly pulls back to reveal a monitor on a picnic table at the scene. The announcer's voice-over about Walker continues over nontelevisual shots of the preparation of the Parthenon. The temporary identification of Altman's discourse with that of the TV (which is, of course, as fictional as the film in which it is contained) underlines the status of the film and its audience as equally culpable participants in the politics of the spectacle. There is no difference, no "moral" difference, between the production of the spectacle within the film and of the film itself; *Nashville*'s audience watches the same thing as the audiences, real and implied (e.g., the TV audience), within *Nashville*.

In the aftermath of the violence, Albuquerque, the aspiring singer (Barbara Harris), sings "It Don't Worry Me" with the gospel choir, a song that has been heard in fragments periodically throughout the film. The lyrics—"I don't care if I ain't free; It don't worry me / They say that life's a one-way street but it don't worry me"—are a perverse spiritual and an anthem to apathy. The crowd of mostly white families, happy to have something to watch, sway to the rhythm and the camera pans up, past the screen-size flag, to the sky. Before it does, a quick camera movement is inserted, which follows a female security guard wearing dark glasses moving through the crowd. It is an ominous and disconcerting shot, suggesting a fascistic underside to the passive, homogeneous Nashville crowd.

The very last shot of the film, a tilt up from a long shot of the Parthenon hung with red, white, and blue iconography to the sky, is not unlike those unbroken shots of sea and sky that Godard employs. The emptying out of the image has, in this case, a slightly different effect, however. As a loss of the spectacle of performance, the last trace of differentiation is diminished—that between spectator and spectacle. The passive gaze of the viewer, which has met its mirror image several times in the course of the film, finally encounters the giant gap of an empty sky.

Although the "awesome machinery of ritual" does *contain* the spectacle of violence, insofar as the show does go on, order is restored, and the crowd is pacified, the mythic content of the ritual is impossible to realize. The family of America is represented as a consuming "mass" in which sexual and racial differences are radically suppressed.

Haven Hamilton's claim that "this doesn't happen in Nashville" is clearly a pathetic attempt to restore an ideological facade over the explosion of contradiction and disharmony. In *Nashville*'s apocalyptic ending, the nonviability of either the mythic harmony of the family or the salvation of fidelity is registered. And yet a simple ideological reading can go only so far in explaining the function of death in the film. Ideological contradictions remain unaddressed, restricted to Opal's obsessive muttering, and the reconstitution of the spectacle and the show is unhampered by blood. The film has been criticized for Altman's failure to take a position on the "issues" raised by the narrative and for the ideological complicity of his unrelenting realist style.[59] But it is precisely this realism, continuous even through the unstylized representation of death, that produces an allegory of theatrical ritual.

The teleology of the musical putting on of the "show" becomes a discourse of fatalism through the social experience and recent memory of political assassination. At one point, Opal offers a "theory of assassination," which is that "people who carry guns are the real assassins. They stimulate other people who are perhaps innocent, but who pull the trigger." In keeping with Opal's theory, Kenny emerges as much a victim as does Barbara Jean. After the shooting, their bodies are carried off the scene in a short series of matched shots, both splayed with arms outstretched in Christ-like postures. Barbara Jean's death ties up all the narrative threads of *Nashville* by virtue of the presence of all the characters at the scene of the crime. Triplette's efforts to assemble all the singers in the film for Walker's rally constitutes the film's major connective story line. What we believed was an epic text is suddenly dramatic, in terms that are less Brecht's than Barthes's:

> Disclosure is then the final stroke by which the initial "probable" shifts to the "necessary": the game is ended, the drama has its denouement, the subject correctly "predicated" (fixed) ... what is shown is shown in one stroke, and at the end: it is the end which is shown.[60]

Narrative mortality is produced as the allegory of "the show" of American cultural homogeneity. It is allegory rather than critique because the extensive mortification of social values and public institutions remains within a circuit of realist image production in which the myth of the real is never really lost. The impotence of cultural criticism within a realist mode is itself allegorized within the film's mortification of entertainment. Barbara Jean's death is the final stroke in the film's demystification of the Hollywood musical. The movement of the narrative toward the grand finale of the political rally at the Parthenon emulates "the type of unifying finale which has characterized the folk musical ever since *Oklahoma!*"[61] However, if the dominant myths of the musical are those of romance, familial and national unity, and the ease with which an ideal world can be realized from the contradictory world of work and social differences, in *Nashville* every relationship is irrevocably fraught with contradiction and disharmony. This discursive tension is then radically subverted by the narrative strategies deployed to achieve a closing image of startling unification and frightening homogeneity.

The attempt to address violence and its representation is extremely difficult within a realist cinematic mode. Any representation is inevitably a contribution to the mimetic circuit that violence has inscribed in American culture. If "the mimetic attributes of violence are extraordinary,"[62] the ultimate sacrifice would be the image itself, but while representations of death often involve a dissolution of realism through such techniques as spatial fragmentation and temporal retardation, the image is ultimately "saved" by the very theme of death. The paradox implied in the Bazinian "myth of total cinema" is sustained through violence; Cawelti's "moral necessity" is displaced onto the image itself. The regeneration of the image after the sacrifice may be a restoration of "order"—a curtailment of the potential spread of violence—but it is also a resurrection of the binding principle of death, and the metaphoric, mimetic pleasure of narrative closure.

The transgressive potential of Bataille's theory of sacrifice is alluded to in the shock of the event, and yet it cannot be realized in the commodified form of narrative realism. Barbara Jean's violent death closes the story of a "good film," a performance of sacrifice, a theatrical gesture of meaningful meaninglessness. Narrative mortality is the allegory of a desire for sacrificial purification, the shocking discovery that this is the death that was wanted all along, but also the knowledge that such an act cannot be merely a performance but must also be part of history. The final shots of the film, the Saturday afternoon audience, restore the sign of history in an abrupt shift to a documentary mode. It is only because the death has been theatrical but not excessive (the special effects of *Bonnie and Clyde* and *The Wild Bunch* are conspicuously absent) that this shift to the "historical" audience is possible. The spectacle of death is effectively framed within a total system of consumption, which is characterized as a homogeneous "mass" that swallows the film's own spectator.

Even the eroticism of sacrifice is nullified within the system of commodified ritual. The dialectic of "continuity" and "discontinuity," which Bataille identifies in ritual sacrifice, is given over entirely to the ongoing facade of "the show must go on." The political transformation that Hal Phillip Walker has called for is, of course, never going to take place — in his populist terms or any other. The "realistic" representation of violence in *Nashville* co-opts narrative mortality within the codes of performance instrumental to the maintenance of the entertainment industry. The gender codes, as we have seen, also inscribe the death within the institution of the oedipal family, refiguring political violence as domestic violence.

In contrast, in *The Wild Bunch,* in which violence becomes a form of writing, an inscription of excess within a sacrificial mode, the necessity of historical change is implied. (The violence of that massacre is also "staged" insofar as the heroes shoot from Mapache's "podium" into the audience of the village.) Its eroticism contains the shock necessary for historical imagination, even if the film's utopian ideation is in turn mystified as revolutionary heroism. The spectacular departure from realism at the end of *Bonnie and Clyde* offers no spectatorial position other than empathetic identification with the dying characters. The "shock" of discontinuity is thereby entirely closed off by coherent subjectivity, limiting the film's historical discourse to endless repetition. Although *Nashville* also succumbs to repetition and homogeneity, history is not mystified but visibly "emptied" through the event of sacrificial crisis. The blue sky at the end is "not the blue sky at the end of the *Wizard of Oz*";[63] it has no utopian dimension, nor any critical perspective, but simply drains the spectacle of the residue of violence.

In *Nashville,* the sacred character of sacrifice is mortified in a narrative in which death as closure becomes a spectacle in and for itself. The erotic power of sacrifice is alluded to on several levels, but the film is only an allegory of transgressive desire, fully conscious of the limits of Hollywood realism and the society of the spectacle. Barbara Jean's death cannot be rationalized and Kenny's action is unpremeditated, and yet it fulfills the viewers' expectation of spectacle — collapsing performance, assassination, and political discourse onto a single falling body. As such it suggests that the narrative teleology is itself a "ruin" of a lost myth of closure, an arbitrary adherence to a convention of desire. Girard's claim that a desire for violence in and for itself informs such a myth seems to be borne out by *Nashville*:

> The notion of an instinct (or if one prefers, an impulse) that propels men toward violence or death — Freud's famous "death wish" — is no more than a last surrender to mythological thinking, a final manifestation of that ancient belief that human violence can be attributed to some outside influence — to gods, to fate, to some force men can hardly be expected to control.[64]

Perhaps the random violence of terrorism and assassination, like the car accident, is an uncontrollable, infectious *disease* of violence that the enactment of ritual sacrifice can only reduplicate. Jean Baudrillard claims that "we live in a situation where cataclysm never occurs. We live in a situation of only virtual catastrophes which are *eternally* virtual."[65] Apocalypse, in other words, has been mystified in sacrificial crisis, and is rendered impotent. In postmodern culture, the visionary dimension of apocalypse reveals nothing but its own status; and this is its catastrophe. The utopian potential of narrative mortality is to grasp this catastrophe as a passage, a bridge or threshold onto another history, one in which memory serves as the guarantee of transformation and temporal difference.

It may be that *Nashville* goes as far in this direction as it is possible for a Hollywood film to go; that is, the dialectic of memory and desire, loss and expectation, upon which narrative mortality depends, can only take place in the cinema with an allegorical treatment of the image itself. Although in *Nashville* many of the actors and actresses write their "own" songs, the distinction between actor and character is by this means further blurred and not — as in Wenders's and Godard's use of performance — incorporated as a discursive fragmentation. Although the star system is in a sense allegorized by stars "playing" stars, the industrial apparatus that such a system supports is actually reinforced. The visionary impetus of Benjamin's "dialectical images" depends on a mortification of the symbolic desires on which visual pleasure feeds. What we have seen in the three films discussed here is a refusal to forego such pleasure and a consequent compromise of apocalyptic vision. With nothing really lost after all, there is nothing to redeem.

CONCLUSION

THE SENSELESSNESS
OF ENDING

● ─────────────────────────────────────

> I know the delirium of mourning. When the dead one with all its gigantic
> body invades the heart of the one left alive, a savage explosion drives
> the living to obliterate all limits, in a dangerous intoxication.
> —CATHERINE CLÉMENT[1]

Many of the films discussed in this book end with images of sky
and water, blue expanses broken only by a horizon or a cloud
(*Le Mépris, Pierrot le fou, Lightning Over Water, Nashville*). Visibility
itself is stripped to its most essential form of seeing, and yet there is
nothing to be seen. If "nothing" is the threat of death, it is also the
potential of narrative to create a void, a desire for meaning. In the
empty image of sea, sky, or both, nature provides the background
for a historiography of catastrophe in which nothing and everything
happens. Natural history is, for Benjamin, a history of decay and
transience, privileging the present moment as being always at the
limit of history. The film spectator, who is left with a closing image of
emptiness and perceives it as a ruin of visibility, may therefore "see"

the condition of the cinema, and also the condition of historical imagination.

These allegories of eternity demonstrate the impossibility of representing eternity, and they do so through a radical form of address. Insofar as the frame is empty, without being blank, point of view is made redundant. The last shot of *Night Moves* (Penn, 1975) is an extreme high angle of a boat in which the protagonist is left to die turning slow circles on a blue ocean; the name on the back of the boat is "Point of View." The otherness of the screen and the spectacle returns the gaze as a reflection of the projector beam, so that the loss of the image and the lost transparency of the image are redeemed in an intersubjectivity of looks. Although this formulation, drawn from Benjamin, may have mystical overtones, it is also true that the "look" produced by these images exists in a present tense. The allegorical representation of history is grounded in an experience of the present because it is only possible to imagine the history of the future on the blank screen of eternity.

Despite the intertextual fragmentation of these films, their discourse of history may be more properly modernist; it becomes "postmodern" through the mortifying gaze of allegory. Fredric Jameson notes that the allegorical method "is very much what is demanded and mobilized by the periodizing schema of the modernism/postmodernism break as such."[2] The break between the modern and the postmodern may, in other words, be accomplished through allegorized reading, rather than any formal properties of the text. It is, moreover, really more of a fracture than a break. Narrative mortality becomes increasingly irrelevant as an interpretive structure in films like Godard's *King Lear* (1987), a film that "shoots itself in the back," or Atom Egoyan's *Family Viewing,* which shoots itself in the living room.

Frank Kermode claims that "the sense of an ending" is "endemic to what we call modernism," as is the perception of historical time as "eternal transition, perpetual crisis."[3] Now that another fin de siècle is upon us, we need to apprehend the limits of modernism. As mortality has become a virtual function of representation, violence in contemporary culture has become disturbingly banal. Apocalypse has been rendered boring through repetition, and in the age of AIDS apocalyptic fantasies have given way to a more politicized view of mortality, as in Derek Jarman's *Edward II* (1991). The cynical apprehension of narrative mortality is epitomized in films such as *Tetsuo* (Shinya Tsukamoto, 1989) and *The Falls* (Peter Greenaway, 1980), films that sustain their ironic and apocalyptic discourses from start to finish, ending at fairly arbitrary points of narrative exhaustion. Closure is completely robbed in this postmodern cinema of both imminence and immanence.

The films with which this book is concerned contain the indices of sacrificial crisis, but they cannot be characterized as either modern or postmodern. They might be said to occupy a certain threshold between modernist desire and its postmodern annihilation. Although they may be open to various postmodern readings, narrative mortality persists as the trace and limits of modernism within the postmodern. As Benjamin puts it,

> Once modernism has received its due, its time has run out.
> Then it will be put to the test. After its end it will become
> apparent whether it will ever be able to become antiquity.[4]

Benjamin's fascination with the limits of modernism was a relentless effort to conceive the present as historical, and to conceive the future neither as "progress" nor as utopian, but as the obverse side of memory, as a space of desire and imagination. The reading of these films as allegories of narrative mortality may be described as an attempt to redeem the historiography of modernist film practice. At the same time, it is evident that the filmmakers themselves—Lang, Oshima, Godard, Wenders, and Altman—locate themselves at the limits of various modernisms. Beyond these limits, narrative mortality is still legible in postmodern cinema, though in significantly altered forms.

The Consumption of Transgression

Wild at Heart (David Lynch, 1990) and *The Cook, the Thief, His Wife and Her Lover* (Peter Greenaway, 1989), made more than twenty years after the bloody ballets and tableaux of Vietnam-era cinema, suggest that history in postmodern crisis cinema has become a discourse of decay and decadence, which the aesthetic practice of auteurs such as Greenaway and Lynch is designed to purify. A comparison of these two films with *Weekend* (Godard, 1968) will indicate how narrative mortality appears within the postmodern aesthetic of excess. In

Wild at Heart, Sailor and Lulu come across a wounded girl in a still-smoldering car accident who is more concerned about her lost pocketbook and credit cards than her dead boyfriend and bloody head. In *Weekend,* Corinne emerges from a car wreck screaming "Help! My Hermes bag!" Perhaps this intertextual motif is an incidental point of contact between two films that might seem to have very little in common. Where Godard's film ends with the titles "End of Story/End of Cinema," Lynch's ends with a deus ex machina of redemption. And yet both are road movies featuring multiple fire and car accidents, both are about a couple, a dead father and a bad mother, and both narratives are constantly interrupted by stories and corpses. *The Cook, the Thief, His Wife and Her Lover* is divided, like *Weekend,* into days of the week and (like the 1967 film) shifts to the French Revolution for its codification of time. It also shares with *Weekend* a cannibalistic ending and an anti-Hollywood ambition.[5] Historical discourses figure quite critically in both *Wild at Heart* and *The Cook, the Thief,* but there is a sense in which violent excess and spectacular death are closely linked to a failure of narrative to redeem history.

The respectively cold and hot performances of *The Cook, the Thief* and *Wild at Heart* are highly stylized. And yet both these films are centered around a core of believability, a sign of authenticity anchoring all of their respective excesses, in the discourse of romance and true love. Both Greenaway and Lynch are engaged in a resanctification of decadent and debased worlds, Greenaway through the iconography of the garden and the ritual of Communion, Lynch resorting to a mélange of Elvis and the Wizard of Oz, an American iconography of pleasure and resurrection. In both cases, this truth-value is eroticized, its indubitability ironically guaranteed by its invisibility. The bodies of the lovers in both films are the harbors of goodness; and intercourse in secret, secluded spaces is the only escape from the evil of their unbearable, inhospitable worlds.

Historical references in *The Cook, the Thief* operate on so many levels that they are reduced to an accumulation of signifiers with little allegorical potential. If the library contains the traces of the French Revolution, the parking lot is Margaret Thatcher's England. A seventeenth-century Dutch painting of bourgeois mastery hangs over the dining room, and on yet another textual axis is a characterological figura-

tion of the French Revolution. The history of the European bourgeoisie is thus alluded to in a virtually random fashion. The dispossessed kitchen staff may be liberated from their feudal existence at the
end of the film, and yet Albert's death is brought about not by revolution but by an act of vengeance drawn from seventeenth-century
English drama. Greenaway's refusal to distinguish between bourgeois
greed and the historical terror performed against it is symptomatic of
his allegorical technique, in which history becomes discursive style.
The ideological significance of the Girondist and Jacobin periods of
the French Revolution loses its impetus when they are collapsed into
a single character (Alfred). Greenaway's purpose may be to reinvest
the ruins of history with new meaning, which is indeed the potential
of Benjaminian allegory, and yet the effect is a redemption of bourgeois cultural consumption and mastery.

Greenaway is, in Benjamin's words, "at home in the fall." *The Cook,
the Thief* avoids the existential anxiety and nostalgia of modernist art
cinema and, despite the reflexivity, there is no crisis of representation.
The crisis is, rather, one of aesthetics. The "hell" that is depicted in
The Cook, the Thief is not the void that lies beyond representation,
because this "void" is filled by the aesthetics of consumption; the
signified "content" of romantic love and good taste is preserved in
the fetish of the lover's corpse. Michael's body, as it is finally glazed
and garnished by the cook, is revealed in a close-up lateral tracking
shot, not unlike those that have displayed the laden tables of culi-
nary materials and products throughout the film.

The lover's body is a metaphor for the body of the film; an objet
d'art prepared by a master craftsman.[6] In the process of remystifying
a debased culture, Georgina's feminist vengeance is displaced onto
Michael's prairie oysters: the male genitals perched cockily atop the
corpse like a flag. The male body is finally raised to the status of those
beautiful women's and children's bodies that Albert has so cruelly dis-
figured and symbolically castrated. Although the narrative structure
of *The Cook, the Thief* takes the form of apocalypse, its alliance of purification and aestheticization redeems the transient body of history
with the aura of art. The scatological is cleansed with the pleasures
of the erotic body, the mortal flesh itself is redeemed as good taste,
and the Rights of Man are given visual and carnal representation.

The body of the film, like the body of the lover, is a "cooked" image, one prepared and served up for the purpose of visual consumption, a signifier of desire that is indeed inaccessible because it is only the look of death: like the black food that Richard (the cook) serves, it is not death itself. And yet we are left again on the verge of allegory because this ironic consciousness is ultimately lost to the ritual of film narrative, the desired image of the desired end. For Bataille, the erotic importance of beauty is its befoulment, and the power of death is its ugliness, a power of which it is robbed in the final moments of *The Cook, the Thief*. Greenaway, like the cook, has made death safe for visual consumption by transforming mortal flesh into a sacrament of moral justice, and, given the film's sumptuous production values, he has indeed charged a lot for it. The image of sacrifice in this film has the effect of closing history off from that which cannot be represented, which for Girard is the sacred, and for Benjamin the theological and the difference of historical change.

Connie's pleasure in eating her husband in the final shots of *Weekend* suggests that the ritual of cannibalism has caused that film's violence to be reappropriated by bourgeois culture and the aesthetics of "good taste." The film itself, however, remains a "bad" film, in bad taste, transgressing the conventions of visual consumption. Transgression, of course, often only confirms the social codes that are broken, and ritual sacrifice is the institutionalization of such transgression. But Bataille's transgression, or the properly surrealist dynamic,[7] involves the eroticization of death, the pleasure of murder, and it is this potential that is subversively linked with Third World revolution in *Weekend*. The film itself is only an allegory of pleasure and desire, of which the conflagrations of smashed cars are the signifiers. The body of the film itself, signified by the rabbit, whose lifeless eye returns our gaze as fixedly as those of the immigrant laborers, is the auteur's sacrifice and signature of historical transformation.

The closure of representation is also the theological force informing *Wild at Heart,* although here it is American popular culture that is redeemed from a hell ruled by a monstrous mother. Death in *Wild at Heart* is not in itself allegorical, for it is inscribed quite securely within an ideology of failure. It only happens to other people, which, in *Wild at Heart,* includes a black man, a number of anonymous strangers, Johnnie the incompetent detective, Lulu's cuckolded father,

and the very bad Willem Defoe character, Bobby Peru. Sailor's redemption at the end of the film by the good (white) witch is more
fully allegorical, especially when he incarnates Elvis's immortality,
singing "Love Me Tender" on the hood of Lulu's car. The iconographic
artifice of *Wild at Heart*, epitomized in Sailor's repeated comment
about his snakeskin jacket and its representation of his identity,
involves a redemption of signification and a recovery of meaning.
Sailor's "identity" is finally secured through the mythology of family
romance.[8]

Lynch is also preoccupied with forcing the viewer to look at transgressive imagery of the body, from grotesque deformities and accident victims to vomit and disabilities, symptoms of the "hell" in which
Sailor and Lulu find themselves. The discourse of the grotesque
reaches its climax in *Wild at Heart* with the death of Bobby Peru,
and yet the decapitation and amputation of this scene is "contained"
within the generic conventions of the splatter film. Tania Modleski
has argued that the "terror of pleasure" fundamental to the horror film
may constitute an "other" aesthetic in postmodern culture. She suggests that "perhaps the contemporary artist continues to be subver-
sive by being nonadversarial in the modernist sense, and has returned to our pop cultural past partly in order to explore the site
where pleasure was last observed."[9] Certainly this return is accomplished in *Wild at Heart*, with the effect of transforming crisis into
an aesthetic of excess, but is this recovery of pleasure really worth
the price?

Modleski evokes the terms of Benjaminian allegory, and yet where
she, like Benjamin, is concerned with historical difference and the
potential of postmodernism to break quite radically with the cultural
assumptions of modernism, *Wild at Heart* fails to realize this potential because of its cultural affirmation and closure of history. The work
of the text blurs the distinction between "classic" American popular
culture and the 1990s on all levels. From cars and costume to rock
music, the difference between the 1950s and the 1990s is lost to the
universalizing discourse of Americana. If the radical potential of allegory is the inscription of history in the ruins of signification, these
ruins become the foundation in *Wild at Heart* for a mystification of
American cultural history. The representation of death and violence
does not open up representation onto the void of the future, or mark

the limits of representation, but becomes the signifier of a weirdness that the film manages to bring under control through a discourse of belief.[10]

In *Weekend,* car accidents and traffic jams are signifiers of the ruins of desire in commodity culture, and the trajectory of the film is toward the preautomotive realm of nature for a redemption of historical desire. The traffic jam at the end of *Wild at Heart* is a symbolic desire for progress in a stagnant culture, and Sailor and Lulu fulfill this desire through an allegory of resurrection. Their romantic reunion — with child — is a transcendence of the stagnation. If the film's trajectory is toward Los Angeles, it is a Western in which the morality of the wilderness has been fully eclipsed by the civilizing force of the nuclear family.

In their capitulation to resurrection, both *Wild at Heart* and *The Cook, the Thief* fail to realize the historical potential of allegory. The allegories of these films "fill out and deny the void in which they are represented, just as, ultimately, the intention does not faithfully leap forward to the idea of resurrection."[11] Neither Lynch nor Greenaway can allow allegory to go away "empty-handed" either. Evil in Benjamin's *Trauerspiel* "means precisely the non-existence of what it presents ... evil as such reveals itself to be a subjective phenomenon,"[12] but in these films evil remains a necessary characteristic of worlds rife with class and racial tensions. Class and race may not themselves be demonized, but they are key characteristics of the hellish worlds within which white bourgeois couples can take on the aura of transcendence.

Perhaps what neither Lynch nor Greenaway fully appreciates is the effect of narrativity and its powers of closure on their allegorical, painterly imagery. Despite the historical regression and bodily transformation that takes place in their work, neither one is able to reach back to the prehistoric of the profilmic material. Their refusal to violate representation to this extent constitutes a closure of history and cinema within the limits of the visible and knowable. Their allegorical stylistics inscribe a desire to transgress these limits, but the body of the film itself will not be sacrificed. In both the European and the American contexts, it may be authorship itself that is being preserved from the threat of history. The discourse of gender in the two films suggests that the crisis at hand is one of male mastery, and the abstraction of belief that the narratives strive to salvage from the ruins of representation is, on some level, a belief in patriarchy.

In the end, their transgressive imagery is not so different from the excessive violence of *Bonnie and Clyde* or *The Wild Bunch,* still contained within the limits of a spectacle that is now disguised as the aesthetic, auteurist production of images. For both directors the body is the site of transience, semiosis, and transformation, and the most potent symptoms of decay are Lynch's flies on vomit and Greenaway's maggot-ridden meat. And yet the body is also eroticized, the decay corrected, and historical temporality closed off in the symbolization of transcendence, resurrection, and immortality. This is also true of Penn's and Peckinpah's genre revisionism, in which myths of romance and nostalgia are inseparable from the spectacular bodies of actors and actresses: the repressed homoeroticism of *The Wild Bunch* and the destiny of the couple in *Bonnie and Clyde* are only realized in the fantastic and violent destruction of those bodies. The discourses of historical utopia in the earlier films have, however, decayed into the ruins of theatrical settings for narratives of redemption in the late 1980s, and are thereby quite incapable of being themselves redeemed.

At the "end of cinema" in 1967 Godard offers a demonstration that the historiographic potential of cinematic allegory depends on the temporal relation between the filmic discourse and that which was filmed. Of course cinema had to continue to be made, and while Godard has continued to work more or less within this historical dialectic, as have other filmmakers, one finds in the films of Lynch and Greenaway a capitulation of transgression to transcendence. In this respect, they perpetuate the desperate auteurism of Wim Wenders, without his preoccupation with film history and ontology. *Weekend* may be a dead film, insofar as its political rhetoric is a somewhat naïve appreciation of postcolonial culture, and yet its use of violence is in the service of a historiography that, in Benjamin's terms, conceives the present tense as the death of the past.

Fin de Millennium Dystopias

In the mid 1990s, the body counts of contemporary cinema seem to be on the rise, on a number of a different fronts. The increased popularity of Hong Kong cinema in North America indicates an expanding international market for highly stylized violence predicated on thin narrative premises. The proliferation of martial arts and action-hero films and TV series have spawned renewed debates about media violence. On the margins of these developments, a number of independent filmmakers have produced dystopian responses to the excess of social and media violence. Ostensible critiques of the macho culture of violence, these films challenge the spectator to participate in sadomasochistic viewing experiences, with varying degrees of success in distancing themselves from the exploitation with which they flirt.[13] The "end of the cold war" and accompanying proclamations of the "end of history" at the end of the century have brought renewed significance to questions of terminality, closure, and narrative mortality, both in Europe and North America. Both continents have witnessed extreme racial and ethnic violence erupt in the context of the New World Order declared in the aftermath of communism.

Two of the recent "ultraviolent" films merit consideration as indications of yet another development of narrative mortality as a politics of representation.[14] Less consumable than the films of either Greenaway or Lynch, *C'est arrivé près de chez vous* (Rémy Belvaux, André Bonzel, and Benoît Peolvoorde, 1991 — *Man Bites Dog* is the English release title) and *Henry: Portrait of a Serial Killer* (John McNaughton, 1986, released 1990) explore psychotic personalities in realist styles that are evocative of the documentary impetus of the New Wave cinemas. They are, however, entirely fictional. Stripped of any allegorical sense of history, they rework narrative mortality as an infinite present tense.

In fausse-vérité style, Ben, the psycho hero of *Man Bites Dog,* talks incessantly to the camera, explaining the techniques of serial killing and boasting arrogantly about his atrocities. Benoit Peolvoorde's virtuoso performance and the film's mastery of direct cinema conventions lends the violence a surreal quality.[15] In black and white, the blood and gore are easily accommodated into the "everyday" reality of Ben's suburban existence. However, as the nonlinear structure of the film moves from one setting to another with little motivation, the murders are often emphasized by violent cutting. The shock effect of the random killing consistently interrupts the banal suburban reality, which nevertheless absorbs the murders by allowing Ben to continue his killing spree unchallenged.

The narrative continuity of *Man Bites Dog* is provided only by Ben's omnipresent face in front of the camera, but the film crew's escalating complicity with his actions lends the narrative a teleological thrust. Ben and the filmmakers are eventually shot by an unknown hand. Someone is tracking Ben throughout the film, although the details of this "other" story remain outside the purview of the narrative, which refuses to explain anything more than meets the eye. The film's final shot, a canted angle from the perspective of the dead cameraman, evokes the ending of *The State of Things*. This shot, of the crumbling walls of an abandoned building, is more radically empty than Wenders's though, especially since we never actually see the cameraman's face in the film (although we do hear his voice). The static shot is held until the film "runs out." Narrative mortality emerges here as a surrealist discourse of shock, disruption, and violent transgression that has the capacity of emptying cinematic representation of its pretensions of realism and closure. We are far from Wenders's anxieties of subjectivity and identity, and, as the French title's second-person address suggests, the film constitutes an assault on the spectator.

One scene in particular seems to depict the crisis of spectatorship that narrative mortality, as a discourse of believability, negotiates. At one point in the film, Ben is hospitalized after a boxing accident. The filmmakers and Ben's friends hold a small birthday party for him when he comes home, and Rémy (the "director") presents Ben with a gun holster as a gift. After putting it on, Ben turns his back to the group, swings around, and shoots the man at the other end of the table, provoked by minor jealousy and insecurity when the man whispers to Ben's girlfriend behind his back. A moment of silence follows, while the party guests, splattered with blood, contemplate the abrupt turn of events. For the spectator, it opens a space in the narrative flow for someone to call Ben's bluff, to call the film's bluff, and plead for an end to the carnage. The camera rests on the two women, Ben's girlfriend and his mistress, who flank the dead man, but the moment passes, and both party and film recover their momentum. The film depicts a world where no one is safe unless they fill a subservient role to Ben's monstrous ego. His bigotry identifies the discourse of power as white chauvinist supremacy, and allusions to the holocaust (Ben dumps his victims in a reservoir, which drains to reveal heaps of corpses) historicize the narrative as the persistence of a historical nightmare.

As a critique of media violence, *Man Bites Dog* goes too far beyond the scope of believability and good taste to make an "ethical" intervention into yellow journalism. By plunging the viewer into a dystopian realm of gratuitous violence, it suggests instead that mortality is a critical function of narrative realism. Any critique of violence must first come to terms with the techniques of realist representation that the media exploits. The challenge of wedging death and realism apart is as difficult as facing up to "Ben" and his control over the film. That he is not, in the end, brought to justice, but killed by the specter of vengeance that lurks within the ruined landscape, suggests that the terror he has personified is a historical terror. The film cannot imagine another history, or provide an end to the terror it depicts, but this total failure may in fact be the means by which it is most allegorical, subjecting history absolutely to the natural logic of decay.[16]

Like *Man Bites Dog, Henry: Portrait of a Serial Killer* opens with horrifying imagery of blood and violence, in this case color tableaux of female corpses. Again, apocalyptic narrative conventions are deflected by sustaining a high level of violence throughout this film, although here, the full gamut of horror-film techniques is deployed: eerie music, camera movements, and point-of-view editing to build suspense at critical moments.

The detailed realism of *Henry* locates his "portrait" within the historical context of a poor Chicago neighborhood, and Henry's "problem" is analyzed as an oedipal nightmare of sexual abuse. Instead of offering any kind of therapeutic cure, though, the film spins out Henry's misogyny as an endless series of dead bodies. Henry and his friends Otis and Becky, who he draws into his routine of random violence, are victims of poverty, isolated within an insular world of incest, racism, and institutional neglect. The big battered 1970s cars that Otis and Henry drive are the film's most potent images of the ruins of capitalism within which the serial killer plies his trade. In the virtual absence of any sign of the law, Henry's confidence in his work distinguishes the film from any other American thriller. With no moral authority to lose, this film, like *Man Bites Dog,* deploys narrative mortality as a discourse of infinite repetition, in which death serves only to distinguish killer from victim. It becomes a mechanism of power cut off from any historical necessity. The excess and repetition rob death, finally, of its redemptive potential in narrative, as the reality test is repeatedly tried and relentlessly passed. The final shot of *Henry,* a suitcase (which we assume conceals Becky's body) sitting on the side of the highway, reduces the banality of nothingness that we have seen in so many other films to trash.

Because we do not see Becky's murder, the heavy, blood-soaked suitcase makes demands on our imagination that the opening imagery of *Henry* prevents. It is a powerful image precisely because of the absence of a body. Corpses in this film, especially female corpses, are robbed of any allegorical potential. Stylized by color, lighting, and camera movements, the opening tableaux can only represent violence against women in bold symbolic fashion. Symbolism finally gives way to allegory in the film's final shot, but there is no sacrifice here, nor anything to redeem. Henry's world is governed by a power greater than his own, and "believability" is a believability only in the invisible corpse that sustains the image. The image is not freed by the representation of death, but weighted down by the burden of reality.

Henry and Otis shoot one of their most vicious atrocities — the desecration of a domestic scene (also the height of violence in *Man Bites Dog*) — on video, and Otis watches the footage at home over and over again. Instrumental to the dystopian imagination of history in these films is the way they are cut off from the profilmic. Both films incorporate filmmaking practices — low-end, low-tech technology operated by fictional characters — that produce a second level of reality within each text. Not only is this second order of reality equally fictional, but the filmic gaze that is inscribed in these films is characterized as the desire to see death and violence. This thorough mortification of the gaze finally aligns the art-film spectator with the snuff-film spectator in a dialectical relationship.

Benjamin describes the surrealists as having opened up an "image sphere" in which political materialism and physical nature share the inner man, the psyche, the individual ... with dialectical justice, so that no limb remains unrent. Nevertheless — indeed, precisely after such dialectical annihilation — this will be a sphere of images and, more concretely, of bodies.... [The surrealists] exchange, to a man, the play of human features for the face of an alarm clock that in each minute rings for sixty seconds.[17]

In the serial-killer films' dangerous evocation of the snuff film, the unfilled desires of surrealist practice have become monstrous. The depiction of an eternal present tense is truly alarming, and yet the representation of "now" is divorced from any historical index of the image. The repressed violence of *Beyond a Reasonable Doubt* has returned with a vengeance that annihilates even the dynamics of catastrophe. A mortification of visibility itself takes place in these films, which come even closer than *Weekend* to apprehending the "end of cinema." The utopian thrust of the New Wave cinemas is inverted by way of a narrative mortality turned in on itself, consuming cinematic pleasure and narrative desire in dystopian affirmations of cinematic realism.

The Gender of Narrative Mortality

Writing about *Reservoir Dogs* (Tarantino, 1992), Amy Taubin comments, "It's the privilege of white male culture to destroy itself, rather than to be destroyed by the other."[18] Narrative mortality emerges in the latter part of the twentieth century as a partner to feminist discourse, clearing the way for cinematic representation that might redeem the annihilated desires of so many female characters and spectators. Its manifestation in postmodern cinema as a discourse very specifically aligned with male violence indicates that the traces of modernism are the traces of a "boy's" cinema in decay, and that this deterioration may have been reified in the perpetual delay of its final disappearance. *Reservoir Dogs,* in which no woman characters appear at all, revives a motif from *Double Indemnity* in which the time of the film is the time of a man bleeding to death. The femme fatale may be reduced to a single bullet from an anonymous woman (who is herself killed by her victim, Tim Roth/Mr. Orange), but her abstract disembodiment confirms her necessity to this cinema of decay.[19] Mary Ann Doane has suggested that

> as soon as the relation between vision and knowledge becomes unstable or deceptive, the potential for a disruption of the given sexual logic appears. Perhaps this disruptiveness can define, for feminist theory, the deadliness of the femme fatale.[20]

The triumph of the riddling question of the Sphinx in the fractured story of Oedipus implicit in *Beyond a Reasonable Doubt* is made possible by the virtual abstractions of the femme fatale as a form of textual logic. It is ultimately over the dead body of Patty/Emma that the contradictions of capital law and "classical Hollywood cinema" are mortified and deauthorized. Both Godard and Oshima mobilize the narrative potential of double suicide for historical desires. The woman's body remains the image of desire, but, in the transposition from melodrama to allegory in *Cruel Story of Youth,* that body becomes the sign of a desire for social change and not sexual or emotional fulfillment. Mako's abortion in the middle of the narrative becomes an allegorical loss of family and motherhood, a sign of the ruins of Japan, which are not mourned but mortified.

For his part, Godard's women display a proximity to popular culture constitutive of modernist cultural anxieties. The lack of distance between women and their culture (Bardot is discovered sunbathing with an open book resting on her naked posterior) is characteristic of countless theories of mass media — including Benjamin's, as we have seen.[21] And yet, from the perspective of narrative mortality, Bardot in *Le Mépris* and Karina in *Pierrot le fou* effectively destabilize the existential anxieties of their male counterparts. The double deaths that end each film evoke a romance of double suicide that confronts the meaninglessness of modernist suicide. It is by way of the desires of the women that the narratives are able to transcend the end of history and imagine a different future.

In contrast, the cruel disfigurement of Faye Dunaway in *Bonnie and Clyde,* tied to the gearshift, and the assassination of Barbara Jean/Ronnee Blakeley in *Nashville* curtail any redemptive potential by submitting totally to the tyranny of narrative realism, in which the spectacle of violence is a violence predominantly against women. Wim Wenders's inability to represent women or work within romantic narrative structures is constitutive of his inability to "go home"—or remember German history. As a perpetual detour, narrative mortality is an allegory in his cinema of the failure of documentary and narrative realisms to come together in the interests of auteurist mastery. Women in his films about filmmaking are always on the sidelines, awkwardly caught in a gaze that kills without desire, helplessly outside history.

The serial-killer films of the 1990s adopt this mortifying gaze in an escalated violence that is no longer able to distinguish image from reality. In the postmodern arena, the annihilation of the real robs narrative mortality of its redemptive potential and reifies it as a function of historical amnesia and horror. The independent art cinema may still be dominated by white men, but it is significant that the excess of violence is perpetrated within "the men's room," and within very legible languages of misogynist bigotry in which nothing is hidden except the women themselves. The film history traced in this book has located a mortification of realist aesthetics and politics in a cinema of masters for whom romanticism and baroque decadence are aesthetic choices in a library of styles.

Peter Greenaway and David Lynch demonstrate that heterosexual romance remains a vital discourse in the resurrection of art cinema, but at the same time that the narrative scenario of threat and rescue, in which women are the eternal victims, confuses the dynamics of corporeality with those of the eroticized female body. Beyond the New Wave cinemas, identity politics has redefined the categories of subjectivity and desire within a global politics of competing voices. Women's desire can no longer be co-opted for utopian discourses that fail to ruin the historical coding of gender, class, and race.

Oshima's preoccupation with rape within the drama of rebellion is an attempt to embrace the romance of heterosexual desire on the verge of its annihilation. Especially in the Japanese context, "freedom" for women has meant only the freedom to choose a husband, marking the limits of the discourse of melodramatic desire. Rape does not produce victims and villains in Oshima's cinema, but a narrative structure in which sexual desire cannot be read as an allegory of closure. In the theme of double suicide, "marriage" and death are uncannily united, potentially splitting open the sense of closure precisely by doubling it.

In the ruins of the master's house, cinema might yet redeem itself and its historiographic nature in the interests of new subjectivities. Especially in the age of AIDS, death can no longer be taken for granted, as the condition of "meaning." Death wields a very special power, as Derrida has said,[22] and it yields it to the critic of a text: the power of textual death is precisely in its deconstruction of an ideology of presence. To mortify a film is to go beyond its perpetual present tense and illuminate it as a discourse of history. Benjamin's theory of historiographic vision insists on a redemption of belief from its modernist destruction, a belief in history free of mythical limits, including the limits of Benjamin's own modernism.

Visibility in narrative film produces a dialectics of seeing in which death is always an allegorical option, insofar as the images register a past tense. The cinema, in this sense, may have been postmodern all along, and narrative mortality is the process by which it becomes aware of this state and produces a dialectical spectator, one who both believes and disbelieves, a crucial position for the feminist spectator looking for pleasure in the cinema.[23] When the void against which representation defines itself is not mystified but is articulated as impossible to represent, death comes into its own as the sign of the fragility of the present tense.

In addition to bodies, a great number of dead cars were discovered littering the preceding pages, rusting by the wayside of a discussion about dead characters and dying narratives. Not only do these shattered automobiles, as the emblems of collision and decay, register a collapse of accident and necessity; not only do they signify the false promises of consumer capitalism; they will never completely return to nature. This impossibility of total decay undermines the very principle of death as closure as a form of narrative desire. History is indexically embedded in these ruins, restricting desire and its construction of the future from imagining eternity; the image of the future becomes a history of the future. It is loss and not return that is inscribed in dead cars, the loss, moreover, of desirable commodities. The allegorical potential of narrative mortality lies precisely in its mortification of commodification and loss.

The spectacle of death keeps death somewhere else, a strategy essential to a disavowal not only of our own death but of the claim history has made on nature. Narrative mortality maintains the subject's tenuous claim on time, but, in the work of many filmmakers, it has become a structure upon which to reassert that claim, to reverse it, or to explode it. At stake is the redemption of history from the ruined mythologies of capitalism and Marxism. Once death is understood as something other than closure, as the vehicle of expressing the very impossibility of closure, it stands as a threat to commodification, on the threshold of the discovery of historical difference.

NOTES

Introduction: Narrative Mortality

1. Robert Kolker has written about this period as "Contemporary International Cinema" (*The Altering Eye* [Oxford University Press, 1983]), and I used "International Postwar Cinema" in an earlier version of this project. However, neither "contemporary" nor "postwar" labels convey the sense of a historical period distinct from the present.

2. Peter Brooks, *Reading for the Plot: Design and Intention in Narrative* (New York: Vintage Books, 1985).

3. Stephen Heath, *Questions of Cinema* (Bloomington: Indiana University Press, 1981).

4. See George Steiner's introduction to *The Origins of German Tragic Drama,* trans. John Osborne (London: New Left Books, 1977), and Susan Buck-Morss, *The Dialectics of Seeing: Walter Benjamin and the Arcades Project* (Cambridge, Mass.: MIT Press, 1989).

5. Walter Benjamin, "The Storyteller," in *Illuminations,* ed. Hannah Arendt, trans. Harry Zohn (New York: Schocken Books, 1969), p. 97.

6. "Our image of happiness is indissolubly bound up with the image of redemption. The same applies to our view of the past, which is the concern of history. The past carries with it a temporal index by which it is referred to redemption" ("Theses on the Philosophy of History," in *Illuminations,* p. 254).

7. Jügen Habermas, "Consciousness-Raising or Redemptive Criticism: The Contemporaneity of Walter Benjamin," *New German Critique* 17 (Spring 1979), p. 56.

8. Benjamin, "Theses on the Philosophy of History," p. 262.

9. Habermas, "Consciousness-Raising or Redemptive Criticism," p. 59.

10. Fredric Jameson, *The Political Unconscious: Narrative as a Socially Symbolic Act* (Ithaca, N.Y.: Cornell University Press, 1981).

11. Fredric Jameson, *Postmodernism or, the Cultural Logic of Late Capitalism* (Durham, N.C.: Duke University Press, 1991), p. 168.

12. For example, *Citizen Kane* (Welles, 1941), *Lolita* (Kubrick, 1962), *Gandhi* (Attenborough, 1982), *Vagabond* (Varda, 1986). Raymond Bellour has even labeled narrative return a "law" of classical film: that the end must reply to the beginning. His work on *Psycho* (Hitchcock, 1960) demonstrates the "monstrosity" of the detour that Hitchcock's narrative takes in order to meet this requirement ("Psychosis, Neurosis, Perversion," *Camera Obscura* 3/4 [Summer 1979]).

13. Jameson, *The Political Unconscious,* p. 82.

227

14. George Gerbner, "Death in Prime Time: Notes on the Symbolic Function of Dying in the Mass Media," *The Social Meaning of Death,* The Annals of Political and Social Science, vol. 47, 1980.

15. Philippe Ariès, *The Hour of Our Death,* trans. Helen Weaver (New York: Vintage Books, 1982), pp. 582–83.

16. Benjamin notes that "dying has been pushed further and further out of the perceptual world of the living" ("The Storyteller," p. 94).

17. Ernst Becker, *The Denial of Death* (New York: Free Press, 1973). Becker draws on the post-Freudian thought of Norman O. Brown and Otto Rank to delineate the mechanisms of the repression of death, but breaks with Freud himself on the primacy that he (Becker) attributes to the fear of death.

18. The "denial of death" is likewise assumed by most clinical thanatologists. Repression theories of death often assume a "healthy" relationship to death. Ariès makes the important point that psychologists of mourning, in which he includes the Freud of "Mourning and Melancholia," assume that the model of "the beautiful death" is a natural rather than a historical attitude toward death. Repression, and the corresponding tactics of the psychologist to heal the bereaved's "wound" take for granted the "affectivity" that became bound with death as love was to sex in the nineteenth century (Ariès, *The Hour of Our Death,* p. 581.

19. Michel Foucault, *The History of Sexuality,* vol. 1: *An Introduction,* trans. Robert Hurley (New York: Vintage Books, 1980).

20. Linda Williams objects to the facile inclusion of "snuff" within the pornography genre, pointing out that it involves very different forms of power and pleasure. She does note that snuff violence offers a high visibility quotient that may compensate for the invisibility of sexual pleasure. It is precisely this contradictory spectacularization of death that challenges its ostensible denial. See Linda Williams, *Hard Core: Power, Pleasure, and the Frenzy of the Visible* (Berkeley: University of California Press, 1989), p. 194. See also Geoffrey Gorer, "The Pornography of Death," in *Identity and Anxiety: Survival of the Person in Mass Society,* ed. Maurice R. Stein, Arthur J. Vidich, and David Manning White (New York: Free Press, 1960).

21. Herbert Marcuse, "The Ideology of Death," in *The Meaning of Death,* ed. Herman Feifel (New York: McGraw-Hill, 1959), p. 66.

22. Ibid., p. 74.

23. At the time of writing, Dr. Jack Kevorkian in the United States and Gaile Rodriguez in Canada have been bringing euthanasia politics into the public arena, demonstrating that the desire to die one's own death constitutes a challenge to social norms of mortality. In both countries, assisted suicide has been legislated against.

24. Foucault argues against "the hypothesis that modern industrial societies ushered in an age of increased sexual repression." He convincingly demonstrates that "never have there existed more centers of power; never more attention manifested and verbalized; never more circular contacts and linkages; never more sites where the intensity of pleasures and the persistency of power catch hold, only to spread elsewhere" (p. 49). He effectively counters Marcuse's premise of *Eros and Civilization* in which Thanatos is conceived as a repressive force.

25. Fredric Jameson, *Marxism and Form: Twentieth-Century Dialectical Theories of Literature* (Princeton, N.J.: Princeton University Press, 1971), p. 111.

26. Herbert Marcuse, *Eros and Civilization: A Philosophical Inquiry into Freud* (New York: Vintage Books, 1955), p. 29.

27. Walter Benjamin, *Charles Baudelaire: A Lyric Poet in the Era of High Capitalism,* trans. Harry Zohn (London: Verso, 1983), p. 118.

28. Rick Altman, *The American Film Musical* (Bloomington: Indiana University Press, 1989), p. 360.

29. "Ressentiment" is the "ideologeme" par excellence of Jameson's second stage of textual interpretation, in which the symbolic act is situated within the arena of its social consumption. Jameson's concept derives from Nietzsche, for whom "ressentiment" originates in a "slave revolt in manners" dating from Roman times: "All truly noble morality grows out of triumphant self-affirmation. Slave ethics, on the other hand, begins by saying *no* to an 'outside,' an 'other,' a non-self, and that *no* is its creative act" (Friedrich Nietzsche, "The Genealogy of Morals," in *The Birth of Tragedy and the Genealogy of Morals,* trans. Francis Golffing [New York: Doubleday, 1956], p. 171). In Golffing's translation, "ressentiment" is translated as "rancour."

30. Catherine Clément, *Opera, or the Undoing of Women,* trans. Betsey Wing (Minneapolis: University of Minnesota Press, 1988), p. 174.

31. Roland Barthes, *Mythologies,* trans. Annette Lavers (Toronto: Granada Publishing, 1973). Benjamin actually anticipates Barthes's theory of myth in the Arcades Project. He says, "what matters here is the dissolution of 'mythology' into the space of history." And at another place he advocates a release of "the enormous energy of history that lies bonded in the 'Once upon a time' of classical historical narrative. The history which showed things 'as they really were' was the strongest narcotic of the century" (Walter Benjamin, "N [Theoretics of Knowledge; Theory of Progress]," trans. of *Passegen-Werk* by Leigh Hafrey and Richard Sieburth, *The Philosophical Forum* 15:1–2 [Fall–Winter 1983/84], p. 32).

32. By "apparatus" theory I am referring to the body of work that appeared in *Screen* in the 1970s, especially that of Christian Metz, Laura Mulvey, Jean-Louis Baudry, and Stephen Heath. This work has been anthologized and reprinted in numerous places. It finds one of its purest forms in *Apparatus: Selected Writings,* ed. Theresa Hak Kyung Cha (New York: Tanam Press, 1980). Baudry, for example, writes: "Film lives on the denial of difference: the difference is necessary for it to live, but it lives on its negation" ("Ideological Effects of the Basic Apparatus," p. 29).

33. Jacques Lacan, *The Four Fundamental Concepts of Psychoanalysis,* trans. Alan Sheridan (New York: W. W. Norton, 1978), p. 28.

34. Ibid., p. 89.

35. Teresa de Lauretis, *Alice Doesn't: Feminism, Semiotics, Cinema* (Bloomington: Indiana University Press, 1984), p. 28.

36. Hélène Cixous, "Castration or Decapitation?" trans. Annette Kuhn, *Signs* 7:11 (Autumn 1981), p. 45.

37. Ibid., p. 53.

38. See Miriam Hansen, "Benjamin, Cinema and Experience: 'The Blue Flower' in the Land of Technology," *New German Critique* 40 (Winter 1987): 179–224.

39. Walter Benjamin, "Notes to the Theses on History," *Gesammelte Schriften,* vol. 1, p. 1231, quoted and translated by Susan Buck-Morss, *The Dialectics of Seeing,* p. 339.

40. Benjamin, "The Storyteller," p. 102.

41. Benjamin, *The Origins of German Tragic Drama,* p. 217.

42. Michel Foucault, "What Is an Author?" [1969], trans. Donald F. Bouchard and Sherry Simon, repr. in *Critical Theory since 1965,* ed. Hazard Adams and Leroy Searle (Tallahassee: University Presses of Florida, 1986), p. 140.

43. Maurice Blanchot, "Literature and the Right to Death" [1949], *The Gaze of Orpheus and Other Literary Writings,* trans. Lydia Davis, ed. P. Adams Sitney (Barrytown, N.Y.: Station Hill, 1981), p. 55.

44. Jameson, *The Political Unconscious,* p. 99.

45. Williams, *Hard Core,* pp. 56–57.

46. "Snuff film" refers to the documentation of actual human death as it is contextualized and exploited through fiction, marketing, and exhibition to become a consumable spectacle. However, when the spectacle of death becomes an end in itself—in films that few people have actually seen or desire to see—we have a virtual mortification of visibility.

47. Benjamin, *Gesammelte Schriften,* vol. 5, p. 417, quoted in Buck-Morss, *The Dialectics of Seeing,* p. 197.

48. Buck-Morss, *The Dialectics of Seeing,* p. 201.

49. Guy Debord, *Society of the Spectacle* (Detroit: Black and Red, 1983), p. 158.

50. Frank Kermode, *The Sense of an Ending: Studies in the Theory of Fiction* (New York: Oxford University Press, 1966), p. 47.

51. Ibid., p. 132. Because the "duration" of the film *Last Year at Marienbad,* for example, "is the ninety minutes passed in watching it," this text is merely a matter of "rigor," a formal tendency that could "destroy the novel" (p. 151).

52. Roland Barthes, *Camera Lucida: Reflections on Photography,* trans. Richard Howard (New York: Hill and Wang, 1981), p. 9.

53. The question of video specificity and the possibility of reading narrative mortality in videotexts will be deferred to chapter 2, although it has to be said that this book cannot do justice to the question.

54. Richard John Neupert, *The End: Notions of Closure in the Cinema* (Ph.D. diss., University of Wisconsin at Madison, 1986), p. 58. Neupert defines narrative discourse as an "umbrella term" for the totality of discursive operations in a text (p. 43), but does not actually clarify how it can be open or closed. In his film analyses, it is said to be "open" when "the device is laid bare" (e.g., *Tout va bien*) or the plurality of narrative voices remain fragmented (e.g., *Weekend*), and "closed" when it is "unified, directed and homogeneous" (e.g., *The 400 Blows*).

55. Although Neupert notes that repetition on the discursive level is a means by which "a Closed text brackets itself off from the endless fictional world" (p. 93) and that "ending on marriage in a classical narrative goes beyond mere story logic," there is no acknowledgment of those (identical) processes by which a text is "bracketed" from nonfictional reality, or any questioning of why certain endings "go beyond story logic."

56. Heath cites an Apollinaire story about some ambitious early filmmakers who kidnap three unsuspecting performers off the Paris streets. On camera, "the gentleman is forced, under threat of himself being killed, to murder the young lovers. The crime is sensational ... the film a spectacular box-office draw" (*Questions of Cinema,* p. 111). The Apollinaire story is called "Un beau film."

57. Fernando Solanas and Octavio Gettino, "Towards a Third Cinema," *Afterimage* 3 (1971), in *Movies and Methods,* vol. 1, ed. Bill Nichols (Berkeley: University of California Press, 1976).

58. Kaja Silverman argues that the protagonist of *Peeping Tom* is brought down by the female aural control of Mark's womb/cave/projection room, negating the gaze with the power of sound (*The Acoustic Mirror: The Female Voice in Psychoanalysis and Cinema* [Bloomington: Indiana University Press, 1988], pp. 32–41).

59. Other examples of the "mortifying gaze" literally reproduced in narrative film can be found throughout the history of cinema. They include *Falsely Accused!* (Biograph, 1907), *The Machine to Kill Bad People* (Rossellini, 1948), *Blow-Up* (Antonioni, 1967), *Good Morning Babylon* (Paulo and Vittorio Taviani, 1987).

60. Noël Carroll, "Interpreting Citizen Kane," *Persistence of Vision* 7 (1989), pp. 51–62.

61. See Dana Polan, *Power and Paranoia: History, Narrative and the American Cinema, 1940–1950* (New York: Columbia University Press, 1986).

62. Jacques Rivette, "Notes on a Revolution," *Cahiers du Cinéma* 54 (Christmas 1955), trans. Liz Heron, repr. in *Cahiers du Cinéma: The 1950's,* ed. Jim Hillier (Cambridge, Mass.: Harvard University Press, 1985), p. 95.

63. Buck-Morss, *The Dialectics of Seeing,* p. 233.

64. Benjamin, "N [Theoretics of Knowledge; Theory of Progress]," p. 32. Benjamin is quoting from Monglod's *Le préromantisme français,* vol. 1, *Le héros préromantique* (Grenoble, Èditions B. Arthaud, 1929).

Chapter 1. Beyond Pleasure: Lang and Mortification

1. Sigmund Freud, "Reflections upon War and Death" [1915], in *Character and Culture,* trans. E. Colburn Mayne (New York: Collier Books, 1963), p. 122.

2. Walter Benjamin, "The Storyteller," in *Illuminations,* ed. Hannah Arendt, trans. Harry Zohn (New York: Schocken Books, 1969), p. 101.

3. Jacques Rivette, "The Hand," in *Rivette: Texts and Interviews,* ed. Jonathan Rosenbaum, trans. Amy Gateff and Tom Milne (London: British Film Institute, 1977). Originally published in *Cahiers du Cinéma* 76 (November 1957).

4. The Venice Film Festival had been held annually since 1934, although it was suspended from 1943 to 1946 and revamped in 1947; Japanese film made a splash there in 1951 with *Rashomon.* The Berlin festival was established in 1951 as a direct result of the cultural isolation of West Berlin after World War II. The Moscow festival was inaugurated in 1935 and became biennial after 1957. With the establishment of Cannes in 1946, a competitive atmosphere emerged between these different European forums, which developed in the late 1950s into a strong international film culture.

5. The postwar French interest in American film is said to have been spawned by the flooding of the French market with all the Hollywood films banned during the occupation. See Dudley Andrew, *André Bazin* (New York: Oxford University Press, 1978), p. 97.

6. See André Bazin, "The Myth of Total Cinema" and "The Evolution of Film Language," in *What Is Cinema?* vol. 1, trans. Hugh Gray (Berkeley: University of California Press, 1967).

7. See Andrew, *André Bazin,* for an intellectual biography. For a discussion of the Christian existentialist dimension of Bazinian neorealism, see Bazin's colleague Amédée Ayfre, "Neo-Realism and Phenomenology," *Cahiers du Cinéma* 17 (November 1952), trans. Diana Matias, in Jim Hillier, ed., *Cahiers du Cinéma: The 1950's* (Cambridge, Mass.: Harvard University Press, 1985), pp. 182–91.

8. André Bazin, "An Aesthetic of Reality" [1948], in *What Is Cinema?* vol. 2 (1971), p. 27.

9. The paternal relations of the *Cahiers du Cinéma* collective are most explicit in the biographical legends of Bazin and François Truffaut, a relationship memorialized

in Truffaut's first film, *The 400 Blows* (1960). See also Truffaut's introduction to *What Is Cinema?* vol. 1.

10. Jacques Rivette, "Letter on Rossellini," *Cahiers du Cinéma* 46 (1955), trans. Tom Milne, in Hillier, ed., p. 198.

11. Jacques Rivette, "Notes on a Revolution," *Cahiers du Cinéma* 54 (Christmas, 1955), trans. Liz Heron, in Hillier, ed., p. 95. Rivette is writing specifically about the films of Nick Ray, Richard Brooks, Anthony Mann, and Robert Aldrich.

12. Luc Moullet, "Sam Fuller: In Marlowe's Footsteps," *Cahiers du Cinéma* 93 (March 1959), in Hillier, ed., p. 148; Jean-Luc Godard, in an editorial board discussion of *Hiroshima mon Amour, Cahiers du Cinéma* 97 (July 1959), in Hillier, ed., p. 62.

13. Moullet, "Sam Fuller," p. 148.

14. The editors of *Cahiers du Cinéma*, "John Ford's *Young Mr. Lincoln*," *Cahiers du Cinéma* 223 (August 1970), trans. in *Screen* 13:3 (Autumn 1972).

15. Dana Polan, *Power and Paranoia: History, Narrative and the American Cinema, 1940–1950* (New York: Columbia University Press, 1986).

16. As far as I can determine, no print longer than the eighty-minute version that is currently in distribution ever existed.

17. Charles Higham and Joel Greenberg, *The Celluloid Muse: Hollywood Directors Speak* (London: Angus and Robertson, 1969), p. 123.

18. Lang is quoted as saying that "every film should be a documentary of its time" in Peter Bogdanovich, *Fritz Lang in America* (New York: Praeger/Movie Magazine, 1967), p. 19.

19. Walter Benjamin, *The Origins of German Tragic Drama,* trans. John Osborne (London: New Left Books, 1977), p. 166.

20. Ibid., p. 234.

21. Ibid., p. 75.

22. Benjamin best presents his theory of literary criticism in the "Epistemo-Critical Prologue" to the *Trauerspiel* book. To explain its philosophical basis is beyond the scope of this chapter. See Charles Rosen, "The Ruins of Walter Benjamin," in *On Walter Benjamin,* ed. Gary Smith (Cambridge, Mass.: MIT Press, 1991).

23. Stephen Jenkins, "Lang: Fear and Desire," in Stephen Jenkins, ed., *Fritz Lang: The Image and the Look* (London: British Film Institute, 1981), p. 115.

24. Garrett Stewart, "Photo-gravure: Death, Photography and Film Narrative," *Wide Angle* 9:1 (1987).

25. Raymond Bellour, "The Pensive Spectator," trans. Lynne Kirby, *Wide Angle* 9:1 (1987), p. 9.

26. Reynold Humphries, *Fritz Lang: Genre and Representation in His American Films* (Baltimore: Johns Hopkins University Press, 1989), p. 66.

27. See, for example, Walter Benjamin, "A Short History of Photography" [1931], trans. Stanley Mitchell, *Screen* 13 (Spring 1972).

28. Sigmund Freud, "The Uncanny" [1919], in *Studies in Parapsychology* (New York: Collier Books, 1963), p. 40. Freud uses Otto Rank's "Der Doppelgänger" as a key source.

29. This is how Vivian Sobchack uses the term. She points out that the semiosis of the body is "difficult to contain in cultural vision" because of taboos against and denials of death ("Inscribing Ethical Space: Ten Propositions on Death, Representation and Documentary," *Quarterly Review of Film Studies* [Fall 1984], p. 293).

30. Charles Sanders Peirce, *Collected Papers,* vol. 2, p. 228, quoted by Teresa de Lauretis, *Technologies of Gender* (Bloomington: Indiana University Press, 1987), p. 39.

Peirce's semiotics provide de Lauretis with the "'missing link' between signification and concrete action," giving "the sense of a certain weight of the object in semiosis, an overdetermination wrought into the work of the sign by the real" (p. 41).

31. Umberto Eco, *The Role of the Reader: Explorations in the Semiotics of Texts* (Bloomington: Indiana University Press, 1979). See also Teresa de Lauretis, "Gaudy Rose: Eco and Narcissism," in *Technologies of Gender*, pp. 51–69.

32. These are the terms used by Jean-Louis Comolli and François Géré to describe Lang's *Hangmen Also Die* in "Two Fictions concerning Hate," in Jenkins, ed., *Fritz Lang*, p. 146.

33. Rivette, "The Hand," p. 65.

34. Higham and Greenberg, *The Celluloid Muse*, p. 124.

35. A typical death in film noir consists of a crumpled grey suit, a suddenly heavy body, followed by an emotionally charged reaction shot, or by a metaphoric image, such as a falling bowling pin, or a synecdochic image, such as a dropped object. Corporeality is, for the most part, repressed. Challenges to the production code were beginning to survive in 1956, and there are some important exceptions, including films by Lang and Hitchcock as well as Kubrick's *The Killing* (1956).

36. Motion Picture Producers and Distributors Association Production Code, 1939, reprinted in Ruth A. Inglis, *Freedom of the Movies* (Chicago: University of Chicago Press, 1974), p. 206.

37. Michel Foucault, *The Order of Things: An Archaeology of the Human Sciences* (New York: Vintage Books, 1973), p. 8.

38. Nick Browne, "The Spectator in the Text: The Rhetoric of *Stagecoach*," in *Movies and Methods*, vol. 2, ed. Bill Nichols (Berkeley: University of California Press, 1985), p. 468.

39. Michel Foucault, *Discipline and Punish: The Birth of the Prison*, trans. Alan Sheridan (New York: Vintage Books, 1979), p. 200.

40. Foucault argues that the system of surveillance embodied in panopticism originated in the containment of the plague in the late Middle Ages, when entire towns were compartmentalized and subdivided so as to thwart the chaos of death and disease with the analytical discipline of power (ibid., pp. 195–200).

41. Comolli and Géré, "Two Fictions concering Hate," p. 146.

42. Benjamin, *The Origins of German Tragic Drama*, p. 232.

43. Hugo Adam Bedau, "Introduction" to *The Death Penalty in America: An Anthology*, ed. Hugo Adam Bedau (Chicago: Aldine, 1964), p. v.

44. D. N. Rodowick, "Madness, Authority and Ideology: The Domestic Melodrama of the 1950s," in *Home Is Where the Heart Is: Studies in Melodrama and the Woman's Film*, ed. Christine Gledhill (London: British Film Institute, 1987), p. 277.

45. Paul Arthur, "Shadows on the Mirror: Film Noir and Cold War America, 1945–1957" (Ph.D. diss., New York University, 1985), p. 56.

46. *Beyond a Reasonable Doubt* comes toward the end of Arthur's periodization of film noir, which he terminates with *Touch of Evil* in 1958, and indeed, by 1956, cold war hysteria had dissipated somewhat with Stalin's death and the end of the Korean War. The domestic conflicts in this film, like those of the family melodramas of the period, indicate the synecdochic nature of "domesticity" in American cold war ideology, and also the overlap of genres. Arthur and Rodowick both identify narrative conflicts in the mid-fifties — rocking the "domestic" boat — between individual and institutional values, which are conceived of as state, judicial, and corporate institutions in film noir, and as the patriarchal nuclear family in the melodrama.

47. Arthur, "Shadows on the Mirror," p. 76.

48. Jenkins, *Fritz Lang*, p. 122.

49. Claire Johnston, *"Double Indemnity,"* in *Women in Film Noir,* ed. E. Ann Kaplan (London: British Film Institute, 1980), p. 102.

50. Lotte H. Eisner, *Fritz Lang* (New Yor k: Oxford University Press, 1977), p. 359.

51. Mark Vernet provides a particularly phallocentric reading in his analysis of the "black hole" of film noir. He provocatively argues that the noir text seeks to fill the void of an opening murder, but I would take issue with his assumptions that (1) this "hole" is a textual "castration" and (2) the fiction successfully restores the defensive structures against this threat of castration (Mark Vernet, "The Filmic Transaction: On the Openings of Films Noirs," trans. David Rodowick, *The Velvet Light Trap* 20 [Summer 1983]).

52. Laura Mulvey, *Visual and Other Pleasures* (Bloomington: Indiana University Press, 1989), p. 179. Mulvey equates the first part of Oedipus's story, his travels to Thebes, with Propp's model of the fairy tale. The subsequent investigation that Oedipus undertakes to free Thebes from the plague is organized by a hermeneutic code such as that of the detective story. Mulvey notes the parallels between the noir protagonist's questioning of identity and his narrative trajectory with the structure of the Oedipus story. Both the proairetic code (the code of actions) and the hermeneutic code (the code of enigmas) are developed by Roland Barthes in *S/Z,* trans. Richard Miller (New York: Hill and Wang, 1974).

53. Shoshana Felman, "Beyond Oedipus: The Specimen Story of Psychoanalysis," in *Lacan and Narration: The Psychoanalytic Difference in Narrative Theory* (Johns Hopkins University Press, 1983), pp. 1029–30.

54. Jacques Lacan, *Le Séminaire, livre 2, Le Moi dans la théorie de Freud et dans la technique psychoanalytique* (Paris: Seuil, 1978), pp. 271–72; quoted by Felman, "Beyond Oedipus," p. 1032.

55. Jacques Lacan, "Desire and the Interpretation of Desire in *Hamlet,"* *Yale French Studies* 55/56 (1977), p. 19.

56. *Hamlet* is also a privileged text for Benjamin, who sees in it the redemption of melancholy that the German baroque poets were never able to achieve (*The Origins of German Tragic Drama,* p. 158).

57. See *The Ego and the Id* (1923), standard edition, vol. 19, pp. 58–59, where Freud describes the fear of death as a "development" of the fear of castration.

58. Stuart Schneiderman, *Jacques Lacan: The Death of an Intellectual Hero* (Cambridge, Mass.: Harvard University Press, 1983), p. 58.

59. Ibid., p. 76.

60. An example of this tendency in film criticism is Mark Vernet's analysis of film noir ("The Filmic Transaction").

61. Comolli and Géré, "Two Fictions concerning Hate," p. 132.

62. Mulvey, *Visual and Other Pleasures,* p. 200.

63. See Johnston, *"Double Indemnity."*

64. Lacan, "Desire," p. 45.

65. Rivette's description of the film's "objective mise-en-scène" is strikingly close to Benjamin's description of *Trauerspiel*: "It is up to the spectator to assume responsibility not only for the thoughts and 'motives' of the characters, but for this movement from the Interior, grasping the phenomenon solely on its appearances; it is up to him

to know how to transform its contradictory moments into the concept" (Rivette, "The Hand," p. 68).

66. Peter Brooks, *Reading for the Plot: Design and Intention in Narrative* (New York: Vintage Books, 1985), p. 22.

67. Jean-François Lyotard, "Fiscourse Digure: The Utopia behind the Scenes of the Phantasy," trans. Mary Lydon, *Theatre Journal* 35:3 (October 1983), p. 356.

68. D. N. Rodowick, *The Difficulty of Difference: Psychoanalysis, Sexual Difference and Film Theory* (New York: Routledge, 1991), p. 94.

69. Ibid.

70. Barbara Klinger, "'Cinema/Ideology/Criticism' Revisited: The Progressive Text," *Screen* 25:1 (January–February 1984), p. 44. The initial theorization of the "progressive text" is the Comolli/Narboni *Cahiers du Cinéma* editorial of 1969: "Cinema/Ideology/Criticism," trans. in *Screen* 12:1 (Spring 1971). Klinger lists the key articles that have endorsed this position.

71. Raymond Bellour, "On Lang," in Jenkins, ed., *Fritz Lang.*

72. Benjamin evokes *Beyond the Pleasure Principle* in his discussion of the Proustian *mémoire involontaire* (see chapter 4). "Memory traces" in the unconscious protect the psyche against traumatic experiences, but in modernity, when "the shock experience has become the norm," experience becomes highly conscious, a constant meeting of stimuli and expectation. Poetry produced in such a context is highly "conscious" (as opposed to "memory traces"): "It would suggest that a plan was at work in its composition.... There is something odd about speaking of a raison d'etat in the case of a poet; there is something remarkable about it: the emancipation from experience" (Benjamin, *Charles Baudelaire: A Lyric Poet in the Era of High Capitalism,* trans. Harry Zohn [London: Verso, 1983], p. 116).

73. Brooks, *Reading for the Plot,* p. 58.

74. Jacques Lacan, *The Four Fundamental Concepts of Psychoanalysis,* trans. Alan Sheridan (New York: W. W. Norton, 1978), p. 55.

75. Comolli and Géré, "Two Fictions concerning Hate," p. 132.

76. Lacan, *The Four Fundamental Concepts,* p. 89.

77. Benjamin, "The Storyteller," p. 87.

78. See Barbara Klinger, "Much Ado about Excess: Genre, Mise-en-Scène and the Woman in *Written on the Wind," Wide Angle* 11:4 (October 1989).

79. Lang left Hollywood shortly after completing *Beyond a Reasonable Doubt,* saying, "I looked back over the past—how many films had been mutilated—and since I didn't have any intention of dying of a heart attack, I said, 'I think I'll step out of this rat race.' And I decided not to make pictures here any more" (Bogdanovich, *Fritz Lang in America,* p. 110).

Chapter 2. Wim Wenders: Film as Death at Work

1. André Bazin, "Mort tous les après-midi," *Qu'est-ce que le cinéma?* vol. 1, *Ontologie et langage,* Éditions du Cerf, 1969, p. 68; my translation.

2. Thomas Elsaesser, *New German Cinema: A History* (New Brunswick, N.J.: Rutgers University Press, 1989); Eric Rentschler, *West German Film in the Course of Time: Reflections on the Twenty Years since Oberhausen* (Bedford Hills, N.Y.: Redgrave, 1984).

3. Timothy Corrigan, *New German Film: The Displaced Image* (Austin: University

of Texas Press, 1983), p. 39. Corrigan also demonstrates Lang's similar role in Alexander Kluge's and Werner Herzog's conceptions of cinematic nationalism (pp. 95, 139).

4. *La politique des auteurs* was developed in *Cahiers du Cinéma* in the 1950s as a policy of privileging the role of the director in film criticism. See François Truffaut, "Une certaine tendance du cinéma français," *Cahiers du Cinéma* 31 (January 1954), and André Bazin, "De la politique des auteurs," *Cahiers du Cinéma* 70 (April 1957).

5. Kathe Geist, *The Cinema of Wim Wenders: From Paris, France, to "Paris, Texas"* (Ann Arbor: UMI Research Press, 1988), p. 89.

6. Quoted by Geist, ibid., p. 89, from Alain Masson and Hubert Nioget, "Entretien avec Wim Wenders," *Positif* (October 1977), p. 24.

7. Vivian Sobchack, "Inscribing Ethical Space: Ten Propositions on Death, Representation and Documentary," *Quarterly Review of Film Studies* (Fall 1984), p. 292.

8. I would like to thank Paul Arthur for pointing this out to me.

9. This term comes from Amos Vogel, "Grim Death," *Film Comment* 16:2 (March–April 1980), p. 78; quoted by Sobchack, "Inscribing Ethical Space," p. 283.

10. Walter Benjamin, *The Origins of German Tragic Drama*, trans. John Osborne (London: New Left Books, 1977), p. 178.

11. Two versions of *Lightning Over Water* exist. One was screened at Cannes in May 1980 under the title (or subtitle, depending on the source; see conflicting reports in *Sight and Sound* [Spring 1981]) *Nick's Film*. Wenders subsequently reedited it and added voice-over and soundtrack for rerelease in the summer of 1981, under the title *Lightning Over Water*. Pacific Arts Video has unfortunately released the first version as *Lightning Over Water*. I will be referring throughout to Wenders's (second) reedited version, and its transcription in *Nick's Film: Lightning Over Water*, by Wim Wenders and Chris Sievernich (Zweitausendeins, 1981).

12. Ron Burnett, "Wim Wenders, Nicholas Ray and Lightning Over Water," *Cine-Tracts 14/15* 4:2/3 (Summer–Fall 1981), p. 13.

13. The conception of film as "la mort au travail" can be traced to Jean Cocteau, cited by Stephen Heath in *Questions of Cinema* (Bloomington: Indiana University Press, 1981), p. 114. He refers to "Entretien avec Jean-Marie Straub and Danielle Huillet," *Cahiers du Cinéma* 223 (August 1970), pp. 53–55, for the source of the comment. It was also elaborated upon by Godard in a 1962 *Cahiers du Cinéma* interview (*Godard on Godard*, ed. Jean Narboni and Tom Milne, trans. Tom Milne [New York: Da Capo Press, 1972], p. 181).

14. Harold Bloom, *The Anxiety of Influence: A Theory of Poetry* (New York: Oxford University Press, 1973), p. 10. Bloom characterizes anxiety of influence as a "fear of death that is a personified superego."

15. Geist claims that "when it came time to edit, Wenders lacked sufficient footage and was forced to use the videotaped material" (*The Cinema of Wim Wenders*, p. 84). And yet the omnipresence of Farrell and his camera in almost all the scenes suggests some level of purposiveness on Wenders's part during the shooting.

16. Ivone Margulies, "Delaying the Cut: The Space of Performance in *Lightning Over Water*," *Screen* 34:1 (Spring 1993), p. 59.

17. Timothy Corrigan, "Cinematic Snuff: German Friends and Narrative Murders," *Cinema Journal* 24:2 (Winter 1985), p. 11. In this passage he is quoting Julia Kristeva, "The Father, Love, Banishment," in *Desire in Language: A Semiotic Approach to Literature and Art*, ed. Leon S. Roudiez (New York: Columbia University Press, 1980), pp. 150–51.

18. It is significant that Wenders does not read the two lines that follow these in

the diary, also scrawled on the screen, which continues: "and the will to find all the places to work down the love … (indecipherable) … silent thoughts."

19. Bernardo Bertolucci, "The Boundless Frivolity of People About to Die," in Wenders and Sievernich, *Nick's Film,* p. 5.

20. Corrigan, "Cinematic Snuff," p. 16.

21. Margulies, "Delaying the Cut," p. 61.

22. Bazin develops these thoughts in relation to "le petit mort" in "Marginal Notes on Eroticism in the Cinema," in *What Is Cinema?* vol. 2, trans. Hugh Gray (Berkeley: University of California Press, 1971), 169–175.

23. Bazin, "Mort tous les après-midi," p. 69.

24. Philip Rosen, "History of Image, Image of History: Subject and Ontology in Bazin," *Wide Angle* 9:4 (1987), p. 14.

25. Bazin, *What Is Cinema?* vol. 1 (1967), p. 10.

26. Rosen, "History of Image," p. 18. Rosen quotes Bazin from *What Is Cinema?* vol. 1, p. 15.

27. Annette Michelson, review of the English translation of *What Is Cinema? Artforum* 6 (September 1968), p. 70.

28. Rosen, "History of Image," p. 17. The best discussion of Bazin's Catholicism is Dudley Andrew's in *André Bazin* (New York: Oxford University Press, 1978).

29. Pamela Falkenberg, "'The Text! The Text!': André Bazin's Mummy Complex, Psychoanalysis and the Cinema," *Wide Angle* 9:4 (1987), p. 36.

30. Margulies, "Delaying the Cut," p. 67.

31. Ibid.

32. James Naremore argues that Nick's participation in the film was "genuine behavior" because "the actor's body is different from the social construct we call the actor's 'self.'" But in another sense *Lightning,* like most movies, tends [ultimately] to put biology in the service of character" (James Naremore, "Film and the Performance Frame," *Film Quarterly* 38:2 [Winter 1984/85], p. 15).

33. Ray was a close colleague of Elia Kazan and shared the responsibility for introducing method acting to Hollywood in the 1950s. (See Bernard Eisenshitz's biography of Ray in Wenders and Sievernich, *Nick's Film.*)

34. Geist, *The Cinema of Wim Wenders,* p. 88.

35. Stephen Heath, "Film Performance," in *Questions of Cinema,* p. 115.

36. Geist has remarked on the parallel these images bear with the depiction of death as "passage" in Romantic painting. She notes especially Caspar David Friedrich, and points out that one German word for eternity, *das Jenseits,* translates as "the other side" (Geist, *The Cinema of Wim Wenders,* p. 88).

37. Sigmund Freud, "Mourning and Melancholia" [1917], trans. Joan Riviere, in *General Psychological Theory: Papers on Metapsychology* (New York: Collier Books, 1963), p. 164.

38. Paul Virilio, *War and Cinema: The Logistics of Perception* [1984], trans. Patrick Camiller (London: Verso, 1989), p. 67.

39. Freud, "Mourning and Melancholia," p. 178.

40. If film is a "death mask," a mummification to which death poses an ontological challenge, the instantaneous video image is equally damaging to the preservative capacity of the Bazinian image (Falkenberg, "'The Text! The Text!'" pp. 45–47). The distinction between "living" TV and dead photographic mediums is problematic, especially when the video imagery has been transferred to film.

41. Jon Jost, "Wrong Move," *Sight and Sound* 50:2 (Spring 1981), p. 96.

42. Susan Sontag, *Illness as Metaphor* (New York: Vintage Books, 1979), p. 8.

43. Ibid., pp. 32, 35.

44. Eric L. Santer, *Stranded Objects: Mourning, Memory and Film in Postwar Germany* (Ithaca, N.Y.: Cornell University Press, 1990). Wenders's melancholia is more international in scope than the other German films Santer analyzes.

45. Elsaesser, *New German Cinema*, p. 215.

46. *The American Friend* and *Paris, Texas* are perhaps the best examples of this equation of woman and an originary home.

47. Sigmund Freud, "The Uncanny" [1919], in *Studies in Parapsychology* (New York: Collier Books, 1963), p. 51. See also Mary Ann Doane, *The Desire to Desire: The Woman's Film of the 1940's* (Bloomington: Indiana University Press, 1987), pp. 139–40, for a discussion of the Freudian uncanny in relation to the gaze.

48. Margulies notes the play of the uncanny in the film's representational strategies ("Delaying the Cut," p. 3).

49. Elsaesser, *New German Cinema*, p. 116.

50. Ibid., p. 49

51. Greg Kahn, "Territorial Rites: Ruiz, Jost and Wenders in Portugal," *Framework* 15/16/17:103 (Summer 1981). According to Kahn, Jost had planned to document Ruiz's production, but was once again ousted by Wenders.

52. Wim Wenders, "Interview with Patrick Bauchau," *Jungle* 7 (1984), p. 55.

53. See interviews with Bauchau and Isabelle Wiengarten in "Dossier on Wim Wenders; L'Etat des choses," *Jungle* 7 (1984).

54. Wenders, "Interview with Patrick Bauchau," p. 55.

55. Wenders, interview in pressbook.

56. Wenders, "Interview with Patrick Bauchau," p. 55.

57. Ibid., pp. 52–53.

58. Walter Benjamin, "The Storyteller," in *Illuminations,* ed. Hannah Arendt, trans. Harry Zohn (New York: Schocken Books, 1969), p. 94.

59. Ibid., p. 87.

60. In the first scene of what I call the Portuguese segment of the film, Fritz gives Anna (Isabelle Wiengarten), one of the actresses on *The Survivors*' set, a copy of *The Searchers* by Alan Le May. Anna reads a passage about "survivors," which she repeats in a subsequent scene. Later, after a piece of driftwood crashes through his window, Fritz reads a passage from the book about reading such uncanny signs. In Los Angeles, he drives by a movie marquee where *The Searchers* is playing.

61. Geist quotes Wenders's address to a New York audience on 21 May 1982: "An American production, shot in Hollywood, inside a studio, with a producer who understands himself as the center of the film ... The tradition was such a myth for me, the American cinema had haunted me for so long, that it was an enormous challenge and opportunity when Francis Coppola invited me to come over and make *Hammett* for him" (Geist, *The Cinema of Wim Wenders,* p. 82.)

62. Wenders, "Interview with Patrick Bauchau," p. 55.

63. J. Laplanche and J.-P. Pontalis, *The Language of Psychoanalysis,* trans. Donald Nicholson-Smith (New York: W. W. Norton, 1973), p. 256.

64. Freud, "Mourning and Melancholia," p. 173. See also "On Narcissism: An Introduction" [1914], trans. Cecil M. Baines, in *General Psychological Theory.*

65. The casting of Sam Fuller and the hiring of Robert Kramer as screenwriter might be regarded as means by which Wenders attempted to offset his directorial vi-

sion. But since these directors are relegated to their specific tasks, they function more as support for Wenders's valorization of directorial vision, in which his own is unambiguously privileged.

66. Stephen Heath, "Film Performance," p. 121.

67. Santer, *Stranded Objects,* p. 31.

68. The fictional filmography appearing on a computer screen reads as follows: 1969, *Schauplätze* (the title of Wenders's own first short film); 1970, *Der Lange Brief;* 1971, *A Stranger Here Myself;* 1972, *Le Visage Vert;* 1973, *Rule Without Exception* (the working title of *The American Friend*); 1976, *Shadow of a Man;* 1977, *No Incident;* 1978, *Trapdoor;* 1989, *The American Hunter.*

69. Walter Benjamin, *The Origins of German Tragic Drama,* p. 185.

Chapter 3. Oshima Nagisa: The Limits of Nationhood

1. Georges Bataille, *Erotism: Death and Sensuality,* trans. Mary Dalwood (San Francisco: City Lights Books, 1986), p. 144.

2. Peter B. High, "Oshima: A Vita Sexualis on Film," *Wide Angle* 1:4 (1977), p. 62.

3. Oshima Nagisa, "Authorial Asthenia," in *Cinema, Censorship, and the State: The Writings of Nagisa Oshima,* trans. Dawn Lawson, ed. Annette Michelson (Cambridge, Mass.: MIT Press, 1992), p. 46. In keeping with Asian convention, all Japanese names will be printed with the last name first.

4. Oshima Nagisa, "Beyond Endless Self-Negation: The Attitude of the New Filmmakers," in *Cinema, Censorship, and the State,* p. 48.

5. Joan Mellen, *Voices from the Japanese Cinema* (New York: Liveright, 1975), p. 264.

6. An extreme example of the prostitution of the body is the buying and selling of blood in *The Sun's Burial* (1960). The sweat that is emphasized in the film's mise-en-scène visually underscores the "milking" of the characters by their corrupt environment.

7. Ian Buruma, *Behind the Mask: On Sexual Demons, Sacred Mothers, Transvestites, Gangsters, Drifters and Other Japanese Cultural Heroes* (New York: Pantheon, 1984), p. 166.

8. Herbert Marcuse, *Eros and Civilization: A Philosophical Inquiry into Freud* (New York: Vintage Books, 1955), pp. 203–16.

9. Marcuse, *Eros and Civilization,* p. 136.

10. Noël Burch, *To the Distant Observer: Form and Meaning in the Japanese Cinema* (Berkeley: University of California Press, 1979).

11. Noel Burch introduces this term into his discussion of Oshima, using Jindrich Honzl's definition in "la mobilité du signe théâtral" in *Travail Théâtral* 4 (July–September 1971), developing it in terms of theatrical and cinematic specificity (Burch, *To the Distant Observer,* p. 336). The use of the term here is intended to emphasize Oshima's allegorical approach to traditional "presentational" Japanese aesthetics. David Desser also uses the term in a similar sense in *Eros Plus Massacre: An Introduction to the Japanese New Wave Cinema* (Bloomington: Indiana University Press, 1988), pp. 171–91.

12. Stephen Heath, "The Question Oshima," in *Questions of Cinema* (Bloomington: Indiana University Press, 1981), p. 153.

13. Peter Lehman, "The Mysterious Orient, the Crystal Clear Orient, the Non-existent

Orient: Dilemmas of Western Scholars of Japanese Film," *Journal of Film and Video* 39 (Winter 1987), p. 10.

14. See Desser for a more complete explanation of the historical underpinnings of the Japanese New Wave (*Eros Plus Massacre,* pp. 13–38).

15. *Zengakuren* are associations of Japanese students formed in the 1950s with close ties to the Japan Communist party.

16. The successful Korean uprising in the spring of 1960 was a source of inspiration to the Japanese *zengakuren* (Richard Storry, *A History of Modern Japan* [Penguin, 1984], p. 275).

17. The *michiyuki* is a theatrical device found in Noh drama, puppet theater, and Kabuki. During the passage, the lovers "mature," or become dignified, while the narrator indulges in his most poetic language (Donald Keene, *The Major Plays of Chikamatsu* [New York: Columbia University Press, 1961], p. 24). That the couple always travels *away* from their village or home indicates the choice they have made of love (*ninjo*) over duty (*giri*).

18. Tadao Sato describes the *feminisuto* tradition: "The image of a woman suffering uncomplainingly can imbue us with admiration for a virtuous existence almost beyond our reach, rich in endurance and courage. One can idealize her rather than merely pity her, and this can lead to what I call the worship of womanhood, a special Japanese brand of feminism" (*Currents in Japanese Cinema,* trans. Gregory Barrett [New York: Kodansha International, 1982], p. 78).

19. Desser points out that, given the historical exclusion of women from the Japanese stage and screen, their presence in the films of the 1920s was already political, and in the 1960s the erotic emphasis replaced the "transcendental" for a more psychological politics (*Eros Plus Massacre,* pp. 108–44).

20. See, for example, Oshima's essay on *Violence at Noon,* "The Wounds of Those with Shame," in *Cinema, Censorship, and the State,* pp. 114–22. For a more thorough discussion of sexuality in Oshima's films, see Maureen Turim, "Signs of Sexuality in Oshima's Tales of Passion," *Wide Angle* 9:2 (Spring 1987).

21. Audie Bock claims that Oshima regarded American films as "the enemy" (*Japanese Film Directors* [New York: Kodansha International, 1987], p. 315) but even in the essay she cites (translated in *Cinema, Censorship, and the State*) there is far more wrath directed at the Japanese cinema, its repetitive engagement with certain genres, and its high production values than at foreign films. In fact, I cannot find any reference to the American cinema in Oshima's translated writing.

22. Maureen Turim, "Oshima's Cruel Tales of Youth and Politics," *Journal of Film and Video* 39 (Winter 1987), p. 50. My reading of the melodramatic structure of *Cruel Story* is indebted to Turim. Oshima apprenticed at Shochiku's Ofuna studio. Under the direction of Kido Shiro, Ofuna specialized in humanist formula pictures known for their sentimental "flavor."

23. Peter Brooks, *The Melodramatic Imagination: Balzac, Henry James, Melodrama, and the Mode of Excess* (New York: Columbia University Press, 1976), p. 141.

24. The costumes are credited to M. Hinae, who was to become a major fashion designer.

25. Oshima has described melodrama as the most traditional form of cinema in Japan (*Cinema, Censorshp, and the State,* p. 28). The abbreviated discussion of Western and Japanese melodrama that follows has been developed in "Insides and Outsides: Cross-Cultural Criticism and Japanese Film Melodrama," *Melodrama and Asian Cinema,* ed. Wimal Dissanayaki (New York: Cambridge University Press, 1993). See

also Yoshimoto Mitsuhiro, "Melodrama, Postmodernism and Japanese Cinema," *East-West Film Journal* 5:1 (January 1991), p. 44.

26. Thomas Elsaesser, "Tales of Sound and Fury: Observations on the Family Melodrama," in *Movies and Methods,* vol. 2, ed. Bill Nichols (Berkeley: University of California Press, 1985).

27. Roland Barthes, *Empire of Signs,* trans. Richard Howard (New York: Hill and Wang, 1982), p. 62.

28. Ibid., p. 49.

29. The *bunraku* puppet plays and Kabuki plays of Chikamatsu Monzaemon (1653–1725) are not usually described as melodrama, probably because of the discredit the label tends to bear, and yet these are narratives of great emotional intensity, heightened by music, gesture, and mise-en-scène.

30. The term "moral occult" is central to Brooks's theory of melodrama. It refers to the invisible realm of moral feeling that is not transcendent or handed down from above, but comes from within melodramatic personae, with equivalent authority to that of divine law.

31. The different psychoanalytic structure of Japanese culture is, however, only one explanation for the differences between Japanese and Western melodrama's performances of suffering. Doi Takeo has mapped the Japanese psychoanalytic terrain in terms of *amae,* or "the anatomy of dependence." His work suggests that when Freudian terms are applied to the Japanese psyche (and, of course, there is no reason to believe this should or can be done), the Japanese subject appears to be terminally preoedipal and overwhelmingly male (*The Anatomy of Dependence,* trans. John Bester (New York: Kodansha International, 1981).

32. Ibid., p. 33.

33. Buruma, *Behind the Mask,* p. 176.

34. Alan Wolfe, *Suicidal Narrative in Modern Japan: The Case of Dazai Osamu* (Princeton, N.J.: Princeton University Press, 1990), p. 38.

35. The "I-novel" was an early twentieth-century genre of first-person narrative. Its most well known exponent is Soseki Natsume, who died in 1915.

36. Wolfe, *Suicidal Narrative,* p. 34.

37. Walter Benjamin, *The Origins of German Tragic Drama,* trans. John Osborne (London: New Left Books, 1977), p. 184. Further references will be included in the text.

38. Turim, "Oshima's Cruel Tales," p. 46.

39. Bock, *Japanese Film Directors,* p. 231.

40. "For it was absolutely decisive for the development of this mode of thought [allegory] that not only transitoriness, but also guilt should seem evidently to have its home in the province of idols and the flesh" (Benjamin, *The Origins of German Tragic Drama,* p. 224).

41. Dana Polan, *The Political Language of the Avant-Garde* (Ann Arbor: UMI Research Press, 1985), pp. 114–15.

42. Oshima's thematics have been described by Dana Polan as an opposition between "an enclosed inside … and an historically reflexive outside" (ibid., p. 34). Noël Burch poses Oshima's problematics as "What is the relation between this *me* and the struggle *out there?*" (*To the Distant Observer,* p. 327). Maureen Turim has also isolated the conflict between the personal and the political in Oshima's films ("Rituals, Desire, Death in Oshima's Ceremonies," *Enclitic* 5:2/6:1 [Fall 1981/Spring 1982] and "Oshima's Cruel Tales").

242 Notes to pages 123–33

43. Peter N. Dale, *The Myth of Japanese Uniqueness* (London: Cromm Helm, 1986), p. 105. Dale specifically links *giri* and *ninjo* to Japanese perceptions of social outsides and more personable insides, and further, to Japaneseness and non-Japaneseness.

44. Michel Foucault, *The History of Sexuality*, vol. 1: *An Introduction,* trans. Robert Hurley (New York: Vintage Books, 1980), p. 140.

45. As the boy lists the places through which the family has traveled, three grainy black-and-white photographs of his face fill the screen, followed by two color stills of him lying on the pavement, and one of a red taillight, and then three more black-and-white photos of him with other boys.

46. Walter Benjamin, "The Storyteller," *Illuminations,* ed. Hannah Arendt, trans. Harry Zohn (New York: Schocken Books, 1969), p. 94.

47. Joan Mellen claims that the boy's sense of responsibility for the girl's death is evidence of the survival of his "moral sense," and it is the means by which "Oshima pleads for the valuable humanity being trampled ... in Japan" (*The Waves at Genji's Door: Japan through Its Cinema* [New York: Pantheon Books, 1976], p. 353). Adam Knee argues that the boy blames his parents for the accident, which is why the memory of the girl precipitates his confession ("Criminality, Eroticism and Oshima," *Wide Angle* 9:2 [Spring 1987]).

48. Garrett Stewart, "Photo-gravure: Death, Photography and Film Narrative," *Wide Angle* 9:1 (1987), p. 22.

49. The four point-of-view shots are (1) a pan shot of the horizon from a moving ferry (one of the only camera movements in the film), which ends when it reaches the boy's parents; (2) his glimpse of some bullies in an alley, who, seeing him see them, turn on him violently; (3) his voyeuristic peek at his parents singing drunken folk songs with some geishas at an inn; and (4) his accidentally seeing his mother leave the doctor's office, where she was supposed to have gone to have an abortion (she slaps him and later bribes him to keep quiet).

50. Kristin Thompson and David Bordwell have exhaustively and convincingly documented and demonstrated Ozu's alterity vis-à-vis the classical Hollywood model ("Space and Narrative in the Films of Ozu," *Screen* 17:2 [Summer 1976]).

51. Bataille, *Erotism,* p. 22.

52. Oshima, *Cinema, Censorship, and the State,* pp. 170–72.

53. Ibid., p. 172. Oshima's adaptation of this "true story" went to some lengths to preserve an ethnographic quality. He stresses the efforts he and his crew went to in casting the boy (who was himself an orphan and not a professional actor), and their travels around Japan visiting orphanages. He also points out that the film was shot in chronological order, with cast and crew following the wandering trail of the family across and around Japan.

54. H. D. Harootunian, *Things Seen and Unseen: Discourse and Ideology in Tokugawa Nativism* (Chicago: University of Chicago Press, 1988), p. 410.

55. Ibid., p. 413.

56. David Bordwell describes Ozu's narratives as "liberal protests" against the "broken promise of Meiji" (*Ozu and the Poetics of Cinema* [Princeton, N.J.: Princeton University Press, 1989], p. 42). Although Bordwell recognizes the importance of history in Ozu's narrative structure, there is little evidence that Ozu or his characters have or ever had any historical desires or expectations of social transformation.

57. Oshima notes that shooting the film in chronological order meant that the boy matured over the course of the shoot. However, he became too dependent on the

"family" of the crew, a dependency that Oshima tried to break. "And in order to do the important scene in which the boy becomes isolated and independent, I thought that 'Tetsuo' had to throw away dependency and become able to stand on his own in reality as well" (*Cinema, Censorship, and the State,* p. 180).

58. Stephen Heath, "Anata Mo," *Screen* 17:4 (Winter 1976/77). The words "anata mo" (and you) are repeated over and over again by the voice-over that concludes *Death by Hanging.*

59. Harootunian, *Things Seen and Unseen,* p. 410.

60. Doi, *The Anatomy of Dependence,* p. 95.

61. Desser, *Eros Plus Massacre,* p. 199.

Chapter 4. Jean-Luc Godard: Allegory of the Body

1. Walter Benjamin, *The Origins of German Tragic Drama,* trans. John Osborne (London: New Left Books, 1977), p. 166.

2. Jean-Luc Godard, *Godard on Godard,* ed. Jean Narboni and Tom Milne, trans. Tom Milne (New York: Da Capo Press, 1972), p. 217.

3. Mark Poster, *Existential Marxism in Postwar France: From Sartre to Althusser* (Princeton, N.J.: Princeton University Press, 1975), p. 104.

4. Jean Collet, *Jean-Luc Godard: An Investigation into His Films and Philosophy,* trans. Ciba Vaughan (New York: Crown Publishers, 1970), pp. 35–36.

5. Godard, *Godard on Godard,* p. 174.

6. Susan Sontag, "Godard," in *A Susan Sontag Reader* (New York: Farrar, Straus & Giroux, 1982), p. 255.

7. Mikhail Bakhtin, *Problems of Dostoevsky's Poetics,* trans. and ed. Caryl Emerson (Minneapolis: University of Minnesota Press, 1984), p. 290.

8. Belmondo's blurry vision as he "dies" at the end of *A bout de souffle* may be a representation of death "from the inside," but it is highly ironic, suggesting the absurdity of this point of view within the film's otherwise *vérité* style.

9. Maurice Merleau-Ponty, *Sense and Non-Sense,* trans. Hubert L. Dreyfus and Patricia Allen Dreyfus (Evanston, Ill.: Northwestern University Press, 1964), p. 58. Godard refers extensively to Merleau-Ponty, both directly and indirectly, in *Two or Three Things I Know About Her* (1967).

10. Poster, *Existential Marxism in Postwar France,* p. 148.

11. The best discussion of the film as an adaptation, which takes into account the ironic aspect of the novel, is Marsha Kinder's "Thrice-Told Tale: Godard's *Le Mépris,*" in *Modern Filmmakers and the Art of Adaptation,* ed. Andrew S. Horton and Joan Margretta (New York: Ungar, 1981).

12. Walter Benjamin, "The Work of Art in the Age of Mechanical Reproduction," in *Illuminations,* ed. Hannah Arendt, trans. Harry Zohn (New York: Schocken Books, 1969), p. 242.

13. Yvonne Baby, "Shipwrecked People from the Modern World: Interview with Jean-Luc Godard on *Le Mépris,*" in *Focus on Godard,* ed. Royal S. Brown (Englewood Cliffs, N.J.: Prentice Hall, 1972), p. 37.

14. For the mythic dimensions of "aura," see Winfried Menninghaus, "Walter Benjamin's Theory of Myth," trans. Gary Smith, in *On Benjamin,* ed. Gary Smith (Cambridge, Mass.: MIT Press, 1988), p. 316.

15. Benjamin, "The Work of Art," p. 233. In Harry Zohn's translation the word

"orchid" replaces "blue flower." Miriam Hansen claims that the latter is the correct translation, and points out the resonance of "blue flower" to the German Romantic tradition (Miriam Hansen, "Benjamin, Cinema and Experience: 'The Blue Flower in the Land of Technology,'" *New German Critique* 40 [Winter 1987], p. 204).

16. Benjamin, *The Origins of German Tragic Drama,* p. 165.

17. Benjamin, quoted and translated in Menninghaus, "Walter Benjamin's Theory of Myth," p. 321.

18. Ibid., p. 320.

19. Benjamin, *The Origins of German Tragic Drama,* p. 108.

20. Walter Benjamin, "The Storyteller," in *Illuminations,* p. 98.

21. Walter Benjamin, *Charles Baudelaire: A Lyric Poet in the Era of High Capitalism,* trans. Harry Zohn (London: Verso, 1983), p. 114.

22. Walter Benjamin, "N [Theoretics of Knowledge; Theory of Progress]", trans. of *Passagen-Werk* by Leigh Hafrey and Richard Sieburth, *The Philosophical Forum* 15:1–2 (Fall–Winter 1983/84), pp. 8–9.

23. Menninghaus, "Walter Benjamin's Theory of Myth," p. 315.

24. Richard Allen, "The Aesthetic Experience of Modernity: Adorno, Benjamin and Contemporary Film Theory," *New German Critique* 40 (Winter 1987), p. 230; Jürgen Habermas, "Conscious-Raising or Redemptive Criticism: The Contemporaneity of Walter Benjamin," *New German Critique* 17 (Spring 1979), pp. 48–49; Miriam Hansen, "Benjamin, Cinema and Experience: 'The Blue Flower' in the Land of Technology," *New German Critique* 40 (Winter 1987), pp. 195–96.

25. Walter Benjamin, "On the Mimetic Faculty," in *Reflections: Essays, Aphorisms, Autobiographical Writings,* trans. Edmund Jephcott, ed. Peter Demetz (New York: Schocken Books, 1986), p. 334.

26. Hansen, "Benjamin, Cinema and Experience," p. 222.

27. Collet, *Jean-Luc Godard,* p. 90.

28. The best examples of this attempt to transgress the limitations of perception are Karina in *Vivre sa vie* and *Le Petit Soldat* and Godard's description of Belmondo in *A bout de souffle* as "a block to be filmed to discover what lay inside" (*Godard on Godard,* p. 175).

29. *Letter to Jane* even includes references to Henry Fonda as an icon of American ideology—a far cry from Godard's 1957 essay on *The Wrong Man,* in which he wrote that "essence intrudes on existence" in the "beauty of Henry Fonda's face" (ibid., p. 49).

30. Benjamin, *Charles Baudelaire,* p. 149.

31. Ibid., p. 148.

32. Hansen, "Benjamin, Cinema and Experience," pp. 213–15.

33. Benjamin, *Charles Baudelaire,* p. 147.

34. Laura Mulvey, "Visual Pleasure and Narrative Cinema," *Screen* 16:3 (Autumn 1975), repr. in Laura Mulvey, *Visual and Other Pleasures* (Bloomington: Indiana University Press, 1989).

35. As Colin McCabe and Laura Mulvey put it, "Godard slides continually between an investigation of the images of woman and an investigation which uses those images," compromising, in their opinion, his feminism ("Images of Woman, Images of Sexuality," in Colin McCabe, *Godard: Images, Sounds, Politics* (Bloomington: Indiana University Press, 1980), p. 87.

36. Benjamin, *The Origins of German Tragic Drama,* p. 55.

37. Although neither section of the film is set entirely outside or inside, the exteriors in Rome include only high-walled clearings in claustrophobic city streets and a furnished garden; the interiors in Capri have huge windows through which the landscape continues to overwhelm the characters. It should also be noted that Godard has reversed the proponents of the two theories in his adaptation. In Moravia's *Il Disprezzo*, it is the German director who proposes the modern "neurotic" interpretation, and the screenwriter who wants to stick to the classical Homeric version.

38. In Eric Auerbach's analysis of Homer, the Greek epic had no secrets, no morals, and no meanings to divulge; detail had the status simply of detail (Erich Auerbach, *Mimesis: The Representation of Reality in Western Literature,* trans. Willard R. Trask [Princeton, N.J.: Princeton University Press, 1953], p. 13.

39. Benjamin, "The Storyteller," p. 99.

40. George Lukács, *The Theory of the Novel: A Historical-Philosophical Essay on the Forms of Great Epic Literature,* trans. Anna Bostock (Cambridge, Mass.: MIT Press, 1971), p. 47.

41. Raymond Bellour, "On Fritz Lang" [1966], in *Fritz Lang: The Image and the Look,* ed. Stephen Jenkins (London: British Film Institute, 1981), p. 29.

42. Benjamin, *The Origins of German Tragic Drama,* p. 223.

43. Lang's first words in the film, addressed to Prokosch while watching rushes of "his film," interpret Homer's *Odyssey* as a "fight of the individual against circumstances ... a fight against the gods." As is made clear later in the film, when Camille reads from a book on Lang, these sentiments echo Lang's own treatment of the theme of destiny in his films. Bardot/Camille reads aloud from what looks like Luc Moullet's monograph on Lang, and Lang has repeated similar ideas in his interviews with Bogdanovich and Eisner.

44. Godard, *Godard on Godard,* p. 201.

45. Ibid., p. 175.

46. Bill Simon pointed out to me the monumentality of Godard's mise-en-scène and its resonance in the Langian intertexts.

47. Godard, *Godard on Godard,* p. 201.

48. Benjamin, *Charles Baudelaire,* p. 132.

49. Godard says that "it's not that she (Bardot) can do many things. She can only do certain things. Just don't ask her to do more.... She couldn't think about what she was doing, do it, and make it work" (Collet, *Jean-Luc Godard,* p. 90). He also says of Jack Palance that he was "very disagreeable" to work with because "he didn't have to act, just the fact of his being there was already a kind of performance" ("Excerpt from an Interview with Richard Grenier and Jean-Luc Godard" by James Blue, in *Jean-Luc Godard,* ed. Toby Mussman [New York: E. P. Dutton, 1968], p. 250).

50. Walter Benjamin, *Gesammelte Schriften,* vol. 5, p. 444, trans. and quoted by Susan Buck-Morss, *The Dialectics of Seeing: Walter Benjamin and the Arcades Project* (Cambridge, Mass.: MIT Press, 1989), p. 195.

51. Benjamin, quoted in Buck-Morss, *The Dialectics of Seeing,* p. 195. Buck-Morss quotes from Benjamin's text "Zentralpark" (1939–40), a "fragmentary text formulated specifically with reference to Benjamin's planned book on Baudelaire."

52. Andreas Huyssen, *After the Great Divide: Modernism, Mass Culture, Postmodernism* (Bloomington: Indiana University Press, 1986), p. 209.

53. Two Hollywood gangster/noir films, *They Live by Night* (Nicholas Ray, 1948) and *Gun Crazy* (Joseph H. Lewis, 1949), seem to be fairly close to the surface of

Pierrot le fou, especially the latter in terms of the prevalence of automobiles and the femme fatale who is responsible for the hero's increased criminal involvement. The pastoral interlude of Lang's *You Only Live Once* (1937), as well as the romantic double death with which that film ends, suggest that it also belongs to the "popular" narrative sources of *Pierrot le fou.*

54. Bakhtin, *Problems of Dostoevsky's Poetics,* p. 127.

55. Mikhail Bakhtin, *Rabelais and His World,* trans. Hélène Iswolsky (Bloomington: Indiana University Press, 1984), p. 70.

56. Bakhtin, *Problems of Dostoevsky's Poetics,* pp. 114–18.

57. The term "metaphysical materialism" is used by Terry Eagleton with reference to the common theoretical ground of Bakhtin and Benjamin (*Walter Benjamin or Towards a Revolutionary Criticism* [London: New Left Books, 1981]).

58. Marie-Claire Ropars Wuilleumier, "Form and Substance, or the Avatars of Narrative," in Brown, ed., *Focus on Godard,* p. 101.

59. Ibid., p. 102.

60. Georges Bataille, *Erotism: Death and Sensuality,* trans. Mary Dalwood (San Francisco: City Lights Books, 1986).

61. Benjamin, "N [Theoretics of Knowledge]", p. 10.

62. Benjamin, *Charles Baudelaire,* pp. 75–76.

63. Eagleton, *Walter Benjamin,* p. 150.

64. Walter Benjamin, "On Surrealism," in *Reflections,* p. 192.

65. Benjamin, "N [Theoretics of Knowledge]," p. 13.

66. Eagleton, *Walter Benjamin,* p. 155.

67. Godard, *Godard on Godard,* p. 219.

68. Andreas Huyssen, "Mass Culture as Woman: Modernism's Other," in *After the Great Divide,* pp. 44–64.

69. Rick Altman, *The American Film Musical* (Bloomington: Indiana University Press, 1989), p. 360.

70. Paul de Man, "The Rhetoric of Temporality," in *Critical Theory since 1965,* ed. Hazard Adams and Leroy Searle (Tallahassee: University Presses of Florida, 1986), p. 209.

71. Charles Baudelaire, "De l'essence du rire," in *Curiosités esthétiques: L'Art romantique et autres Œuvres critiques,* ed. H. Lemaître (Paris: Garnier, 1962), quoted in de Man, "The Rhetoric of Temporality," p. 214, trans. eds. of *Critical Theory since 1965.*

72. Benjamin, *The Origins of German Tragic Drama,* p. 178.

73. Buck-Morss, *The Dialectics of Seeing,* p. 179, quoting Benjamin from "Zentralpark," pp. 658, 660.

74. Godard, *Godard on Godard,* p. 215.

75. Luc Moullet's "Sam Fuller: In Marlowe's Footsteps" (*Cahiers du Cinéma,* March 1959) is perhaps the seminal appreciation of Fuller's violence. Godard's own commentary on *Forty Guns* is basically a euphoric description of the film's most violent scenes. See also James Hillier's Introduction to part 2 of *Cahiers du Cinéma: The 1950's* (Cambridge, Mass.: Harvard University Press, 1985), p. 79.

76. Benjamin quotes Marx in the Arcades project: "'The reformation of consciousness lies *solely* in the awakening of the world ... from its dreams about itself.'" ("N [Theory of Knowledge]," p. 1; quoted from *Der historische Materialismus: Die Frühschriften Leipzig* [1932], vol. 1, p. 226).

77. Arthur Rimbaud, "Une Saison en Enfer" (1873), trans. J. S. Watson, Jr., in *A Season in Hell: The Life of Arthur Rimbaud*, by Jean-Marie Carr (New York: Macaulay, 1931), pp. 301, 304; italics in source.

78. Allusions to Rimbaud have been isolated by both Milne (*Godard on Godard*, p. 279) and Ropars Wuilleumier ("Form and Substance," p. 101).

79. Maurice Blanchot, "Literature and the Right to Death" [1949], in *The Gaze of Orpheus and Other Literary Writings*, trans. Lydia Davis, ed. P. Adams Sitney (Barrytown, N.Y.: Station Hill, 1981), p. 55.

80. Bakhtin, *Problems of Dostoevsky's Poetics*, p. 290.

81. Benjamin, *The Origins of German Tragic Drama*, p. 218.

82. Benjamin, "The Storyteller," p. 102.

83. Benjamin, *The Origins of German Tragic Drama*, p. 178.

84. Ibid.

85. Benjamin, *Charles Baudelaire*, p. 172.

86. "The necessity to be modern" is a theme that runs throughout the essays that Jim Hillier has collected in his volume of writings from the 1950s. See especially Jacques Rivette, "Notes on a Revolution" (*Cahiers du Cinéma* 54 [Christmas 1955]) and Godard, "Nothing but Cinema" (February 1957), in Jim Hillier, ed., *Cahiers du Cinéma: The 1950's* (Cambridge, Mass.: Harvard University Press, 1985).

Chapter 5. American Apocalypticism: The Sight of the Crisis

1. Maurice Blanchot, *The Writing of the Disaster,* trans. Ann Smock (Lincoln: University of Nebraska Press, 1976), pp. 1–2.

2. Timothy Corrigan, *A Cinema without Walls: Movies and Culture after Vietnam* (New Brunswick, N.J.: Rutgers University Press, 1991), p. 138.

3. In his survey of research into screen and TV violence, André Glucksmann notes that violence in sociological and psychological studies is rarely defined with any precision. It is generally assumed to be acts that "*if carried out in reality,* would be illegal, immoral or simply brutal" (*Violence on the Screen: A Report on research into the effects on young people of scenes of violence in films and television,* trans. Susan Bennett [London: British Film Institute, 1971], p. 16; italics in source).

4. Glucksmann cites Edgar Dale (1935) as the first quantitative analysis of violence in film. This study, like some subsequent studies, distinguishes between murder and other crimes, but not between death and violence (Glucksmann, *Violence on the Screen,* p. 23.)

5. The relationship between violence and formal innovation is implied, if not stated, in William Faure's collection of stills and frame enlargements, *Images of Violence* (London: Studio Vista, 1973).

6. Eisenstein notes that Griffith's bourgeois representation of society demands that the anticipated violence be perpetually postponed. American society "perceived only as a contrast between the haves and the have-nots, is reflected in the consciousness of Griffith no deeper than the image of an intricate race between two parallel lines" (*Film Form,* ed. Jay Leyda [New York: Harcourt and Brace, 1949]), p. 234.

7. Vivian Sobchack, "Inscribing Ethical Space: Ten Propositions on Death, Representation and Documentary," *Quarterly Review of Film Studies* (Fall 1984), p. 289.

8. Paul Virilio, *War and Cinema: The Logistics of Perception* [1984], trans. Patrick Camiller (London: Verso, 1989).

9. Yuri Rubinsky and Ian Wiseman, *A History of the End of the World* (New York: William Morrow, 1982).

10. Frank Kermode, *The Sense of an Ending: Studies in the Theory of Fiction* (New York: Oxford University Press, 1966), p. 5.

11. Jo Ann James, "Introduction" to *Apocalyptic Visions Past and Present*," ed. Jo Ann James and William J. Cloonan (Tallahassee: Florida State University Press, 1988), p. 3.

12. Guy Debord, *Society of the Spectacle* (Detroit: Black and Red, 1983), p. 126.

13. See, especially, Jean Baudrillard, *Fatal Strategies*, trans. Phillip Beitchman and W. G. J. Niesluchowski, ed. Jim Fleming (New York: Semiotext[e], 1990).

14. Corrigan, *A Cinema without Walls*, p. 138.

15. William J. Free, "Aesthetic and Moral Value in *Bonnie and Clyde*," in *Focus on Bonnie and Clyde*, ed. John G. Cawelti (Englewood Cliffs, N.J.: Prentice Hall, 1973), p. 104.

16. Arthur Penn himself invokes a line from *Macbeth* to describe the violence: "Who would have thought the old man could have had so much blood in him?" Interview with Arthur Penn by Jean-Louis Comolli and André S. Labarthe, in *Focus on Bonnie and Clyde*, p. 17.

17. Ibid., p. 16.

18. Roland Barthes, "The Third Meaning," in *Image Music Text*, trans. Stephen Heath (New York: Hill and Wang, 1977), p. 61.

19. Roland Barthes, *Empire of Signs*, trans. Richard Howard (New York: Hill and Wang, 1982), p. 49.

20. Pauline Kael, "Crime and Poetry," from *Kiss Kiss Bang Bang* (1967); repr. in *The Bonnie and Clyde Book*, comp. and ed. Sandra Wake and Nicola Hayden (London: Lorimer, 1972), p. 167.

21. Steve Neale, "Melodrama and Tears," *Screen* 27:6 (November–December 1986), p. 19. Neale is quoting from Peter Brooks, *The Melodramatic Imagination: Balzac, Henry James, Melodrama, and the Mode of Excess* (New York: Columbia University Press, 1976), p. 67.

22. Corrigan, *A Cinema without Walls*, p. 150.

23. Penn interview, *Focus on Bonnie and Clyde*, p. 18.

24. Robert Phillip Kolker, *A Cinema of Loneliness: Penn, Kubrick, Scorsese, Spielberg, Altman*, 2d ed. (New York: Oxford University Press, 1988), p. 52.

25. Ibid., p. 53.

26. Lawrence Alloway, *Violent America: The Movies 1946–1964* (New York: Museum of Modern Art, 1971), p. 57.

27. Kolker, *A Cinema of Loneliness*, p. 55.

28. In comparing the representation of death in documentary and fiction film, Vivian Sobchack claims that the general cultural toleration of narrative death (as opposed to documented death) is due to its containment "in a range of formal and ritual simulations … thus simulated, it simply 'doesn't count' " ("Inscribing Ethical Space," p. 291).

29. Garrett Stewart, "Photo-Gravure: Death, Photography and Film Narrative," *Wide Angle* 9:1 (1987), p. 22.

30. Stewart writes: "Into the (metonymic) chain of contiguity, of continuous motion,

of sequence, of plot, breaks the radical equation *stasis equals death,* the axis of substitution, the advent of metaphor" (ibid.).

31. Philippe Ariès, *The Hour of Our Death,* trans. Helen Weaver (New York: Vintage Books, 1982), p. 116.

32. Much of the violence preceding this massacre is directed against women, who
are represented as unfaithful and brutal intruders in an all-male world. The homoerotic aspect of the narrative of *The Wild Bunch* has been developed by Terrance
Butler in *Crucified Heroes: The Films of Sam Peckinpah* (London: Gordon Fraser, 1979).

33. Richard Slotkin, *Regeneration through Violence* (Middleton, Conn.: Wesleyan
University Press, 1973).

34. John G. Cawelti, "Myths of Violence in American Popular Culture," *Critical Inquiry* 1:3 (March 1975), p. 529.

35. The representation of "Che" in *The Hour of the Furnaces* (Solanas, 1967) involves a similar conflation of heroism and revolutionary ideology. It is also an inter-
esting example of narrative mortality and the representation of death in the duration
of the still photo of Guevara's face held silently on-screen for several minutes.

36. David A. Cook, *History of Narrative Film* (New York: W. W. Norton, 1981), p.
632.

37. Gérard Lenne, *La Mort à voir* (Éditions du Cerf, 1977), p. 27.

38. Georges Bataille, *Erotism: Death and Sensuality,* trans. Mary Dalwood (San
Franciso: City Light Books, 1986), pp. 82–83.

39. René Girard, *Violence and the Sacred,* trans. Patrick Gregory (Baltimore: Johns
Hopkins University Press, 1977), p. 19.

40. Ibid., p. 47.

41. The Christian orientation is made more explicit in René Girard's *Things Hidden
Since the Foundation of the World,* trans. Stephen Bann and Michael Metteer (London:
Athlone, 1987).

42. See, in particular, Christopher Sharrett, "The American Apocalypse: Scorsese's
Taxi Driver," *Persistence of Vision* 1 (Summer 1984); Garrett Stewart, "Coppola's Conrad: The Repetitions of Complicity," *Critical Inquiry* 7:3 (Spring 1983); and Christopher Sharrett, "Apocalypticism in the Contemporary Horror Film: A Typological Survey of a Theme in the Fantastic Cinema, Its Relation to Cultural Tradition and Current
Filmic Expression" (Ph.D. diss., New York University, 1983), p. 301.

43. H. Dale Crockett, *Focus on Watergate: An Examination of the Moral Dilemma
of Watergate in the Light of Civil Religion* (Macon, Ga.: Mercer University Press, 1982),
p. 98.

44. Barbara Jean's frailty and the black funeral wreath in her hospital room, the
several discussions of guns, Linnea's cocktail chat about violent death, and Kenny's
skulking around the Walker campaign headquarters can all be read retrospectively as
hints of the narrative denouement.

45. "The poet brings the sacrificial crisis back to life; he pieces the scattered fragments of reciprocity and balances elements thrown out of kilter in the process of being 'mythologized.' He whistles up a storm of violent reciprocity, and differences are
swept away in this storm just as they were previously dissolved in the real crisis that
must have generated the mythological transfiguration" (Girard, *Violence and the Sacred,*
pp. 64–65.

46. Sharrett has suggested that Watergate was a mythic apparatus constructed to
displace violence, but that the "sacrifice of Nixon failed as ritual, not only because it

was incomplete, but because it was revealed as ritual per se and one that did not genuinely respond to a consensus." The mystification of violence in contemporary America removes it from a political/historical dimension ("The American Apocalypse," p. 61).

47. Glucksmann, *Violence on the Screen,* p. 59.

48. Ibid., p. 60.

49. See Amy Lawrence, "The Aesthetics of the Image: The Hanging of Colonel Higgins: A CBS NewsBreak," *Wide Angle* 12:2 (April 1990).

50. Girard, *Violence and the Sacred,* p. 291.

51. Kenny rents a room from Mr. Green (Keenan Wynn); Kelly becomes something of a confidant for Mr. Green as they both stand vigil at the hospital—Kelly for Barbara Jean, Mr. Green for his wife. Kenny and Kelly's status as replaceable sons for Mr. Green is made clear when Green tells Kelly in church that he lost a son his age in the South Pacific.

52. Girard, *Violence and the Sacred,* p. 36.

53. Catherine Clément, *Opera, or the Undoing of Women,* trans. Betsey Wing (Minneapolis: University of Minnesota Press, 1988), p. 45.

54. Ibid., p. 52. Carmen's death is played out "in a space between two theaters: the opera theater and the fictional amphitheater."

55. Rick Altman, *The American Film Musical* (Bloomington: Indiana University Press, 1989), p. 318.

56. Girard's project in *Violence and the Sacred* involves a revision of psychoanalytic epistemology, and the restoration of myth through the scapegoating process involves a demarcation of Self and Other as fundamental as sexual difference. The "otherness" of the sacrificial victim is the key to the mythic apparatus of ritual.

57. Crockett, *Focus on Watergate,* p. 108.

58. Thomas Elsaesser, "*Nashville:* Putting on the Show," *Persistence of Vision* 1 (Summer 1984), p. 42.

59. Kolker, for example, argues that it "falls short of the notion of the open narrative, in which the viewer is asked to participate in, question, and respond to new forms of expression" (*A Cinema of Loneliness,* p. 319). Other negative reviews of *Nashville* include Penelope Gilliatt in the *New Yorker* (16 June 1975), pp. 107–9; Steven Abrahams in *Jump Cut* 9 (October–December 1975), pp. 7–8; and Robert Mazzocco in the *New York Review of Books* 22:12 (17 July 1975), pp. 18–20.

60. Roland Barthes, *S/Z,* trans. Richard Miller (New York: Hill and Wang, 1974), p. 188.

61. Altman, *The American Film Musical,* p. 324.

62. Girard, *Violence and the Sacred,* p. 31.

63. Altman, *The American Film Musical,* p. 327.

64. Girard, *Violence and the Sacred,* p. 145.

65. Jean Baudrillard, "Panic Crash!" trans. Faye Trecartin and Arthur Kroker, *Panic Encyclopedia: The Definitive Guide to the Postmodern Scene,* ed. Arthur Kroker, Marilouise Kroker and David Cook (Montreal: New World Perspectives, 1989), p. 65.

Conclusion: The Senselessness of Ending

1. Catherine Clément, *Opera, or the Undoing of Women,* trans. Betsey Wing (Minneapolis: University of Minnesota Press, 1988), p. 177.

2. Fredric Jameson, *Postmodernism or, the Cultural Logic of Late Capitalism* (Durham, N.C.: Duke University Press, 1991), p. 168.

3. Frank Kermode, *The Sense of an Ending: Studies in the Theory of Fiction* (New York: Oxford University Press, 1966), p. 98.

4. Walter Benjamin, *Charles Baudelaire: A Lyric Poet in the Era of High Capitalism*, trans. Harry Zohn (London: Verso, 1983), p. 81.

5. "Food for Thought," Peter Greenaway interviewed by Gavin Smith, *Film Comment* (May–June 1990), p. 58.

6. Kathy Acker has pointed out that Michael's body is the body of the host, transforming "violent political vengeance into the ritual of eating and drinking Christ. The transformation of death into life" (Kathy Acker, "The Color of Myth: The World According to Peter Greenaway," *Village Voice* [17 April 1992], p. 67).

7. The political dynamics of transgression are developed by Bataille in his reading of de Sade, whose language, he says, is the means by which violence is apprehended by the conscious mind. His description of de Sade's text is remarkably similar to the experience of watching *Weekend*: both are a means of changing violence into "something else, something necessarily its opposite: into a reflecting and rationalized will to violence" (Georges Bataille, *Erotism: Death and Sensuality*, trans. Mary Dalwood [San Francisco: City of Lights Books, 1986], p. 192).

8. The flashbacks of patricide, Marietta's attempted seduction of Sailor, and Sailor's acquisition of fatherhood are the tokens of an oedipal trajectory of which Marietta, the wicked witch, is both mother and sphinx, brought down by ridicule and ugliness and replaced by Lulu. See Sharon Willis, "Special Effects: Sexual and Social Difference in *Wild at Heart*," *Camera Obscura* 25/26 (January–May 1991), pp. 275–96.

9. Tania Modleski, "The Terror of Pleasure: The Contemporary Horror Film and Postmodern Theory," in *Studies in Entertainment: Critical Approaches to Mass Culture*, ed. Tania Modleski (Bloomington: Indiana University Press, 1986), pp. 164–65. Modleski argues that the violence of representation in the contemporary horror film confounds the critical distinction between modernist and mass culture insofar as visual pleasure is a terrifying, rather than gratifying, experience. She re-poses Hal Foster's question, "How can we break with a program that makes a value of crisis ... or progress beyond the era of Progress ... or transgress the ideology of the transgressive?" She quotes Foster from the Preface to *The Anti-Aesthetic: Essays on Postmodern Culture* (Port Townsend, Wash.: Bay Press, 1983), p. ix.

10. The fantasy of resurrection at the end of *Wild at Heart* evokes an important group of films, categorically built around the disavowal of death. These are the "ghost" films in which the boundary between life and death is crossed and the dead mix freely with those they are supposed to have left behind. In genres from the supernatural to the domestic melodrama, this theme has been engaged with many variations, including *Liliom* (1930 and 1933), *Heaven Can Wait* (1943 and 1978), *Topper* (1937), *It's a Wonderful Life* (1946), *Stairway to Heaven* (1946), *Beetlejuice* (1988), and *Wings of Desire* (1988). These films are not about death but about the capacity of the cinema to transcend death, to penetrate the realm of the unseeable and unknowable; they not only deny death but do so with a melodramatic indulgence in its disavowal.

11. Walter Benjamin, *The Origins of German Tragic Drama*, trans. John Osborne (London: New Left Books, 1977), p. 233.

12. Ibid.

13. In addition to the two films discussed here, other examples of art-house violence produced in the early 1990s include *Benny's Video, Laws of Gravity, Reservoir*

Dogs, and *One False Move.* For discussions of the trend toward excessive violence, see B. Ruby Rich, "Art House Killers," *Sight and Sound* 2:8 (1992), pp. 5–6; Amy Taubin, "The Men's Room," *Sight and Sound* 2:8 (1992): pp. 2–4; "Eight Critics Talk about Violence and the Movies," *Village Voice* (1 December 1992); Devin McKinney, "Violence: The Strong and the Weak," *Film Quarterly* 46:4 (Summer 1993), pp. 16–22.

14. *A Clockwork Orange* (Kubrick, 1971), which remains a repertory cinema staple, is certainly a precedent for the discourses of spectatorship and violence perpetrated against suburban domesticity that occur in the films discussed in this section.

15. It may be the Maysles brothers whom the film emulates most closely, tracking the killer as closely as the investigation of *Salesman,* and also showing the footage to "Ben," catching "Ben" off guard, and including technical "accidents" (three soundmen are accidentally killed, temporarily silencing the film) à la *Gimme Shelter.*

16. "The word 'history' stands written on the countenance of nature in the character of transience. The allegorical physiognomy of the nature-history, which is put on stage in the *Trauerspiel,* is present in reality in the form of the ruin. In the ruin history has physically merged into the setting" (Benjamin, *The Origins of German Tragic Drama,* p. 178).

17. Walter Benjamin, *Reflections: Essays, Aphorisms, Autobiographical Writings,* trans. Edmund Jephcott, ed. Peter Demetz (New York: Schocken Books, 1986), p. 192.

18. Taubin, "The Men's Room," p. 4.

19. *Reservoir Dogs* opens with an ironically misogynist conversation among all the men in which they debate the necessity of tipping waitresses, introducing the characters by way of their various moral stances with respect to this sexism. They are on the "grounds" of absent women.

20. Mary Ann Doane, *Femmes Fatales: Feminism, Film Theory, Psychoanalysis* (New York: Routledge, 1991), p. 14.

21. Andreas Huyssen, *After the Great Divide: Modernism, Mass Culture, Postmodernism* (Bloomington: Indiana University Press, 1986), pp. 44–64; Mary Ann Doane, "Film and the Masquerade: Theorizing the Female Spectator," in *Femmes Fatales,* pp. 17–32; Patrice Petro, *Joyless Streets: Women and Melodramatic Representation in Weimar Germany* (Princeton, N.J.: Princeton University Press, 1989).

22. Jacques Derrida, *Positions,* trans. Alan Bass (Chicago: University of Chicago Press, 1981), p. 6.

23. Judith Mayne's conception of the screen as figure of ambivalence in women's cinema might be read against the threshold of narrative mortality for an articulation of female desire. The difficulties of closure in women's cinema demonstrate "how the female subject is both complicit with the fictions of patriarchy and resistant to them" ("Screen Tests," in Judith Mayne, *The Woman at the Keyhole: Feminism and Woman's Cinema* [Bloomington: Indiana University Press, 1990], p. 85).

BIBLIOGRAPHY

Aesthetics and Politics: Ernst Bloch, George Lukács, Bertolt Brecht, Walter Benjamin, Theodore Adorno. Trans. and ed. Ronald Taylor. London: New Left Books, 1977.

Allen, Richard. "The Aesthetic Experience of Modernity: Adorno, Benjamin and Contemporary Film Theory." *New German Critique* 40 (Winter 1987): 225–40.

Alloway, Lawrence. *Violent America: The Movies 1946–1964*. New York: Museum of Modern Art, 1971.

Altman, Rick. *The American Film Musical*. Bloomington: Indiana University Press, 1989.

Andrew, Dudley. *André Bazin*. New York: Oxford University Press, 1978.

Ariès, Philippe. *The Hour of Our Death*. Trans. Helen Weaver. New York: Vintage Books, 1982.

Artaud, Antonin. *The Theatre and Its Double*. Trans. Mary Caroline Richards. New York: Grove Press, 1958

Arthur, Paul. "Shadows on the Mirror: Film Noir and Cold War America, 1945–1957." Ph.D. diss., New York University, 1985.

Auerbach, Eric. *Mimesis: The Representation of Reality in Western Literature*. Trans. Willard R. Trask. Princeton, N.J.: Princeton University Press, 1953.

Bakhtin, Mikhail. *The Dialogic Imagination: Four Essays*. Ed. Michael Holquist. Trans. Caryl Emerson and Michael Holquist. Austin: University of Texas Press, 1981.

———. *Problems of Dostoevsky's Poetics*. Trans. and ed. Caryl Emerson. Minneapolis: University of Minnesota Press, 1984.

———. *Rabelais and His World*. Trans. Hélène Iswolsky. Bloomington: Indiana University Press, 1984.

Barthes, Roland. *Camera Lucida: Reflections on Photography*. Trans. Richard Howard. New York: Hill and Wang, 1981.

———. *Empire of Signs*. Trans. Richard Howard. New York: Hill and Wang, 1982.

———. *Image Music Text*. Trans. Stephen Heath. New York: Hill and Wang, 1977.

———. *Mythologies*. Trans. Annette Lavers. Toronto: Granada Publishing, 1973.

———. *S/Z*. Trans. Richard Miller. New York: Hill and Wang, 1974.

253

Bataille, Georges. *Erotism: Death and Sensuality*. Trans. Mary Dalwood. San Francisco: City Lights Books, 1986. (First published as *L'Érotisme*, 1957.)

Baudrillard, Jean. *Fatal Strategies*. Trans. Phillip Beitchman and W. G. J. Niesluchowski. Ed. Jim Fleming. New York: Semiotext(e), 1990.

Bazin, André. *Qu'est-ce que le cinéma?* Vol. 1. *Ontologie et langage*. Éditions du Cerf, 1969.

———. *What Is Cinema?* Vols. 1 and 2. Trans. Hugh Gray. Berkeley: University of California Press, 1967, 1971.

Becker, Ernst. *The Denial of Death*. New York: Free Press, 1973.

Bedau, Hugo Adam, ed. *The Death Penalty in America: An Anthology*. Chicago: Aldine, 1964.

Bellour, Raymond. "The Pensive Spectator." Trans. Lyne Kirby. *Wide Angle* 9:1 (1987): 6–10.

———. "Psychosis, Neurosis, Perversion." *Camera Obscura* 3/4 (Summer 1979): 105–29.

Benjamin, Walter. *Charles Baudelaire: A Lyric Poet in the Era of High Capitalism*. Trans. Harry Zohn. London: Verso, 1983.

———. *Illuminations*. Ed. Hannah Arendt. Trans. Harry Zohn. New York: Schocken Books, 1969.

———. "N [Theoretics of Knowledge; Theory of Progress]." Trans. of *Passegen-Werk* by Leigh Hafrey and Richard Sieburth. *The Philosophical Forum* 15:1–2 (Fall-Winter 1983/84): 1–40.

———. *The Origins of German Tragic Drama*. Trans. John Osborne. London: New Left Books, 1977.

———. *Reflections: Essays, Aphorisms, Autobiographical Writings*. Trans. Edmund Jephcott. Ed. Peter Demetz. New York: Schocken Books, 1986.

———. "A Short History of Photography" [1931]. Trans. Stanley Mitchell. *Screen* 13 (Spring 1972): 5–26.

Blanchot, Maurice. *The Gaze of Orpheus and Other Literary Writings*. Trans. Lydia Davis. Ed. P. Adams Sitney. Barrytown, N.Y.: Station Hill, 1981.

———. *The Writing of the Disaster*. Trans. Ann Smock. Lincoln: University of Nebraska Press, 1976.

Bloom, Harold. *The Anxiety of Influence: A Theory of Poetry*. New York: Oxford University Press, 1973.

Bock, Audie. *Japanese Film Directors*. New York: Kodansha International, 1978.

Bogdanovich, Peter. *Fritz Lang in America*. New York: Praeger/Movie Magazine, 1967.

Bordwell, David. "The Art Cinema as a Mode of Film Practice." *Film Criticism* 4:1 (Fall 1979): 56–63.

———. *Ozu and the Poetics of Cinema*. Princeton, N.J.: Princeton University Press, 1989.

Boym, Svetlana. *Death in Quotation Marks: Cultural Myths of the Modern Poet*. Cambridge, Mass.: Harvard University Press, 1991.

Brecht, Bertolt. *Brecht on Theatre: The Development of an Aesthetic*. Ed. and Trans. John Willet. New York: Hill and Wang, 1964.

Brooks, Peter. *The Melodramatic Imagination: Balzac, Henry James, Melodrama, and the Mode of Excess.* New York: Columbia University Press, 1976.

———. *Reading for the Plot: Design and Intention in Narrative.* New York: Vintage Books, 1985.

Brown, Royal S., ed. *Focus on Godard.* Englewood Cliffs, N.J.: Prentice Hall, 1972.

Browne, Nick. "The Spectator in the Text: The Rhetoric of *Stagecoach*." In *Movies and Methods,* vol. 2. ed. Bill Nichols. Berkeley: University of California Press, 1985.

Buck-Morss, Susan. *The Dialectics of Seeing: Walter Benjamin and the Arcades Project.* Cambridge, Mass.: MIT Press, 1989.

Burch, Noël. *To the Distant Observer: Form and Meaning in the Japanese Cinema.* Berkeley: University of California Press, 1979.

Burnett, Ron. "Wim Wenders, Nicholas Ray and Lightning Over Water." *Cine-Tracts 14/15* 4:2/3 (Summer–Fall 1981).

Buruma, Ian. *Behind the Mask: On Sexual Demons, Sacred Mothers, Transvestites, Gangsters, Drifters and Other Japanese Cultural Heroes.* New York: Pantheon, 1984.

Butler, Terrance. *Crucified Heroes: The Films of Sam Peckinpah.* London: Gordon Fraser, 1979.

Carroll, Nöel. "The Future of Allusionism: Hollywood in the Seventies (and Beyond)." *October* 20 (Spring 1982): 51–81.

———. "Interpreting Citizen Kane." *Persistence of Vision* 7 (1989): 51–62.

Cawelti, John G. "Myths of Violence in American Popular Culture." *Critical Inquiry* 1:3 (March 1975): 521–41.

———, ed. *Focus on Bonnie and Clyde.* Englewood Cliffs, N.J.: Prentice Hall, 1973.

Cha, Theresa Hak Kyung, ed. *Apparatus: Selected Writings.* New York: Tanam Press, 1980.

Cixous, Hélène. "Castration or Decapitation?" Trans. Annette Kuhn. *Signs* 7:11 (Autumn 1981): 41–55.

Clément, Catherine. *Opera, or the Undoing of Women.* Trans. Betsey Wing. Minneapolis: University of Minnesota Press, 1988.

Collet, Jean. *Jean-Luc Godard: An Investigation into His Films and Philosophy.* Trans. Ciba Vaughan. New York: Crown Publishers, 1970.

Cook, David A. *History of Narrative Film.* New York: W. W. Norton, 1981.

Corrigan, Timothy. "Cinematic Snuff: German Friends and Narrative Murders." *Cinema Journal* 24:2 (Winter 1985): 9–17.

———. *A Cinema without Walls: Movies and Culture after Vietnam.* New Brunswick, N.J.: Rutgers University Press, 1991.

———. *New German Film: The Displaced Image.* Austin: University of Texas Press, 1983.

Cowan, Bainard. "Walter Benjamin's Theory of Allegory." *New German Critique* 22 (Winter 1981): 110–22.

Crockett, H. Dale. *Focus on Watergate: An Examination of the Moral Dilemma of Watergate in the Light of Civil Religion.* Macon, Ga.: Mercer University Press, 1982.

Dale, Peter N. *The Myth of Japanese Uniqueness*. London: Cromm Helm, 1986.

Dawson, Jan. *Wim Wenders*. Trans. Carla Wartenberg. New York: New York Zoetrope, 1976.

De Lauretis, Teresa. *Alice Doesn't: Feminism, Semiotics, Cinema*. Bloomington: Indiana University Press, 1984.

————. *Technologies of Gender*. Bloomington: Indiana University Press, 1987.

De Man, Paul. "The Rhetoric of Temporality." In *Critical Theory since 1965*, ed. Hazard Adams and Leroy Searle. Tallahassee: University Presses of Florida, 1986: 199–221.

Debord, Guy. *Society of the Spectacle*. Detroit: Black and Red, 1983.

Derrida, Jacques. *Positions*. Trans. Alan Bass. Chicago: University of Chicago Press, 1981.

Desser, David. *Eros Plus Massacre: An Introduction to the Japanese New Wave Cinema*. Bloomington: Indiana University Press, 1988.

Doane, Mary Ann. *The Desire to Desire: The Woman's Film of the 1940's*. Bloomington: Indiana University Press, 1987.

————. *Femmes Fatales: Feminism, Film Theory, Psychoanalysis*. New York: Routledge, 1991.

Doi Takeo. *The Anatomy of Dependence*. Trans. John Bester. New York: Kodansha International, 1981.

"Dossier on Wim Wenders: *L'état des choses*." *Jungle* 7 (1984).

Eagleton, Terry. *Walter Benjamin or Towards a Revolutionary Criticism*. London: New Left Books, 1981.

Eisner, Lotte H. *Fritz Lang*. New York: Oxford University Press, 1977.

Elsaesser, Thomas. "*Nashville*: Putting on the Show." *Persistence of Vision* 1 (Summer 1984): 35–43.

————. *New German Cinema: A History*. New Brunswick N.J.: Rutgers University Press, 1989.

————. "Tales of Sound and Fury: Observations on the Family Melodrama." In *Movies and Methods*, vol. 2, ed. Bill Nichols. Berkeley: University of California Press, 1985: 165–89.

Falkenberg, Pamela. "'The Text! The Text!': André Bazin's Mummy Complex, Psychoanalysis and the Cinema." *Wide Angle* 9:4 (1987): 35–55.

Farrell, Tom. "We Can't Go Home Again." *Sight and Sound* 50:2 (Spring 1981): 92–94.

Felman, Shoshana. "Beyond Oedipus: The Specimen Story of Psychoanalysis." In *Lacan and Narration: The Psychoanalytic Difference in Narrative Theory*. Johns Hopkins University Press, 1983: 1021–53.

Foucault, Michel. *The Archeology of Knowledge and the Discourse on Language*. Trans. A. M. Sheridan Smith. New York: Pantheon Books, 1972.

————. *Discipline and Punish: The Birth of the Prison*. Trans. Alan Sheridan. New York: Vintage Books, 1979.

————. *The History of Sexuality*. Vol. 1: An Introduction. Trans. Robert Hurley. New York: Vintage Books, 1980.

————. *The Order of Things: An Archaeology of the Human Sciences.* New York: Vintage Books, 1973.

————. "What Is an Author?" [1969]. Trans. Donald F. Bouchard and Sherry Simon. Repr. in *Critical Theory Since 1965,* ed. Hazard Adams and Leroy Searle. Tallahassee: University Presses of Florida, 1986: 138–47.

Frampton, Hollis. *Circles of Confusion: Film Photography, Video Texts 1968–1980.* Rochester, N.Y.: Visual Studies Workshop Press, 1983.

Freud, Sigmund. *Beyond the Pleasure Principle* [1920]. Trans. James Strachey. New York: W.W. Norton, 1961.

————. *Civilization and Its Discontents* [1930]. Trans. James Strachey. New York: W.W. Norton, 1962.

————. "Mourning and Melancholia" [1917]. Trans. Joan Riviere. In *General Psychological Theory: Papers on Metapsychology.* New York: Collier Books, 1963: 164–79.

————. "Reflections upon War and Death" [1915]. Trans. E. Colburn Mayne. In *Character and Culture.* New York: Collier Books, 1963: 107–33.

————. "The Uncanny" [1919]. In *Studies in Parapsychology.* New York: Collier Books, 1963: 19–60.

Geist, Kathe. *The Cinema of Wim Wenders: From Paris, France, to "Paris, Texas."* Ann Arbor: UMI Research Press, 1988.

Gerbner, George. "Death in Prime Time: Notes on the Symbolic Function of Dying in the Mass Media." *The Social Meaning of Death,* The Annals of Political and Social Science, vol. 47, 1980.

Girard, René. *Violence and the Sacred.* Trans. Patrick Gregory. Baltimore: Johns Hopkins University Press, 1977.

Gledhill, Christine, ed. *Home Is Where the Heart Is: Studies in Melodrama and the Woman's Film.* London: British Film Institute, 1987.

Glucksmann, André. *Violence on the Screen: A Report on research into the effects on young people of scenes of violence in films and television.* Trans. Susan Bennett. London: British Film Institute, 1971.

Godard, Jean-Luc. *Godard on Godard.* Ed. Jean Narboni and Tom Milne. Trans. Tom Milne. New York: Da Capo Press, 1972.

Gorer, Geoffrey. "The Pornography of Death." In *Identity and Anxiety: Survival of the Person in Mass Society,* ed. Maurice R. Stein, Arthur J. Vidich, and David Manning White. New York: Free Press, 1960: 402–7.

Habermas, Jürgen. "Consciousness-Raising or Redemptive Criticism: The Contemporaneity of Walter Benjamin." *New German Critique* 17 (Spring 1979): 30–59.

————. "Modernism—an Incomplete Project." In *The Anti-Aesthetic: Essays on Postmodern Culture,* ed. Hal Foster. Port Townsend, Wash.: Bay Press, 1983: 3–15.

Hansen, Miriam. "Benjamin, Cinema and Experience: 'The Blue Flower' in the Land of Technology." *New German Critique* 40 (Winter 1987): 179–224.

Harootunian, H. D. *Things Seen and Unseen: Discourse and Ideology in Tokugawa Nativism.* Chicago: University of Chicago Press, 1988.

Heath, Stephen. "Anata Mo." *Screen* 17:4 (Winter 1976/77): 49–66.

———. "Film and System: Terms of Analysis." *Screen,* part 1, 16:1 (Spring 1975): 7–77; part 2, 16:2 (Summer 1975), 91–113.

———. *Questions of Cinema.* Bloomington: Indiana University Press, 1981.

High, Peter B. "Oshima: A Vita Sexualis on Film." *Wide Angle* 1:4 (1977): 62–71.

Higham, Charles, and Joel Greenberg. *The Celluloid Muse: Hollywood Directors Speak.* London: Angus and Robertson, 1969.

Hillier, Jim, ed. *Cahiers du Cinéma: The 1950's.* Cambridge, Mass.: Harvard University Press, 1985.

Horkheimer, Max. *Critical Theory* [1937]. New York: Seabury Press, 1972.

Humphries, Reynold. *Fritz Lang: Genre and Representation in His American Films.* Baltimore: Johns Hopkins University Press, 1989.

Huyssen, Andreas. *After the Great Divide: Modernism, Mass Culture, Postmodernism.* Bloomington: Indiana University Press, 1986.

James, Jo Ann, and William J. Cloonan, eds. *Apocalyptic Visions Past and Present."* Tallahassee: Florida State University Press, 1988.

Jameson, Fredric. *Marxism and Form: Twentieth-Century Dialectical Theories of Literature.* Princeton, N.J.: Princeton University Press, 1971.

———. "Periodizing the 60's" [1984]. In *The Ideologies of Theory: Essays 1971–1986,* vol. 2: *The Syntax of History.* Minneapolis: University of Minnesota Press, 1988: 178–208.

———. *The Political Unconscious: Narrative as a Socially Symbolic Act.* Ithaca, N.Y.: Cornell University Press, 1981.

———. *Postmodernism or, the Cultural Logic of Late Capitalism.* Durham, N.C.: Duke University Press, 1991.

Jenkins, Stephen, ed. *Fritz Lang: The Image and the Look.* London: British Film Institute, 1981.

Jennings, Michael W. *Dialectical Images: Walter Benjamin's Theory of Literary Criticism.* Ithaca, N.Y.: Cornell University Press, 1987.

Jost, Jon. "Wrong Move." *Sight and Sound* 50:2 (Spring 1981).

Kahn, Greg. "Territorial Rites: Ruiz, Jost and Wenders in Portugal." *Framework* 15/16/17:103 (Summer 1981).

Kaplan, E. Ann, ed. *Women and Film Noir.* London: British Film Institute, 1980.

Kastenbaum, Robert, and Ruth Aisenberg. *The Psychology of Death.* New York: Springer, 1972.

Keene, Donald. *The Major Plays of Chikamatsu.* New York: Columbia University Press, 1961.

Kermode, Frank. *The Sense of an Ending: Studies in the Theory of Fiction.* New York: Oxford University Press, 1966.

Klinger, Barbara. " 'Cinema/Ideology/Criticism' Revisited: The Progressive Text." *Screen* 25:1 (January/February 1984): 1–14.

———. "Much Ado about Excess: Genre, Mise-en-Scène and the Woman in *Written on the Wind.*" *Wide Angle* 11:4 (October 1989): 4–22.

Kolker, Robert Phillip. *The Altering Eye: Contemporary International Cinema.* New York: Oxford University Press, 1983.

————. *A Cinema of Loneliness: Penn, Kubrick, Scorsese, Spielberg, Altman.* 2d ed. New York: Oxford University Press, 1988.

Kristeva, Julia. "Women's Time" [1979]. Trans. Alice Jardine and Harry Blake. In *Critical Theory since 1965,* ed. Hazard Adams and Leroy Searle. Tallahassee: University Presses of Florida, 1986: 471–85.

Kunstler, William K. *Beyond a Reasonable Doubt? The Original Trial of Caryl Chessman.* New York: William Morrow, 1961.

Lacan, Jacques. "Desire and the Interpretation of Desire in *Hamlet.*" *Yale French Studies* 55/56 (1977): 11–52.

————. *Écrits.* Trans. Alan Sheridan. New York: W.W. Norton, 1977.

————. *The Four Fundamental Concepts of Psychoanalysis.* Trans. Alan Sheridan. New York: W.W. Norton, 1978.

Lang, Fritz. "Happily Ever After." *Penguin Film Review* 5 (1948): 22–29.

Lang, Robert. *American Film Melodrama: Griffith, Vidor, Minnelli.* Princeton, N.J.: Princeton University Press, 1989.

Lawrence, Amy. "The Aesthetics of the Image: The Hanging of Colonel Higgins: A CBS NewsBreak." *Wide Angle* 12:2 (April 1990).

Lehman, Peter. "The Mysterious Orient, the Crystal Clear Orient, the Non-existent Orient: Dilemmas of Western Scholars of Japanese Film." *Journal of Film and Video* 39 (Winter 1987): 5–15.

Lenne, Gérard. *La Mort à voir.* Poitiers/Liguegé: Éditions du Cerf, 1977.

Lifton, Robert Jay. *Death in Life: Survivors of Hiroshima.* New York: Random House, 1968.

Lukács, George. *The Theory of the Novel: A Historical-Philosophical Essay on the Forms of Great Epic Literature.* Trans. Anna Bostock. Cambridge, Mass.: MIT Press, 1971.

Lyotard, Jean-François. "Fiscourse Digure: The Utopia behind the Scenes of the Phantasy." Trans. Mary Lydon. *Theatre Journal* 35:3 (October 1983): 333–57.

Mann, Paul. *The Theory-Death of the Avant-Garde.* Bloomington and Indianapolis: Indiana University Press, 1991.

Marcuse, Herbert. *Eros and Civilization: A Philosophical Inquiry into Freud.* New York: Vintage Books, 1955.

————. "The Ideology of Death." In *The Meaning of Death,* ed. Herman Feifel. New York: McGraw-Hill, 1959: 64–76.

Margulies, Ivone. "Delaying the Cut: The Space of Performance in *Lightning Over Water.*" *Screen* 34:1 (Spring 1993): 54–68.

Mayne, Judith. *The Woman at the Keyhole: Feminism and Woman's Cinema.* Bloomington: Indiana University Press, 1990.

McCabe, Colin. *Godard: Images, Sounds, Politics.* Bloomington: Indiana University Press, 1980.

Mellen, Joan. *Voices from the Japanese Cinema.* New York: Liveright, 1975.

Menninghaus, Winfried. "Walter Benjamin's Theory of Myth." Trans. Gary Smith. In *On Benjamin,* ed. Gary Smith. Cambridge, Mass.: MIT Press, 1988: 292–328.

Merleau-Ponty, Maurice. *Sense and Non-Sense.* Trans. Hubert L. Dreyfus and Patricia Allen Dreyfus. Evanston, Ill.: Northwestern University Press, 1964.

Metz, Christian. *The Imaginary Signifier: Psychoanalysis and the Cinema*. Trans. Celia Britto et al. Bloomington: Indiana University Press, 1977.

Modleski, Tania. "The Terror of Pleasure: The Contemporary Horror Film and Postmodern Theory." In *Studies in Entertainment: Critical Approaches to Mass Culture*, ed. Tania Modleski. Bloomington: Indiana University Press, 1986: 155–66.

Mulvey, Laura. *Visual and Other Pleasures*. Bloomington: Indiana University Press, 1989.

Mussman, Toby, ed. *Jean-Luc Godard*. New York: E. P. Dutton, 1968.

Naremore, James. "Film and the Performance Frame." *Film Quarterly* 38:2 (Winter 1984/85): 8–15.

Neale, Steve. "Melodrama and Tears." *Screen* 27:6 (November–December 1986): 6–22.

Neupert, Richard John. "The End: Notions of Closure in the Cinema." Ph.D. diss., University of Wisconsin at Madison, 1986.

Nietzsche, Friedrich. *The Birth of Tragedy and the Genealogy of Morals*. Trans. Francis Golffing. New York: Doubleday, 1956.

Oshima Nagisa. *Cinema, Censorship, and the State*. Trans. Dawn Lawson. Ed. Annette Michelson. Cambridge, Mass.: MIT Press, 1992.

———. Interview with Ruth McCormick. *Cineaste* 7:4 (Winter 1976/77): 34–35.

Oudart, Jean-Pierre. "Cinema and Suture." *Screen* 18:4 (Winter 1977/78): 35–47.

Owens, Craig. "The Allegorical Impulse: Toward a Theory of Post Modernism," part 1, *October* 12 (Spring 1980): 67–86; part 2, *October* 13 (Summer 1980): 59–80.

Pasolini, Pier Paolo. "Observations on the Long Take" [1967]. *October* 13 (Summer 1980): 3–6.

Petro, Patrice. *Joyless Streets: Women and Melodramatic Representation in Weimar Germany*. Princeton, N.J.: Princeton University Press, 1989.

Polan, Dana. *The Political Language of the Avant-Garde*. Ann Arbor: UMI Research Press, 1985.

———. *Power and Paranoia: History, Narrative and the American Cinema, 1940–1950*. New York: Columbia University Press, 1986.

Poster, Mark. *Existential Marxism in Postwar France: From Sartre to Althusser*. Princeton, N.J.: Princeton University Press, 1975.

Rentschler, Eric. *West German Film in the Course of Time: Reflections on the Twenty Years since Oberhausen*. Bedford Hills, N.Y.: Redgrave, 1984.

Rivette, Jacques. *Rivette: Texts and Interviews*. Ed. Jonathan Rosenbaum. Trans. Amy Gateff and Tom Milne. London: British Film Institute, 1977.

Rodowick, D. N. *The Difficulty of Difference: Psychoanalysis, Sexual Difference and Film Theory*. New York: Routledge, 1991.

———. "Madness, Authority and Ideology: The Domestic Melodrama of the 1950s." In *Home Is Where the Heart Is: Studies in Melodrama and the Woman's Film*, ed. Christine Gledhill. London: British Film Institute, 1987: 268–82.

Rosen, Charles. "The Ruins of Walter Benjamin." In *On Walter Benjamin*, ed. Gary Smith. Cambridge, Mass.: MIT Press, 1991: 129–75.

Rosen, Philip. "History of Image, Image of History: Subject and Ontology in Bazin." *Wide Angle* 9:4 (1987): 7–34.

Rubinsky, Yuri, and Ian Wiseman. *A History of the End of the World*. New York: William Morrow, 1982.

Said, Edward. *Orientalism*. New York: Vintage Books, 1978.

Santner, Eric L. *Stranded Objects: Mourning, Memory and Film in Postwar Germany*. Ithaca, N.Y.: Cornell University Press, 1990.

Sartre, Jean-Paul. *The Philosophy of Jean-Paul Sartre*. Ed. Robert Denoon Cumming. New York: Vintage Books, 1965.

Sato Tadao: *Currents in Japanese Cinema*. Trans. Gregory Barrett. New York: Kodansha International, 1982.

Schniederman, Stuart. *Jacques Lacan: The Death of an Intellectual Hero*. Cambridge, Mass.: Harvard University Press, 1983.

Schrader, Paul. *Transcendental Style in Film: Ozu, Bresson, Dryer*. Berkeley: University of California Press, 1972.

Sharrett, Christopher. "Apocalypticism in the Contemporary Horror Film: A Typological Survey of a Theme in the Fantastic Cinema, Its Relation to Cultural Tradition and Current Filmic Expression." Ph.D. diss., New York University, 1983.

———, ed. *Crisis Cinema: The Apocalyptic Idea in Postmodern Narrative Film*. Washington, D.C.: Maisonneuve Press, 1993.

Silver, Alain. *The Samurai Film*. New York: Overlook, 1983.

Silverman, Kaja. *The Acoustic Mirror: The Female Voice in Psychoanalysis and Cinema*. Bloomington: Indiana University Press, 1988.

Slotkin, Richard. *Regeneration through Violence*. Middleton, Conn.: Wesleyan University Press, 1973.

Smith, Gary. *On Walter Benjamin: Critical Essays and Recollections*. Cambridge, Mass.: MIT Press, 1988.

Sobchack, Vivian. "Inscribing Ethical Space: Ten Propositions on Death, Representation and Documentary." *Quarterly Review of Film Studies* (Fall 1984): 283–300.

Solanas, Fernando, and Octavio Gettino. "Towards a Third Cinema" [1971]. In *Movies and Methods,* vol. 1, ed. Bill Nichols. Berkeley: University of California Press, 1976: 44–64.

Sontag, Susan. "Godard." In *A Susan Sontag Reader*. New York: Farrar, Straus & Giroux, 1982: 147–89.

———. *Illness as Metaphor*. New York: Vintage Books, 1979.

Stam, Robert. *Reflexivity in Film and Literature: From Don Quixote to Jean-Luc Godard*. Ann Arbor: UMI Research Press, 1985.

Steiner, George. *The Death of Tragedy*. New York: Oxford University Press, 1961.

Stewart, Garrett. "Coppola's Conrad: The Repetitions of Complicity." *Critical Inquiry* 7:3 (Spring 1983): 455–74.

———. *Death Sentences: Styles of Dying in British Fiction*. Cambridge, Mass.: Harvard University Press, 1984.

———. "Photo-gravure: Death, Photography and Film Narrative." *Wide Angle* 9:1 (1987): 11–31.

Thomas, Lewis. "Dying as Failure." In *The Social Meaning of Death*. The Annals of Political and Social Science, vol. 447, 1980.

Turim, Maureen. "Oshima's Cruel Tales of Youth and Politics." *Journal of Film and Video* 39 (Winter 1987): 42–51.

———. "Rituals, Desire, Death in Oshima's Ceremonies." *Enclitic* 5:2/6:1 (Fall 1981/Spring 1982).

———. "Signs of Sexuality in Oshima's Tales of Passion." *Wide Angle* 9:2 (Spring 1987).

Vernet, Mark. "Blinking, Flickering and Flashing of the Black and White Film." Trans. Lee Hildreth. In *Apparatus,* ed. Theresa Hak Kyung Cha. New York: Tanam Press, 1980: 357–72.

———. "The Filmic Transaction: On the Openings of Film Noirs." Trans. David Rodowick. *The Velvet Light Trap* 20 (Summer 1983): 3–9.

Virilio, Paul. *War and Cinema: The Logistics of Perception* [1984]. Trans. Patrick Camiller. London: Verso, 1989.

Weir, Robert F., ed. *Death in Literature*. New York: Columbia University Press, 1980.

Wenders, Wim. *Emotion Pictures: Reflections on the Cinema*. Trans. Shaun Whiteside. London: Faber and Faber, 1986.

———. "Interview with Patrick Bauchau." *Jungle* 7 (1984): 51–58.

Wenders, Wim, and Chris Sievernich. *Nick's Film: Lightning Over Water*. Zweitausendeins, 1981.

Williams, Linda. *Hard Core: Power, Pleasure, and the Frenzy of the Visible*. Berkeley: University of California Press, 1989.

White, Hayden. *The Content of the Form: Narrative Discourse and Historical Representation*. Baltimore: Johns Hopkins University Press, 1987.

———. "The Historical Text as Literary Artifact" [1974]. In *Critical Theory since 1965,* ed. Hazard Adams and Leroy Searle. Tallahassee: University Presses of Florida, 1986: 395–407.

Wolfe, Alan. *Suicidal Narrative in Modern Japan: The Case of Dazai Osamu*. Princeton, N.J.: Princeton University Press, 1990.

Wolfenstein, Martha, and Nathan Leites. *Movies: A Psychological Study*. New York: Free Press, 1950.

Wolin, Richard. *Walter Benjamin: An Aesthetic of Redemption*. New York: Columbia University Press, 1982.

INDEX

Compiled by Hassan Melehy

CATHERINE RUSSELL teaches in the Department of Cinema at Concordia University, Montreal. She has published numerous articles on experimental film, video art, Japanese cinema, ethnographic film, and feminist film theory.